REVOLUTION AT WORK
Mobilization Campaigns in China

Celebrating the Establishment of People's Communes, by the Niuting People's Commune Spare-Time Art Group. [From *Peasant Paintings from Huhsien County* (Peking: People's Fine Arts Publishing House).]

REVOLUTION AT WORK
Mobilization Campaigns in China

CHARLES P. CELL

Department of Sociology
University of Wisconsin–Madison
Madison, Wisconsin

ACADEMIC PRESS   New York   San Francisco   London

A Subsidiary of Harcourt Brace Jovanovich, Publishers

ACADEMIC PRESS, INC.
111 Fifth Avenue, New York, New York 10003

United Kingdom Edition published by
ACADEMIC PRESS, INC. (LONDON) LTD.
24/28 Oval Road, London NW1

Library of Congress Cataloging in Publication Data

Cell, Charles Preston.
　　Revolution at work.

　　(Studies in social discontinuity)
　　Includes bibliographical references.
　　1.　　China—Politics and government—1949–
2.　　Socialism in China.　　I.　　Title.　　II.　　Series.
DS777.55.C3337　　　　309.1'51'05　　　　76-55966
ISBN 0–12–164750–1

To the Chinese people:
  It is their revolution.

This is a volume in

STUDIES IN SOCIAL DISCONTINUITY

A complete list of titles in this series appears at the end of this volume.

Contents

Preface

Mao would have been 83 today. The great transition in leadership witnessed in China during this past year is clearly a watershed event. In the years to come sinologists will undoubtedly speak of China's Mao and post-Mao eras.

When the kernel of this project was originally conceived, in the spring of 1968, it was simply impossible to imagine that the manuscript to come from it would be going to the printer only 4 short months after Mao's death. When the contract with the publisher was signed 3 weeks to the day after Mao's death, it was debated whether major rewriting of the manuscript would be in order. Although parts had been heavily rewritten in the early months of 1976, the data and the conclusions were largely those gathered and developed some 5 years earlier, only four-fifths through the Maoist era. However, after I reread the manuscript, it became clear that except for perhaps including three or four more national campaigns, none of which appeared as important as Agrarian Reform, the Great Leap Forward, or the Great Proletarian Cultural Revolution, the manuscript would not need to be changed. Not only was it quite current, but it would be essentially the same if I were setting out today to do a similar study. Thus, except for a few changes in verb tense and editing for clarity, the manuscript as revised in early 1976 is unchanged.

I did, however, feel that it would be useful and important to add an epilogue, to comment on the significance of the leadership changes, particularly with regard to their impact on the continuance of the mass mobilization campaign. The tumultuous changes that occurred in the final months of 1976 have in some ways made the writing of the epilogue the hardest part of the book. Lacking historical perspective, it is difficult to tread the narrow line between saying so much that it shortly becomes dated and saying so little that it is useless. Hopefully I have been able to map out many of the issues and areas critical to determining China's future. It has not been my intent in the epilogue to predict; rather it has been my goal to provide guidelines to help illuminate the evaluation of China's future.

Over the years that have passed since this project got under way, I have incurred many debts. Although I would like to extend my appreciation to all who assisted me, space will permit the acknowledgment of only a few of the most important. In many ways, the greatest debt I owe is to my parents, my father now only an inspiration of intelligence, mental creativity, and organization, and my mother always active, encouraging, supporting, and loving. More than any others, they nurtured in me the qualities necessary to see this project to its completion. But day by day it has been Davy, Susan, and Bob Goldberg who in countless ways have been there supporting, assisting, and caring.

I am indebted to the Foreign Area Fellowship Program, for the 2 years of financial support they provided during the critical research and writing stages of the project. Also to Martin Whyte, my dissertation advisor, who was always there when frustrating details eluded my grasp. I want to acknowledge Elaine Emling for her steadfast support of this project.

The greatest intellectual debt is to Chuck Tilly. Especially in the early stages of the project, at countless points when ideas, thoughts, and data turned from inspiration to confusion, it was Chuck who helped me back on the road to clarity. It was also he, more than any other, who encouraged me to continue and provided the opportunity for this research to reach the final stage of publication.

Second only to Chuck is Ed Friedman, whose searching and penetrating criticism, coupled with continued praise and encouragement, kept me going where others would have me stop. Many of the improvements to the manuscript's contents must be attributed to the inspiration of Chuck and close reading by Ed.

I want to extend my appreciation to Bill Sewell, who in the later stages of the project provided invaluable advice on how to get from manuscript to book. I also wish to thank my student, John Lo, whose suggestions and helpful criticisms go substantially beyond the meager references in the book. I am especially grateful to my aunt, Cornelia Wolfe, who gave up part of her well-deserved vacation to assist in the indexing.

A word of thanks must also be given to the editorial staff of Academic Press. Somehow all the terrible things I heard about the agony of publishing a book never came to pass, undoubtedly because of their support, encouragement, and hard work.

Finally, but not least of all in this short list but long process of acknowledgment, I cannot forget the secretaries of my department. Mattie Morin, Ginny Rogers, Caroline Werner, Kathy Wildes, Jim Nelson, Edith Wilimovsky, and, above all, Mimi Devaul and Sharon McCarthy were always there with a willing smile, an offer of support, a word of encouragement when the going got tough. In the generally overworked and underpaid life of a secretary, it amazes me how they seem able to keep cheerful. My hand of appreciation remains extended to them.

Storybrook Farm
December 26, 1976   *Brooklyn, Wisconsin*

Chronology of Major Events

CHINESE COMMUNIST MOVEMENT (1921–1949)

July 1921	Founding and First Congress of the Chinese Communist party.
June 1923	Beginning of the First United Front with the Kuomintang (Nationalist party).
March 1926	Coup led by Chiang Kai-shek (then president of China and leader of Kuomintang party) against Communists in Canton.
April 1927	Coup led by Chiang Kai-shek against Communists in Shanghai; end of United Front.
Fall 1927	Movement of rural segment of Chinese Communist party under Mao's leadership to the mountains of Hunan (Chingkanshan).
Summer–Fall 1928	The Party, under Mao and Chu Teh, moves to the Kiangsi–Fukien border area and establishes Chinese Soviets.
October 1934	Kuomintang-led anti-Communist annihilation campaigns begin to succeed; Mao is ill and out of power. The Long March begins.
January 1935	Tsunyi Conference, where Mao assumes leadership of the Party.
October 1935	Remnants of Communist forces arrive in Yenan, Shensi province, and establish a new primary base area.

December 1936   Chiang Kai-shek is kidnapped by his own Nationalist forces in Sian (capital of Shensi province). The Second United Front begins.

February 1942   Mass mobilization campaigns begin in Yenan with a Party rectification campaign.

July 1946   All-out civil war ensues between Communists and Nationalists.

November 1949   Nationalists flee to Taiwan.

PEOPLE'S REPUBLIC OF CHINA (1949–   )

October 1949   The People's Republic of China is proclaimed in Peking.

April 1950   The Marriage Law is passed.

June 1950   The Agrarian Reform Law is passed; the Agrarian Reform campaign begins.

October 1950   China enters the Korean War; the Resist America–Aid Korea campaign begins.

December 1951   Three-Anti and Five-Anti campaigns begin.

July 1955   Mao's speech, "On the Question of Agricultural Cooperation," signals the beginning of the campaign for Higher-Level Agricultural Producers' Cooperatives.

May 1956   The Hundred Flowers campaign is announced.

October 1956   Hungarian revolt takes place.

February 1957   Mao gives the speech entitled "On the Correct Handling of Contradictions among the People."

June 1957   The Anti-Rightist campaign begins in reaction to broad criticism of the Party.

October 1957   Early stages of the Great Leap Forward; decentralization and long-term program to develop agriculture are discussed; the Mass Irrigation campaign begins.

July 1958   Rural commune organization begins, and is formalized in August.

December 1958   Retreat on rural communes and the halting of urban communization take place. Mao Tse-tung resigns as

	chairman of the People's Republic, but remains as chairman of the Party.
August 1959	Further decentralization of rural communes occurs.
August 1960	Soviet technicians are withdrawn from China.
September 1965	Lin Piao's speech, "Long Live the Victory of the People's War," signals China's intention not to become more directly involved in the Indochina war and the need to emphasize domestic issues.
November 1965	Yao Wen-yuan publishes in Shanghai's *Wen Hui Pao* an attack on vice-mayor of Peking Wu Han's play, *Jui Hai Dismissed from Office*—an allegorical attack on Mao's dismissal of Defense Minister Peng Teh-huai in 1959. Seen in retrospect as a prelude to the GPCR.
April–May 1966	Newspaper editorials and articles become increasingly strident in denoucning "backward" forces.
June 1966	The mass activity of the GPCR begins. The first wall poster appears at Peking University. Many national leaders are criticized and eventually removed from office—the most prominent of these are Liu Shao-chi and Teng Hsiao-ping.
January 1967	The army begins to intervene in the GPCR.
February 1967	The first Revolutionary Committee is established and becomes the new institutional form of governance and power at all levels of society.
March 1967	A major effort to denounce Liu Shao-chi begins. Peng Chen and Teng Hsio-ping are officially attacked by name.
September 1968	Mao calls for youth to go to the countryside. A mass exodus begins.
October 1968	Mao's statement that eventually leads to the establishment of May Seventh Cadre Schools is issued.
April 1969	The Ninth Party Congress is held, signaling the end of the GPCR and the consolidation of power under Mao and Lin Piao.
September 1971	Lin Piao falls from power after attempting a coup against Mao. Lin is killed in an airplane crash in Mongolia while trying to flee to Russia.

April 1973	Teng Hsiao-ping, demoted from power and heavily criticized during the GPCR returns as a vice-premier under Chou En-lai.
January 1974	The campaign to criticize Lin Piao indirectly in progress for more than a year is linked to a new effort to criticize Confucius.
January 1975	The Fourth National People's Congress is held; it appears to confirm Teng Hsiao-ping's return to power and the expectation that he will replace the ailing Chou En-lai. Chang Chun-chiao also is seen as important in a post-Chou/Mao leadership. Hua Kuo-feng becomes minister of Public Security.
April 1975	Tung Pi-wu, elder statesman, acting head of state following Liu's downfall, dies.
September–October 1975	National Conference on Learning from Tachai in Agriculture. Hua Kuo-feng, a vice-premier, plays a prominent role.
January 1976	Death of Premier Chou En-lai.
February 1976	Hua Kuo-feng is appointed acting premier. The press begins to denounce Teng Hsiao-ping as an "unrepentant capitalist roader."
July 1976	Death of Chu Teh, elder statesman, close associate of Mao for over half a century, and chairman of the National People's Congress.
September 1976	Death of Chairman Mao Tse-tung.
October 1976	Hua Kuo-feng assumes Mao's position of Party chairman and head of the military; he continues as premier, thus holding the three most powerful positions in China. The "Gang of Four" (Chiang Ching, Chang Chun-chiao, Yao Wen-yuan, and Wang Hung-wen) are denounced, removed from office, and arrested. Criticism against Teng Hsiao-ping is sharply reduced.
December 1976	The Second National Conference on Learning from Tachai begins.

Major Leaders in China

Chang Chun-chiao Rose to national prominence during the GPCR; chairman of the Shanghai Revolutionary Committee. On the national level, he was a member of the Standing Committee of the Party Politburo, a vice-premier and a member of the powerful Military Affairs Commission. At the time of Chou En-lai's death in January 1976, he was seen as rivaling Teng Hsiao-ping as a replacement for Chou and especially Mao. In October 1976 he was denounced as a member of the "Gang of Four," removed from office, and arrested.

Chiang Ching Rose to national prominence during the GPCR; supervised major changes in cultural and artistic spheres of Chinese life. Wife of Mao Tse-tung. In October 1976 she was denounced as a member of the "Gang of Four," removed from office, and arrested.

Chou En-lai Premier of China from 1949 to his death in January 1976. An early supporter of Mao Tse-tung, he participated in the Long March and was a leader of the revolutionary government in Yenan.

Chu Teh The most famous of generals in the Chinese Communist guerilla movement; he was with Mao from the start in the Chingkanshan mountains in 1927–1928. At the time of his death in July 1976, he was a member of the Standing Committee of the Politburo and chairman of the Standing Committee of the National People's Congress.

Hua Kuo-feng A provincial Party leader in Hunan (Mao's native province) until he became minister of Public Security in January 1975. Appointed acting premier in February 1976, and confirmed premier in April. By July 1976, he had become first vice-chairman of the Party. After Mao's death, he assumed (in October 1976) the other two most powerful positions in China of chairman of the Communist party and chairman of the Military Affairs Commission.

Lin Piao

Became defense minister following Peng Teh-huai's dismissal in 1959. He returned the armed forces to a pre-1949 guerilla model of control and operation. They became a model for the GPCR. Second only to Mao during the GPCR, he attempted a coup in September 1971, and was killed in a plane crash in Mongolia while trying to flee to Russia.

Liu Shao-chi

Leader of underground Communist forces in the cities and coastal areas behind Kuomintang and Japanese lines. Became chairman (president) of the People's Republic of China after Mao stepped down in 1958. He was seen as Mao's probable successor, but fell from power with the start of the GPCR.

Mao Tse-tung

At his death in September 1976, Mao was chairman of the Chinese Communist party—a post held since 1935—and chairman of the controlling organ of the military, the Military Affairs Commission. He led the Chinese Communist movement to the countryside in 1927, fell out of favor in the early 1930s, only to reassume control in 1935. He directed the development of the Party and movement in Yenan and the eventual victory in 1949.

Peng Chen

Mayor of Peking and leading figure of the Party at the time of his downfall at the start of the GPCR. He was charged with protecting Wu Han, Peking's vice-mayor, who was an early target of the GPCR.

Peng Teh-huai

Minister of Defense until 1959. He was dismissed, ostensibly because of his attacks on the Great Leap Forward, but possibly also because of his support for the Soviet Union.

Teng Hsiao-ping

Secretary-general of the Communist party until the GPCR, when he was removed, ostensibly for his unwillingness to come to Mao's defense against Liu Shao-chi. He was returned to power by Chou En-lai in April 1973, as a vice-premier. Considered by many as the likely successor to Chou, he was instead denounced and removed from office in February 1976.

Tung Pi-wu | Elder statesman of China. Served as acting chairman (president) of the People's Republic in the years following the GPCR until his death in April 1975.

Wang Hung-wen | Young leader of the GPCR in Shanghai. He became nationally prominent when he was appointed first Party vice-chairman, immediately under Mao, after Lin Piao's downfall. In October 1976 he was denounced as a member of the "Gang of Four," removed from office, and arrested.

Yao Wen-yuan | Early propagandist and leader in the GPCR. He was vice-chairman of the Shanghai Revolutionary Committee, and was heavily involved in propaganda work at the national level. In October 1976 he was denounced as a member of the "Gang of Four," removed from office, and arrested.

Yeh Ching-ying | One of few surviving national leaders from the GPCR. He replaced Lin Piao as defense minister and in October 1976 became Party vice-chairman under Hua Kuo-feng.

Abbreviations

APC   Agricultural Producers' Cooperative

CCP   Chinese Communist Party

GLF   Great Leap Forward

GPCR   Great Proletarian Cultural Revolution

HAPC   Higher-Level Agricultural Producers' Cooperative

KMT   Kuomintang (literally, Chiang Kai-shek's "National People's Party")

MAT   Mutual Aid Teams

PLA   People's Liberation Army

PRC   People's Republic of China

The Chinese system of romanization, *pin yin*, has been followed, except where common usage sanctions a different form (e.g., Mao Tse-tung).

Introduction

The Issues at Stake

> We are now building socialism. Hundreds of millions of people are taking part in a movement for socialist transformation.
>
> —Mao, 1971: 480

A quarter of a century has passed since the founding of the People's Republic of China. Yet China is still a revolutionary society, characterized by high levels of political mobilization and rapid changes in political, social, and economic institutions. Unlike most countries undergoing rapid changes, it is not a country in turmoil, or a country at war with itself or others. It is at peace, confident, optimistic, yet active, energetic, and on the move.

Its goal, at the broadest level, is one sought by most, if not all, developing societies: greater productivity shared by each member in the form of adequate housing, good health care, literacy, and the like, bounded by the conviction that to each person belongs the same rights, respect, and dignity.

Yet to achieve its goal, China has pursued a strategy radically different from those employed by most third world societies, with their capitalist orientations. Its strategy is one of *socialist transformation* through the process of political mobilization.

The fulcrum of this strategy is the mass mobilization campaign, first attempted in the bitter trials of the Kiangsi period, from 1928 to 1934, and then hardened during the Yenan period, beginning in 1936, when it was used to combat the Japanese and the Kuomintang and at the same time build a new society, a new order. The campaign is as important now as it was then. To comprehend how China changed, how it has accomplished so much in so short a time, there is no single institution more important to understand than the campaign.

1

Although analysts of China readily acknowledge the importance of the campaign, there has been no systematic study of it. This work is the first such study of the campaign, its component process of mobilization, and its outcomes, both shortcomings and achievements.

In undertaking such a systematic study, it has become possible for the first time to throw some factual light on one of the major controversies in the field of contemporary Chinese studies: whether the campaign mobilization strategy pursued in China promotes or retards the socialist process of sociopolitical change and especially economic growth. Simply put, is the campaign utilitarian for China's strategy of socialist transformation? Most analysts of contemporary China, at some point, in some way, have considered this question. Few have systematically faced it or the implications involved.[1]

The answer to this question is of tremendous importance to those seeking solutions to the problems of "socioeconomic change." The implications reach far beyond China, a quarter of humankind, to the masses of Asia, Africa, and Latin America. Festering questions of political, social, and economic injustice continue to eat unanswered into the villages of India, the slums of Rio de Janeiro, and the towns of Nigeria. To heal these wounds, which road shall these societies take? The road of capitalism, or the road of socialist transformation? Is yet some third alternative possible, as in present-day Peru, Tanzania, or Algeria?

The penetration of highly industrialized economies into most third world societies has brought modern technology, including such achievements as advanced transportation systems. It has brought modern enclave cities with medical and educational advances, at least for the upper and middle classes. Much of the population of these societies has, however, remained isolated, if not geographically, then in terms of the poverty of services received. Although capitalist development strategies including the mobilization of the economic marketplace and the electoral institutions of the Western Atlantic world have brought benefits to some, many problems remain unresolved. In confronting these unresolved problems, even non-Marxists have questioned, at least in the political arena, whether communist models might be more utilitarian.

> We have already emphasized strongly the failure of Western electoral mobilization and its processes in providing adequate "tools" for the mobilization requirements of developing countries. The communist model, arising as it does from a revolutionary-inheritance situation, is more conducive to adaptation in the Third World [Nettl, 1967: 257].

[1] There a handful of exceptions, most notably Bennett (1973), but none use quantifiable data and most cover only a certain type of campaigns (e.g., rectification, see Teiwes, 1971) or a limited period such as the early years (e.g., Human Resources Research Institute, 1955a, 1955b, 1955c, 1955d, 1955e).

It is at least in part the penetration of "metropolitan" capitalist economies that has caused these third world countries to be caught in a vicious circle of economic dependence, social injustice, and political unrest. Who will break this circle and how will it be broken?

China provides one great example as to how it can be broken. Prior to 1949, China suffered no less than other third world societies do today. A few Chinese in enclave cities benefited, but the masses were left to suffer the usurious rents of tenancy, the poverty of the countryside, and the backbreaking life of coolie labor in the cities.

Yet, every society must make its own choices, build its own institutions. History, culture, and social conditions are too varied between societies to permit blind reproduction from one society to another. The Chinese would be the first to tell us that.

Although this research raises questions in the larger context of the developing world, one must be aware of its limited focus. It is not even a blueprint of the Chinese experience after 1949, let alone an agenda for action elsewhere. It is, rather, a serious effort to begin to understand, in a systematic way, one critical element of the Chinese experience. If some additional light can be shed on the Chinese road to change, then hopefully it can also illuminate our thinking about alternative roads of social, political, and economic change.

1

Which Road to Take?

The bourgeoisie doubts our ability to construct. The imperialists reckon that eventually we will beg alms from them in order to live.
                                                        —Mao, 1967: Vol. 4, 374

On March 5, 1949, Mao Tse-tung concluded his "Report to the Second Central Committee" with this admonition. The session was the last one the Central Committee would have to hold in a rural village to avoid Chiang Kai-shek's Kuomintang (KMT) armies, or the Japanese. The next meeting was held in Peking. The Communist party of China had moved since 1921 from 28 years in opposition, to the leadership of virtually all of China.

Particularly during the years in opposition in Yenan, the Party had forged a comprehensive program of socialist transformation—sociopolitical change and socialist economic construction (Selden, 1969b). The implementation of the program centered on the repeated use of mass mobilization campaigns—the reliance on high levels of mass participation and activism. Would this same program, this same mobilization strategy, transferred to the cities and the entire country, prove successful? Or would, as Mao describes it, the bourgeoisie and imperialists be correct?

This systematic examination of the mobilization campaign and its utility in promoting socialist transformation must begin with an account of the antecedents of the campaign. What impact did the Communist party's pre-1949 experience have on its campaign mobilization program and strategy after liberation (1949 for most areas of China)? What impact did the Russian experience have? What are the characteristics of the mass mobilization campaigns in post-liberation China? How do they relate to Western notions of mobilization? How have Western social scientists—in particular, students of contemporary Chinese society—viewed the campaign? To what extent can their views be systematically evaluated?

5

These are the questions that will be considered in this chapter. I will begin by giving some definitional essentials on (1) the meaning of socialist transformation and (2) the campaign and its importance in contemporary Chinese society. I will then briefly discuss the origins—comparative, historical, and ideological—of the campaign. The stage will then be set for a discussion of how Western social scientists and students of China in particular have viewed the campaign strategy. The most systematic analysis of the campaign to date has been done by anthropologist William Skinner and sociologist Edwin Winckler. This analysis is examined at some length in order to permit the extraction of testable hypotheses. These hypotheses are then juxtaposed to alternate ones which dispute the thoughts of Skinner and Winckler, along with others.

SOCIALIST TRANSFORMATION AND THE CAMPAIGN

Socialist transformation, as Mao and his supporters saw it, holds as its central ultimate goal complete political and economic equality—i.e., total equality in distribution of power and resources throughout the society—ultimately producing a communist state. However, since the achievement of this state is believed to be possible only in the distant future, some inequalities between different groups, especially leaders and led, must be recognized. Thus, the goal is to minimize these differences, to get everyone to think and work in terms of the collective whole, to transform the society from a position of individual thinking and self-advancement to one in which all serve the socialist whole. In practical terms it has meant reining in groups believed to have been consciously trying to sabotage socialist goals, working to bring about in everyone the change from an individualistic to a collective orientation, and building the institutions that can sustain and foster a collectively oriented development of society for the material and ideological benefit of the greatest number. These three immediate goals are at the center of the major types of mass mobilization campaigns examined in this book.

Indeed the hallmark of Chinese Communism is its continuing reliance on the mass mobilization campaign to implement socialist transformation in all facets of Chinese social, political, and economic life. Although observers of China differ widely on the utility of campaigns in China, all will readily attest to their prevalence and importance (e.g., Bennett, 1976: 15; Townsend, 1967: 185). Let two examples suffice:

> The implementation of policy by means of mass mobilization is one of the most distinctive features of the Chinese political process. Since 1949 the Chinese masses have participated in over one hundred mass movements [Gardner, 1969: 477].

> The communists rarely, in fact, try to carry out any important domestic policy without organizing a mass campaign to support it [Barnett, 1964: 135].

The Campaign Defined

In short, campaigns are the central feature in policy implementation, in the effort to fulfill China's goal of socialist transformation. What then is the campaign? Formally defined, the mass mobilization campaign in China is an

> organized mobilization of collective action aimed at transforming thought patterns, class/power relationships and/or economic institutions and productivity.[1]

There is no simple formula for identifying the delimiting parameters of a campaign, or for saying when one begins and when it ends. Often the Chinese will use either *campaign* or *mass movement* to label a series of events. The label is not always used, however, to indicate a campaign. More helpful in identifying a campaign is the concept that all campaigns involve an increased intensity of activity beyond what is expected in regular work and living routines. For example, if factory leaders issue a statement that production should be increased, and the matter is perfunctorily discussed in the course of a regularized study session, it should not be considered a campaign, even though the factory bulletin board may contain some new slogans or articles about raising production. However, if the frequency of study sessions increases, if slogans are mounted over entrances to the factory, if new bulletin boards are erected, if new plans for mass participation are laid in a new and special effort to increase production—if, in short, information and activity indicate special efforts and heightened mass participation and people are mobilized out of their normal work and/or living patterns, then these events are a campaign. The absence of an explicit formula means that for marginal sets of events there may be some disagreement over whether the events actually constitute a campaign. Moreover, what may not start out as a campaign may in due course become one, or vice versa. [Bennett (1976: 17–18) in his monograph on campaigns also admits to the inability to be precise.]

In many cases it is possible to trace the origin and termination points of a campaign to speeches, policy statements, meetings, or conferences. For example, mobilization meetings announcing plans for a campaign are often held at the local level at the commencement of each campaign. However, a few campaigns do not have these demarcation points. (Hence the uncertainty over some dates in Appendix 1.) In spite of the instances of uncertainty, for most campaigns neither the definitional nor the parameter question is a problem.[2]

[1] See *HQ*, November 1, 1959. Different sources refer to *mass movement, mass mobilization campaign, mass campaign*, or just *campaign*. The Chinese in their own translations switch back and forth between some variant of *movement* and *campaign*. In Chinese the referent is always a single term: *qum zhonq yun dong*, literally translated as "mass movement." The term *mass mobilization campaign*, or *campaign* for short, will be used here in order to emphasize the dual components of organization and mass participation.

[2] The process of selecting and researching the campaigns is considered at length in Chapter 3.

Campaign Types

Having considered how to recognize that a series of events is indeed a campaign, and knowing that it is possible to identify clear demarcation points in most cases, we can now look at subtypes of campaigns. Three distinctive subtypes, first mentioned by F. T. C. Yu (1967: 201–202), will be discussed. Even though each type has elements of the others, we can, on the basis of emphasis, classify each campaign as belonging *primarily* to one of the three types.[3]

First are *economic* campaigns. They are usually directed at agricultural, industrial, commercial, and/or medical sectors of the society. Economic campaigns emphasize the improvement of economic conditions directly, or indirectly through building institutions whose establishment is expected to lead to improved economic conditions. Statements issued in the media and at meetings usually make it clear that this campaign type is one aimed primarily at making changes in these institutions and increasing productive output. Leaders talk of "socialist construction," of "still greater efforts" by the masses to break old records and reach new production levels or new standards in physical surroundings. Some of the campaigns classified as economic are the Mutual Aid Teams (MAT) campaign, the campaigns for lower and higher level Agricultural Producers' Cooperatives (APC), the Socialist Reform of Private Business campaign, the Barefoot Doctors campaign, and the Great Leap Forward (GLF) and its associated campaigns such as the Communes and the Backyard Furnaces.

The second type of campaign is primarily *ideological* in character. The ideological campaign is aimed at changing thinking, and cultural and educational standards, correcting erroneous thoughts (i.e., those opposing the prevailing ideological standard), raising each person's general political consciousness, and opposing anti-socialist forces outside the society. In socialist terminology, the primary aim of both ideological and economic campaigns is to resolve non-antagonistic contradictions existing among the people (as opposed to antagonistic contradictions between the people and the enemy). Although the attitudes targeted for change may conflict with "correct socialist thinking," they are not seen as seriously threatening the existing Chinese socialist state. Among the list of ideological campaigns are the Party rectification campaigns, the Resist America–Aid Korea campaign, the 1958 Cultural Revolution, the campaign to Learn from the PLA (People's Liberation Army), and the campaign to Train a Revolutionary Successor Generation.

The third type is the *struggle* campaign, a special type of ideological campaign. Like ideological campaigns, struggle campaigns are aimed at correcting

---

[3] For a discussion of these campaigns see Chapter 2. Listings of the campaigns are found in Appendices 1, 2, and 3.

erroneous thinking, but their focus is on the elimination of the power base and/or class position of enemy classes or groups. They are aimed at resolving antagonistic contradictions. Press reports focus on types of people and individual persons who have seriously erred and must be "struggled" as enemies of the people. The Agrarian Reform campaign, aimed at eliminating the power and position of the landlords, was a struggle campaign, as were the Suppression of Counterrevolutionaries (e.g., Nationalist spies, bandits); the Anti-Rightist campaign, aimed at eliminating the influence of intellectuals and others "opposed" to socialism; and the Great Proletarian Cultural Revolution (GPCR), aimed in part at eliminating the power of the "capitalist roaders."

Why just these three categories? Other typologies were, in fact, examined and found to be less useful.[4] Moreover, this typology has the advantage of distinguishing the two types of contradictions—antagonistic versus nonantagonistic. (As I will argue later, the existence of contradictions and the efforts to resolve them form the major motivating force for and the explanation of the campaigns.) The typology further distinguishes between two clearly very different types of campaigns both aimed at resolving nonantagonistic contradictions—those more attitudinal in thrust and those concerned more with structural, institutional, or production changes.[5]

The typology also corresponds closely with the three goals of sociologist Amitai Etzioni's and with sinologists William Skinner and Edwin Winckler's compliance model, a model that has been the major source for the generation of testable hypotheses (see below). Before turning to the generation of hypotheses, however, it is important to look at the campaign's origins.

THE ORIGINS OF THE CAMPAIGN

Most societies do not show China's high incidence of campaigns as a strategy for policy implementation, for development, or for socialist transformation. What, then, is the campaign's origin? What has been the impact of the Soviet

---

[4] The original rationale for dividing the campaigns into these three types was empirical. In the first section of Chapter 3, several typologies are noted. In the early stages of statistical analysis, it appeared that the economic/ideological/struggle typology was the only one to show significant differences on the three major variables in the study—mobilization, shortcomings, and achievements.

[5] Still, one might ask this question: Even if it is possible to isolate the primary goals of a campaign, is it not true that there are secondary goals as well, and how can they be ignored? The simple answer is that they are *not* ignored. At this point, the effort is merely being made to find a significant and meaningful means to classify the campaigns. Chapters 5 and 6, on shortcomings and achievements, by examining different types of outcomes, integrate the fact that although one goal is primary, multiple goals exist.

experience,[6] of the Chinese Communist experience and ideology, on the development of the campaign strategy in China?

The Soviet Experience

The Soviet Union has, since its beginning, experienced substantial campaign-type activity: e.g., the *Subbotnik* movement (work on Saturday) and Communist Youth Shock brigades during Lenin's years (Sorenson, 1969: 42, 183); the Transformation of Women's Status in Central Asia, Collectivization, and *Stakhanov* movements of Stalin's years (Massell, 1968: 214), and the Virgin Lands and Anti–Social Parasite movements of Khrushchev's years (Armstrong, 1967: 164–171; Cleary, 1965; Nove, 1964: 152–154). Some of the Russian campaigns were similar to mass mobilization efforts in China, but they were characterized more by top-down control, little real mobilization or participation of people, little voluntary compliance, and large doses of coercion to get the campaign carried out. Moreover, in Russia the frequency of campaigns has been lower. Also, in Russia major policies have been more likely to be carried out apart from campaigns.

Thus, beyond the presence of campaign-type activity in Russia, there is little evidence that the Chinese Communists' heavy emphasis on mass mobilization and participation via the campaign is drawn from the Russian experience (Bennett, 1973: 6). Where the Chinese emphasized persuasion, the Russians emphasized coercion—especially during larger mobilization efforts such as collectivization (Bernstein, 1967; Rue, 1966: 1; Schram, 1967: 333–334; Whyte, 1970: 350). Where the Chinese were more likely to use rectification on their ideological enemies, the Russian leaders would turn to physical extermination:

> In Russia there was little group pressure to induce individual self-reform through small group pressures as in China, and no genuine Soviet equivalent of Mao's "curing the illness in order to save the patient." Moreover, particularly under Stalin, Soviet educational measures were marked by extreme routinization, profound cynicism on the part of participants, and generous applications of coercion [Teiwes, 1971: 14].

In China the emphasis seems to have been quite the contrary:

> In both systems persuasive and coercive measures have been intertwined but the Chinese have been more subtle in combining the two methods and have shown a much greater willingness to rely on persuasive techniques [Teiwes, 1971: 16].

[6] Other socialist societies have made use of the campaign strategy as well, particularly Cuba and the Democratic Republic of Vietnam (for Cuba see Goldenberg, 1965; Green, 1970; Matthews, 1969; for Vietnam see Burchett, 1966; Chaliand, 1969; Klein and Weiner, 1959; for a summary of Vietnam and Korea see Bennett, 1973: 6–10).

It is noteworthy that, as in China, the revolutionary movements in both Vietnam and Cuba went through a period of protracted guerilla struggle before liberation (i.e., assuming control of the central government). However, they will not be discussed here, because their origins largely postdate the socialist transformation process in China.

Why the difference? The rise of Russian Communists to power was not marked by a long and protracted guerilla struggle lasting some 20 years. As a consequence, on the eves of Communist victories in both countries, the composition and experience of the leadership of China and Russia stood in marked contrast.

Although in 1917 in Russia and in 1949 in China the population of both countries was at least 80% rural, in Russia only 14.5% of the Party members came from peasant backgrounds (Schapiro, 1959: 234). In China, however, as late as 1956, after 6 years of membership recruitment in the cities, 69% of the Party members came from peasant backgrounds (Lewis, 1963: 108). Moreover, in Russia, at the time of recruitment in 1917, only 2% were actually peasants (Lewin, 1968), although in China in 1956, 58% were actually peasants at the time of recruitment (Schurmann, 1968: 133).

The top Russian leaders had little firsthand knowledge of protracted struggle. Lenin returned from exile after the initial battles had been won. There was no gruelling and tempering Long March, no Yenan in Russia. Party members, cadre leaders in Russia have been largely urban in orientation and experience, in spite of the overwhelming predominance of the rural population.

This lack of orientation and experience in the countryside was soon to take its toll in Russia. The Party was essentially ignorant of rural life (Lewin, 1968: 82). Unlike the Chinese, the Russian leadership penetrated the peasant village with difficulty, found it difficult to mobilize the peasantry, and was frequently faced with disruption and resistance (Whyte, 1970: 286–292). Thus, for example, during the collectivization campaign of the late 1920s, much of the leadership came from the outside to direct the campaign. Prior to the formation of the *kolkhozes* (collectives) there was no leadership training (Bernstein, 1967: 19–20). Party leaders were often weak and corrupt, caring little about the peasants, open to bribery from the *kulaks* (rich peasants), and willing to engage in arbitrary and indiscriminate confiscation and deportation of even poor and middle-class peasants (Fainsod, 1958: 144–145, 246, 278). This is in marked contrast to the Chinese situation where, with little exception, the rural leadership was almost exclusively peasant (see, e.g., Bernstein, 1967; Hinton, 1968).

Administrative solutions by leaders unknowing and even uncaring of the realities of rural life dominated policy implementation in Russia. Careerism and bureaucracy dominated the leadership ranks of Russia:

> By 1921, with the end of the civil war, membership in the Party no longer called for self-sacrifice, and the green light was given to careerists [Schapiro, 1959: 232].

> Decision making in the Soviet Union has been largely of an administrative character, and hence has been in the hands of the bureaucrats. . . .
> The rapid bureaucratization of Soviet society and the extreme centralization of power created a mass level organizational leader very different in nature from the Chinese Communist cadre [Schurmann, 1961: 159, 158].

Not only was there no GPCR to combat the tendencies of bureaucracy and privilege; there was never any concerted effort to carry out thoroughgoing rectification campaigns equivalent to six or seven such campaigns in China (Teiwes, 1971). The rectification campaign Hinton so graphically describes in *Fanshen* (1968), where peasants were encouraged, even implored, by cadres usually of rural or peasant background to criticize their own local Party leaders thoroughly, never could have happened in Russia under a leadership so alienated from peasant countryside.

At best, the Russian leadership paid lip service to identifying and integrating with the rural proletariat. At worst, because of lack of experience and the absence of antidotes to bureaucracy and careerism, the leadership was totally alienated from the majority of the population, especially from the peasants. Their experience, or lack of it, prevented the Soviet leader from developing the ideology and working style characteristic of the Chinese Communist-led revolution. In short, although the form of the Chinese mobilization campaign existed in Russia, the Chinese inspiration for the content must be found elsewhere.

The Chinese Communist Experience: Mao and the Impact of History

The impact of history and the influence of Mao's thought are closely meshed as the two dominant factors in the Party's ideology and working style. The comprehensiveness of Mao's thought and his commitment to its realization were based on the harsh realities of the Communists' long years in opposition.

Mao's early years as a Marxist and member of the new Chinese Communist party (CCP) reflected a traditional Marxist emphasis on the importance of the urban proletariat.[7] At the same time his thinking, at least on the role of the peasantry, was being influenced by Li Ta-chao, Mao's mentor at the Peking University library and one of the founders of the CCP in 1921 (Schram, 1967: 48):

> Li maintained that "our China is a rural nation and a majority of the laboring class is composed of these peasants. If they are not liberated then our whole nation will not be liberated." In 1920 he spoke of the Chinese people as a "proletarian nation," making no distinction between peasant and urban worker. He continued to stress the role of the peasantry and in 1926, without mentioning the lead of the proletariat, called on the peasants to "rely on their own strength" [Harrison, 1969: 45].[8]

[7] In one of his earliest essays, the "Analysis of the Classes in Chinese Society," written in 1926, Mao recognized the existence of a "rural proletariat" in the form of hired "farm labourers" and a "lumpen proletariat" of handicraftsmen and peasants who had lost their land. However, the industrial proletariat was to be "the leading force of the revolution [Mao, 1967: Vol. 1, 18–19]."

[8] For an extended discussion of Mao's ideological mix of Marxism and populism, see Meisner, 1971.

Then in the mid-1920s Mao served as head of the Peasant Institute in Canton. He returned to his native province of Hunan to make an investigation of the peasantry. In his report on the peasant movement, written in 1927, the poor peasants had now become the "vanguard of the revolution [Mao, 1967: Vol. 1, 30–34]." The subsequent rejection of this report was one of the factors accounting for the split in the CCP. This split and the earlier KMT coups against the CCP in March 1926 and June 1927 contributed to Mao's return to the countryside of southern China to begin what was to be nearly a quarter of a century in guerilla opposition. It was during the trials and tribulations of these harsh years that the Communist strategy of socialist transformation through mass mobilization was forged, tested, and developed.

As early as the late 1920s Mao had begun to develop the process of rectification to meet problems such as opportunism, localism, and careerism (Lewis, 1963: 18). The techniques he developed, however, were concentrated on the Party; less emphasis was given to mass participation and involvement.

The small livelihood base encountered in the Chingkiang mountains in 1928–1929 forced the Communists' removal to the Kiangsi–Fukien border areas, where Mao continued to rethink his ideology and working style (Lewis, 1963: 18). Although this period (the early 1930s) witnessed some early efforts to rely more on mass mobilization and participation (Kim, 1969), the strategy was not properly developed to win enough peasant support to ultimately ward off the KMT armies (*PC*, June 16, 1957: 28).

It is from the experience of the trials and tribulations of the Long March that Mao wrote, in 1937, "On Practice" and "On Contradiction" (Mao, 1971). How was the Party to act if it was to win the genuine loyalty of the Chinese people, to survive and grow among them like a "fish in the sea?"

"ON CONTRADICTION" AND "ON PRACTICE"

These two seminal theoretical essays, "On Practice" and "On Contradiction," bring together Mao's comprehension of objective conditions in China, tie in his understanding of Marxist–Leninist thought, and suggest in broad theoretical terms his paradigm of change, of socialist transformation that has guided China:

> Changes in society are due chiefly to the development of the internal contradictions in society, that is the contradictions between productive forces and the relations of production, the contradiction between classes and the contradiction between the old and the new; it is the development of these contradictions that pushes society forward and gives the impetus for the supersession of the old society by the new [Mao, 1967: Vol. 1, 314].

Drawing from Marx, Mao also affirmed the universality of contradictions:

> Contradiction is universal and absolute, it is present in the process of the development of all things and permeates every process from beginning to end.

... there is nothing that does not contain contradictions; without contradiction
nothing would exist [Mao, 1967: Vol. 1, 316, 318].

Contradictions exist at all levels of society. Innumerable contradictions exist
at the same time. The task, therefore, in pushing society forward, in bringing
about change and implementing the socialist transformation program, is to be
able to identify at any given time the most important contradiction.[9] This
principal contradiction will establish the "general line" for the current phase of
transformation in society. The ability to identify the principal contradictions
comes from the ability to integrate knowledge and practice:

> The movement of change in the world of objective reality is never ending and so is
> man's cognition of truth through practice. Marxism—Leninism has in no way ex-
> hausted truth but ceaselessly opens up roads to the knowledge of truth in the course
> of practice. Our conclusion is the concrete, historical unity of the subjective and the
> objective, of theory and practice, of knowing and doing [Mao, 1967: Vol. 1,
> 307–308].[10]

Mao argued that the first stem in the process of the cognition of truth and the
knowledge of contradictions is *perception.* This is the task of going out,
interacting with the people and circumstances around, using all one's senses to
understand the situation thoroughly (Mao, 1967: Vol. 1, 297–302). One's role
is not unlike that of the "participant—observer" interacting with society.

> The second step is to synthesize the data of perception by arranging and reconstruct-
> ing them; this belongs to the stage of conception, judgement and inference. It is only
> when the data of perception are very rich (not fragmentary) and correspond to
> reality (are not illusory) that they can be the basis for forming correct concepts and
> theories [Mao, 1967: Vol. 1, 302].

One should be continually asking questions, trying to understand the relationship of one observation to another, trying to search for the principle behind the
relationship of one thing to another.

> As social practice continues, things that give rise to man's sense perception and
> impression in the course of his practice are repeated many times; then a sudden
> change (leap) takes place in the brain in the process of cognition, and concepts are
> formed. Concepts are no longer phenomena, the separate aspects and the external
> relations of things; they grasp the essence, the totality and the internal relations of
> things [Mao, 1967: Vol. 1, 298].

[9] For an illustrative listing of the important contradictions at the time of the Great Leap
Forward, see Schurmann, 1968: 102–103.
[10] In philosophical terms, one can, of course, trace the relationship of knowing and doing
far back, before the advent of Marxism and Leninism, as far back as the ancient Greeks,
especially Aristotle (Lobkowicz, 1967).

It is from these two steps that one should be able to identify principal contradictions of the time. And how does one know that these are, in fact, the principal contradictions? That is the task of the third stage: verification:

> Marxist philosophy holds that the most important problem does not lie in understanding the laws of the objective world and thus being able to explain it, but in applying the knowledge of these laws actively to change the world. . . . Knowledge begins with practice and must then be returned to practice [Mao, 1967: Vol. 1, 304].

Mao cited, as examples of the verification process,

> the fulfillment of an engineering plan, the verification of a scientific hypothesis, the manufacture of an implement, or the reaping of a crop; or in the process of changing society, take for example the victory of a strike, victory in a war or the fulfillment of an educational plan [Mao, 1967: Vol. 1, 305].

Mao recognized, however, that whether one is engaged "in the practice of changing nature or of changing society, a person's original ideas, theories, plans, or programs are seldom realized without any alteration [Mao, 1967: Vol. 1, 305]." This is due not only to changing natural and social conditions but also to a person's limitation in knowing and understanding a particular process. In short, it is very difficult to master the stages of perception and conception so perfectly that one's theories will be verified without change.[11]

The combining of theory and practice, the realization of the steps of perception, cognition, and verification, comes to fruition in concrete terms with the implementation of the mass line.

THE MASS LINE

Although the difficulties of the late 1920s and early 1930s before the Yenan period (1936–1945) had influenced elements of the mass line, as a working style it fully emerged during Yenan. It is the hallmark of the Yenan period and indeed of even the entire Chinese Communist guerilla movement.[12]

---

[11] It is from this discussion that Mao developed the core definitions of *left* and *right* deviations. Right deviations essentially fail to recognize and move with the changing social conditions. Left deviations, on the other hand, come from proceeding beyond the actual social conditions. Both deviations occur because there has been an alienation from the masses and consequent failure to understand the actual social conditions of a majority of the people (Mao, 1967: Vol. 1, 306–307).

[12] "Although other Communists, both Chinese and Russian, had advocated popular support and the consistency of idea and action, Mao was the first Chinese leader to develop in action a consistent line based not on authority but on the reciprocal and organized relationship between political leaders and the general Chinese population [Lewis, 1963: 22]." This central element of Mao's and ultimately the Party's thinking and practice is portrayed here only in skeletal form. For other explanations see Townsend, 1967: 72–74; Selden, 1971: 274–276; Pfeffer, 1971: 270–271; and especially Lewis, 1963: 70–100.

The great contribution of the Yenan period was the discovery of concrete methods for linking popular participation in the guerilla struggle with a wide-ranging community attack on rural problems. In people's war community action penetrated to every village and every family, and involved every individual. This required new approaches to leadership which were eventually raised to the level of theory as the mass line. . . . The history of the Chinese Communist movement since the Yenan period, particularly its extraordinary record in carrying forward China's economic development and social transformation, has been shaped in large measure by the enduring commitment to the mass line. Enshrined in 1943 as the party's fundamental leadership principle, it remains so to this day [Selden, 1971: 276].

Described as the fundamental political and organization line of the Party, the mass line is based on the belief that "people are the real makers of history" and that they have "boundless creative power." Therefore while Communists should serve and keep close to the people, they cannot take the place of the people or take over from them. "Merely through the efforts of the vanguard and without the genuine consciousness and mobilization of the people themselves," says Liu Shao-chi, "emancipation of the people is impossible, history will not move forward and nothing can be accomplished." Thus the Communists cannot "bestow emancipation" upon the people; they can only lead the people in struggle to emancipate themselves. And they can lead neither by ordering the poeple about ["commandism"] or by trailing behind ["tailism"]; but only by learning from them, systematizing and refining their knowledge and expereince, returning it to them as their own policy and then leading them into action for it. The mass line thus "comes from the masses" and "goes back to the masses," though what comes from them is raw material, what goes back is processed. It arises from and expresses the unity between masses and leaders . . . [Crook and Crook, 1966: 221].[13]

In all the practical work of our Party, all correct leadership is necessarily "from the masses to the masses." This means: take the ideas of the masses (scattered and unsystematic ideas) and concentrate them (through study turn them into concen trated and systematic ideas), then go to the masses and propagate and explain these ideas until the masses embrace them as their own, hold fast to them and translate them into action, and test the correctness of these ideas in such action. Then once again concentrate ideas from the masses and once again go to the masses so that the ideas are persevered in and carried through. And so on, over and over again in an endless spiral, with the ideas becoming more correct, more vital and richer each time. Such is the Marxist theory of knowledge [Mao, 1967: Vol. 3, 119].

[13] In China there are two types of leaders: *activists* or informal leaders who may emerge for a short-term period, usually during a campaign, and *cadres* (*gan bu*) who occupy formal positions with specific responsibilities in government organizations and as leaders of health, education, production, and other units. Not all cadres are Party members. However, virtually all Party members are cadres—possible exceptions being a Party member who is a peasant or factory worker but who does not occupy a formal leadership position. The masses consist of the non-cadre population. Together the masses and cadres combine to form the "people," who are distinguished from the "enemy." The participation of enemy elements in society is not governed by the mass line. For a discussion of the manner of their participation and how it is determined who is or is not an enemy, see the following section of this chapter.

Lewis sees the mass line as containing four progressive stages (1963: 72), two of which closely resemble Mao's stages in "On Practice," except that where "On Practice" is directed at both leaders and masses, the mass line techniques are specifically directed at the relationship *between* leaders and masses.

The first of these stages is that of perception. Cadres should always be interacting with and understanding the views and needs of the masses. They are expected to spend a great deal of time working and interacting with the members of the local unit they serve,[14] in order to carry out the processes of perception and verification correctly. Mao even suggested that cadres select two or three subunits under their jurisdiction for intensive study—a practice that continues to this day (Cell, 1973–1974). Moreover, ever since 1941 higher-level cadres have been "sent down" to villages for extensive periods of work. If cadres open themselves to the feelings of peasants and workers and really seek to understand, they will be able to perceive the objective social conditions correctly—the first stage in the integration of theory and practice.

At all times, but especially when going to lower levels, cadres are expected to submit reports on their observations and to make recommendations for action. This is known as the stage of summarization—the reporting of lower levels up to higher levels and, when necessary, the consolidation of reports to still higher levels.

From these reports comes the stage of authorization—the formulation of new programs, often campaigns, aimed at resolving the problem or contradiction. Minor contradictions may be handled within the unit, but those that affect larger areas are tentatively decided upon at higher levels based on reports, recommendations, and the direct experiences of high-level cadres who have gone to investigate at basic levels of society.[15]

General directives are then sent to the local level for adaptation and implementation on the basis of prevailing conditions. At this point cadres are expected to do more than simply issue orders by use of administrative ma-

[14] A *unit* is an institution for the organization of work, living, learning, and the like. Newspapers, offices, schools, hospitals, and factories are all units. In most rural areas Agricultural Production Teams are the basic production units. In the city, the neighborhood is the basic living unit. (Communes, Production Brigades, Street Committees are also units.) Everyone belongs at least to one unit and most belong to more. Membership is determined by where one lives, works, and/or goes to school on a long-term basis. Hence a patient in a hospital would not belong to the hospital unit, but the entire staff would.

[15] These shorter investigative efforts are not the same as being sent down. Here a cadre goes to a basic-level unit (e.g., rural production team, factory, school, hospital, residence area) for a short period (varying from a few hours to a few days) to observe and gather specific information. When a cadre is sent down (*xia fang*), he is temporarily or permanently suspended from his present position and unit and transferred to a more basic unit, usually agriculture, for a period of time varying from a few weeks or months to several years so that he may obtain a deeper and more general feeling of the prevailing conditions and re-examine their own thinking and attitudes. (See Chapter 4 for additional discussion of *xia fang*.)

chinery.[16] Rather, they are expected to move the masses to a higher state of consciousness (i.e., cognition) by mobilizing, organizing, educating, and convincing them.

This is the final stage of the mass line—verification or the implementation of the program campaign. Implementation may first be attempted on an experimental basis in several localities, or it may begin more or less simultaneously in all areas. In either case, adjustments are made on the basis of prevailing local conditions. As reports are fed back during the process of implementation, many additional adjustments are made, often minor, but sometimes major.

THE ENEMY AND CLASS ANALYSIS

The mass line governs interaction among the people, between the masses and the cadres; it governs the process of resolving nonantagonistic contradictions. However, apart from the masses, there is the enemy. In 1949, for example, the enemy consisted of the KMT leadership, the big capitalists, and the worst of the landlords, all of whom were distinguished by their crimes of excessive usury, rape, brutality, and the like.

In a report commemorating the twenty-eighth anniversary of the Communist party in 1949, Mao took note of the changing class alignments. Enemy, "reactionary" classes were to be dealt with on the basis of coercion. Through persuasion, education, and criticism, these classes were to be given a chance to reform, to become productive members of society. If they refused, they would be coerced as enemies of the people:

> As for members of the reactionary classes and individual reactionaries, so long as they do not rebel, sabotage or create trouble after their political power has been overthrown, land and work will be given to them as well in order to allow them to live and remould themselves through labour into new people. If they are not willing to work, the people's state will compel them to work. Propaganda and educational work will be done among them too, and will be done, moreover, with as much care and thoroughness as among the captured army officers in the past. This, too, may be called a "policy of benevolence" if you like, but it is imposed by us on the members of the enemy classes and cannot be mentioned in the same breath with the work of self-education which we carry on within the ranks of the revolutionary people [Mao, 1967: Vol. 4, 419].

Coercion was not to be used on those not classified as enemies, although there might be a few individual exceptions:

> Here the method we must employ is democratic, the method of persuasion, not of compulsion. When anyone among the people breaks the law, he too should be punished, imprisoned or even sentenced to death; but this is a matter of a few

---

[16] This error is known as *commandism*. The reverse error is *tailism*, the problem of simply responding to the short-term demands of the masses without trying to raise their consciousness. See Liu Shao-chi, 1945.

individual cases, and it differs in principle from the dictatorship exercised over the reactionaries as the class [Mao, 1967: Vol. 4, 417].

Thus struggle campaigns, by definition aimed at the enemy, often involve more abrasive and confrontational kinds of meetings and activities (see Chapter 4 for more detailed description of these events).

Here then, in summary, and in theory, is the Chinese Communist ideology and the mass line work-style. The central strategy utilizing the mass line has been the mass mobilization campaign.

> Instead of mass line techniques being institutionalized as a part of routine decision-making, mass line techniques tended to be embodied primarily in waves of mass campaigns [Pfeffer, 1971: 271].[17]

Indeed, a brief outline of the general pattern of the development of most campaigns suggests there is a link between Mao's notions of the mass line and his ideas on the integration of theory and practice. Although there is no precise number or labeling officially given to the stages most campaigns go through, four stages seem apparent: (1) policy formulation, (2) information dissemination, (3) mass participation, and (4) summation and evaluation.[18]

Policy Formulation. Someone—usually it was Mao himself or one of his supporters—first suggests that a particular campaign is needed. In his essay "On Practice" and as a part of mass line politics, Mao made quite clear the need for constant reporting of conditions up to higher levels in society. For cadres, this is a part of the stage of perception, described earlier. From this kind of reporting May and other leaders were made aware of problems, such as the difficulties experienced in the cooperative organization in agriculture in 1954 and early 1955, and the contradictions relating to agricultural organization and production in the mid-1960s. If the contradictions are deemed to be central enough, proposals are made and circulated for greater mass mobilization to resolve the contradiction. For example, on July 31, 1955, Mao made a speech to Party secretaries attacking the slow pace of cooperativization in the countryside and calling for greater mobilization efforts. This formulation of a mobilization program basically corresponds to the stage of conception in Mao's essay "On Practice," or to the stage of authorization in the mass line.

However, there is no assurance at this point that the campaign will be adopted. There is often opposition requiring that the new policy be discussed and debated. For example, in the case of Mao's 1955 speech, it was not until October 1955 that the speech was published, signaling his victory, and campaign

---

[17] This and subsequent quotes cited to Pfeffer, 1971 are reprinted by permission from Richard Pfeffer, "Mao Tse-tung and the Cultural Revolution," in Norman Miller and Roderick Aya (eds.), *National Liberation,* copyright © 1971 by Free Press, a division of Macmillan Publishing Company.
[18] Skinner and Winckler (1969) suggest that there are six phases to each campaign.

efforts began. Although the GPCR did not begin in earnest until May 1966, or even June, Mao, as far back as January 1965, had come to the conclusion, based primarily on Liu Shao-chi's statements and actions especially after the GLF, that Liu would have to be removed (Schram, 1972: 292; see Chapter 2 for a discussion of the events leading to each campaign). Even though there was never any "blueprint" for the GPCR, the decision that a major mass mobilization effort would have to be made came some time after Mao's January 1965 decision, but prior to the beginning of the GPCR in May 1966. The intervening time was spent building support for the mobilization effort.

Implementation: Information Dissemination. A public statement announcing the campaign is issued, often via a special report, a special combined editorial in the *People's Daily* and *Red Flag,* or the posting of "big character posters." The process has now moved to the point of verification of the policy decision to undertake a campaign.

Although the population is somewhat involved in actually doing things related to the campaign, such as writing letters or essays about the campaign, such activity is generally very low-keyed. The people at this point are more likely to be receivers of information, via mobilization meetings, articles, and editorials discussing the campaign. Study groups begin to meet with greater frequency in order to explain the need for the campaign and generate commitment for the more active phase of the campaign.[19]

Implementation: Mass Participation. The campaign swings into full gear, emphasizing the maximum participation in the campaign by the appropriate sectors of the population. Although the level of mobilization and the kinds of activities vary greatly from campaign to campaign (see Chapter 4), there can be such activities as mass rallies; meetings to criticize, struggle, and condemn; and going to other places, often the countryside, to participate in the campaign.

Summation and Evaluation. The campaign has been completed. There is often an effort to evaluate the results, to determine whether it was basically successful—i.e., whether the contradiction was essentially resolved, and whether new problems or contradictions have emerged. Since resolution is not always forthcoming, the decision must be made whether to delay further efforts to resolve the contradictions, since other contradictions may be considered more important; to move ahead with a new mobilization campaign in the effort to resolve the still existing contradictions; or to undertake yet a new campaign to resolve the new contradictions that arose from the campaign just completed.[20]

Although this summary of the campaigns' origins is brief and skeletal, it is now possible to make some tentative judgment as to which antecedents are more

[19] This phase and the one that follows are two central parts of the mobilization process examined in Chapter 4. Solomon basically agrees on the distinction of these two implementation phases (1971: 348).

[20] This circular pattern is discussed in greater detail in Chapter 2.

important. Although the Russian experience may have had some impact on the form of campaign activity in China, the content of the Chinese-style campaign owes more to the harsh realities of the years in opposition, especially during the Yenan period.[21] To these objective conditions Mao added his understanding of Marxism—Leninism. Nor should we forget Mao's strong ties to and faith in the peasant population. Mao came from peasant stock, mixed well with the peasants of Yenan, and until his death remained a leader of simple tastes (Harrison, 1969: 48–49; Snow, 1972: 187). In short, Mao's own background led him to develop strategies emphasizing direct contact between leader and led, stressing mass participation and mobilization over hierarchical control and bureaucratic management.[22]

The harsh realities of the years in opposition and especially the Yenan experience necessitated these strategies. His understanding of Marxism—Leninism, expressed in his essays "On Practice" and "On Contradiction" and in his development of the mass line as the central operational technique, provided the basis for these strategies. Indeed, in retrospect, given the objective realities of the time, Mao's own background, and his ideological commitment, it is difficult to see what other options there might have been.

THE UTILITY OF CAMPAIGNS: VIEWS FROM THE WEST

Although most Western observers of China agree on the importance of the campaigns in China—and most of them would not seriously disagree with the preceding summary of the relative importance of the antecedents—there is extremely wide disagreement on the utility of campaign mobilization strategies. Because of the prevalence and importance of the campaigns, virtually every observer has at some point reviewed some aspect of the campaigns. To name all such observers and comment on their positions would be an impossible task. Just as every observer has a position, so is every position somewhat peculiar to each observer. There has been little systematic and comparative analysis on the subject of the campaign, and hence little effort to find and sift through the vast number of views, opinions, and positions.

What follows is by no means an effort to discover, identify, and categorize the views of every observer of China. Rather it is an attempt to characterize the three main strands of thought that emerge on the utility of the campaign in a

---

[21] Indeed this will become even clearer in Chapter 2 when a closer look will be given to the Yenan campaigns and their relationship to the ones that followed.

[22] This is in sharp contrast to Liu Shao-chi, who spent most of his years in opposition leading a secret hierarchical underground party behind enemy lines, or to even Chou En-lai, of urban middle-class background, the taskmaster of organization and bureaucracy, who knew how to make the system work on a day-to-day basis.

changing Chinese society. For each strand, illustrations will be given hopefully including what most observers would agree are the most important positions. Reference will be made to important statements by observers of other socialist societies. These two sets, when possible, will then be tied back to more general social science perspectives. This latter task will help to provide some basis for understanding the rationale for these different positions.

What, then, are these three strands? The first argues that campaigns are negative in their utility, that mobilization strategies are designed only to gain the population's acquiescence, not their ideological commitment. Thus little of value for the population comes from the campaign. The second position stakes out an intermediate ground. It suggests that campaigns, and their implied high levels of mobilization, may be beneficial in certain places and at certain times, perhaps for ideological purposes or in the transitional period just after a government has assumed national leadership. The third position sees the campaign mobilization strategy as being of continuing benefit to the society, particularly with reference to the socialist transformation of the society. The next step is to examine each position closely.

Campaign Mobilization Strategies: Negative

The strongest proponents of the negative view of mobilization strategies are often observers of socialist societies other than China. Sociologist, Philip Selznick and Vietnam analyist, Douglas Pike are chief among them. But such views also exist among observers of China, most notably political scientists, Chalmers Johnson and Richard Solomon, and possibly even to a limited extent anthropologist William Skinner and sociologist Edwin Winckler. At first reading one might question how it is possible to lump together a Chalmers Johnson who is dealing with the origins of the Chinese Communist movement, a Douglas Pike who is asking how the Vietnamese Communists work, and a Richard Solomon who is investigating Mao's relationship to authority structures. However, deeper penetration into their respective positions finds them all quite compatible.

Essentially, they all deny that Communism has provided a positive ideology that could win acceptance by the population. They believe, rather, that the Communists came to power and/or have maintained their power through their abilities to organize, manipulate, and/or capitalize on the peasants' built-in fear of authority and foreign aggressors.[23] In short, although each may attempt a somewhat different explanation, all agree on the end result.

---

[23] In the limited goal of maintaining leadership domination over the population, these strategies could be said to have positive utility. But in terms of the mobilization strategy's popular appeal, there is little that is seen as positive. It is in this latter sense that the term *positive* is used.

Sociologist Philip Selznick writing on Russia in *The Organizational Weapon* reveals his message within the tital itself. Although he recognizes the role of mobilization, Selznick sees the work of the Russian Communist party essentially in manipulative and exploitative terms: "The essential characteristic of the mass in bolshevik terms is its manipulability [1952: 83]." He argues that the masses are manipulated into a position of struggle against the old economic and political order; their adherence is sought through the use of slogans like *peace, bread, land,* and *unity* (1952: 10). Selznick believes that only the elite are allowed to know what is happening. Although the content of the mobilization process in Russia is undoubtedly more negative, it is one thing to argue that the party was incapable of forming positive links with the masses, and quite another to argue that prior to 1952 the Communist party never saw its relationship to the masses in positive terms, but rather was always a practitioner of manipulation.

Although a different Communist-oriented organization is under scrutiny, Vietnam analyst Douglas Pike's emphasis on manipulability is virtually identical to Selznick's:

> The social changes brought to the liberated areas were perhaps more apparent than real. The NFL [National Liberation Front] administrative association was more manipulative than participational, and such an arrangement usually carries with it the seeds of its own doom.... [24]
>
> The deeper one plunged into the study of the NLF the stronger became the feeling of being on the edge of a future social morass, only dimly seen. Here, one felt, was tomorrow's society, the beginning of 1984, when peace is war, slavery is freedom, the nonorganization is the organization [1966: 382–383].

Again, the message is eminently clear: The communists in Vietnam mobilized the population not because they wanted to resolve inequalities in the society, not because the leadership and the population had a positive relationship with each other, but because the leadership was able to manipulate the population into believing that what the population really wanted would come with the Communists' victory when, according to Pike, it really would not ("peace is war, slavery is freedom"). In short, the NLF could organize and manipulate, but its ideology was a charade. Thus it was through its ability to organize, not its ideology or mobilization goals, that it was able to endure and achieve what Pike must certainly believe to be a Pyrrhic victory.

Turning to the Chinese scene we find University of California political scientist Chalmers Johnson no less emphatic in his dismissal of the positive character of the Chinese mobilization strategy. In essence, Johnson argues that the Communists' rise to power in the late 1930s and early 1940s was not due to the mobilization strategies of the Yenan period. Rather it was because they

---

[24] The level of popular support achieved by the Chinese is probably exceeded in socialist societies today only by the Vietnamese. Pike's statement is probably a better description of American policy in Indochina.

could manipulate the loyalties of the Chinese peasantry by appealing to their nationalistic spirits in their fight against the Japanese:

> After 1937 [the Communist party] succeeded because the population became receptive to one particular kind of political appeal; and the Communist party—in one of its many disguises—made precisely that appeal: it offered to meet the needs of the people for leadership in organizing resistance to the invader and in alleviating war-induced anarchy in the rural areas [1962: 7].

Johnson is willing to admit that the Communists, in terms of their anti-Japanese program, did have some positive appeal. But he is unwilling to credit them with any significant positive response or loyalty from the peasantry based on the social and economic programs developed in the Yenan period (see Chapter 2, and Selden, 1971).

The fallacies of this argument have been rather thoroughly covered by others (Gillin, 1964; Selden, 1971). But I will raise one rhetorical question. If you were a peasant in northern Shensi province in the late 1930s and early 1940s, would you be more likely to respond to programs to remove the presence of the Japanese, whose destruction you may have heard of but are not likely to have seen, or would you be more responsive to programs striking at the heart of your poverty and misery—programs aimed directly at containing the exploitation and oppression of the landlords?

A more intricate argument, but still one which basically questions the positive utility of the Chinese mobilization is advanced by former Kissinger aide and Rand Corporation Researcher, Richard Solomon. In essence Solomon argues that the Communists, led by Mao, have endured in China because of their ability to capitalize on and channel (i.e., manipulate) the peasant's longstanding fear of authority.

> Mao's particular contribution to the process of promoting social change would seem to be his conception of an institutionalized motivational mechanism for mobilizing a basically conservative and politically reticent peasantry. *Sentiments of aggression,* when *disciplined* in their expression through *organizational* controls and given purposeful direction through a social ideology, became a powerful tool for promoting change where established authority and custom are rooted in personal anxieties. Such emotions apparently are the *only* motive force powerful enough to overcome rapidly the inhibitions which sustained tradition in the personalities of China's peasants [1971: 523; emphasis added].[25]

The validity of Solomon's appeal to the forces of traditional society has been seriously questioned by others (Metzger, 1972; Mote, 1972; see also Kagan,

---

[25] This and subsequent quotes cited to Solomon, 1971 are from Richard Solomon, *Mao's Revolution and the Chinese Political Culture.* Copyright © 1971 by The Center for Chinese Studies, University of Michigan. Reprinted by permission of the University of California Press.

1973). Although he is willing to admit that there is a social ideology,[26] when the content of that social ideology is investigated, it is not so much the social and economic programs that improve the livelihood and appeal in a very direct and positive way to the peasantry. Rather it is, as Selznick and others believe, the ability of the Chinese leadership (specifically Mao) to manipulate the population, in this case, by attacking Mao's enemies (be they intellectuals in the Hundred Flowers campaign or cadre authority in the Socialist Education campaign or the GPCR). In short, the content of the social ideology is negative. Solomon does not seriously consider the possibility that Mao and the Chinese Communists have genuinely appealed to the aspirations and needs of the population, and that through a common bond and direct link between Mao and the Communist leadership and the masses via the mobilization strategy there might be a strong positive and mutual commitment.[27]

C.I.A. analyst Philip Bridgham's views on the mobilization strategy are also negative. Even though he concentrates his critique on the prospects for economic change, a close reading of his views makes it quite clear he is no more convinced about the positive utility of the campaign in other realms of society.

> It is extremely doubtful that the "cultural revolution" will succeed any better than previous political indoctrination campaigns in solving the perennial problem confronting the Chinese leadership—how to persuade the long-suffering Chinese people to produce more and consume less in order to accelerate economic development. The underlying premise of the "cultural revolution,"—that it is possible to cultivate a new "socialist" or "communist" man who voluntarily subordinates individual to collective goals and enthusiastically participates in collective production—appears to be based on a utopian view of human nature. When methods of persuasion fail to achieve the utopian objective, it becomes necessary to rely increasingly on methods of coercion and suppression. If this analysis is correct, then the outlook in Communist China in the years ahead is for the unfolding of a programme of economic and social development featuring increased tension and conflict and patterned increasingly on the Stalinist model of forced-draft economic development of a generation ago [1967: 35].[28]

[26] In fact, like Skinner and Winckler (discussed later) Solomon argues that the mobilization ends up in a negative phase: "excesses are committed by over zealous Party cadres. These excesses produce economic or organizational difficulties [1971: 348]."

[27] Although it is not clear that William Kornhauser's thesis on mass society and the positions presented by Solomon draw from each other, they are certainly compatible. Kornhauser eschews those societies that fail to develop strong secondary associations to mediate between the top and the bottom. The failure to do so produces "extremist movements" with all their so-called negative implications (i.e., for the stability and maintenance of the status quo). China, for Kornhauser, would be an excellent example. Here Mao's emphasis on a direct leader—follower relationship via the mass mobilization campaigns would, in Kornhauser's view, be fraught with all the potential he and those cited in this section see for negative consequences.

[28] Given their negative views regarding the Chinese Communists' social ideology, it is perhaps no coincidence that American intelligence has employed Bridgham and Solomon.

Finally, a brief allusion must be made to Stanford anthropologist, William Skinner and Columbia sociologist, Edwin Winckler (1969). Although their arguments will be more thoroughly explicated and examined in the next section, because I believe the major thrust of their position suggests the campaigns are of limited utility, there is some indication that they may in fact view campaigns as basically negative in impact.

As part of their model, Skinner and Winckler have outlined the phases of the campaign cycle (see Table 1.2). The cycle is one in which each campaign ultimately deteriorates into negative results. For example, the involvement of participants during phase 3 is characterized by "disaffection and ambivalence." The naming of phase 4, *deterioration,* is indicative of their view of events. "Deterioration is a period of impending crisis: lower participants are becoming speedily more alienated [1969: 424–425]." Alienation reaches its peak in phase 5, *retrenchment.* Conditions, according to Skinner and Winckler, improve only with the demise of the campaign and the return to normalcy. Although it is possible they might hold problematic the actual *level* of alienation and negative outcomes of each campaign cycle, they leave little doubt about the direction. In short, campaigns tend to be characterized by terms such as *crisis, alienation, negative feelings, disaffection,* and *ambivalence.* There is little suggestion that they view campaigns as having a potential for positive results, especially when compared with noncampaign periods.

Although in Chapter 7 I will discuss the views outlined here in the light of the data collected, it is difficult to test their validity systematically. It is difficult enough to generate data with which to test the *limited* utility of campaigns, let alone to test hypotheses of no utility. To generate sufficient data one would have to have either a long period of no campaign activity in China, or another society exactly the same as China, but without a campaign mobilization strategy. The latter is simply impossible. The former is not possible because of the presence of national campaigns (not to mention local ones) in at least some sector of the society during every year, if not every month, since 1949. Much more testable are the more widely held views that in one sense or another the campaign mobilization strategy is of limited utility.

Campaign Mobilization Strategies: Limited Utility

Although the arguments upholding the limited utility of campaigns are diverse, two different central strands can be discerned. One position argues that the campaign strategies were of positive value only during the early transitional years. The other argues that campaign mobilization strategies may be useful for realizing certain goals, such as ideological ones, but not others, such as economic ones.

The first argument originates from views dating all the way back to Max Weber (1964), who argued that there were three different types of authority structures: traditional, charismatic, and legal–rational. The middle form, charismatic, with its highly fluid forms of societal organization and leader–follower interaction, was most likely to be found in transitory periods between the other two forms. Contemporary social scientists and especially early observers of the so-called developing world drew from these ideas. Although political scientist David Apter does not specifically allude to Weber's thinking, Apter's description of the "mobilizing system" provides the link between Weber and students of China who adhere to this view of the limited utility of campaigns:

> mobilization systems are most suitable at points of conversion from one system type to another. . . . Examples are the move from dependent to independent status and from the first stages of modernization to major industrialization . . . [1965: 390].

> [However], . . . after the first period of mobilization . . . perhaps four or five years . . . the problem of efficiency becomes paramount. . . . such systems begin to promote unrealistic industrialization goals . . . [and] rely heavily on coercion [1965: 381, 387].

Apter's more general theories of modernization, and the Chinese scene are brought together by A. Doak Barnett, Brookings Institution analyst:

> While the effectiveness of mass campaigns during the early years of revolutionary stuggle in China was indisputable, their suitability and effectiveness now as a basic instrument to create a modernized and developed society is less clear [1968: 437].

Barnett goes on to argue that mobilization campaigns in later stages of a society's development are costly, waste time, misorder priorities, create political excesses, and disrupt regular government functions. Barnett is a believer in stability and bureaucracy. It is no secret that Mao and others who support mass mobilization strategies see bureaucracies and bureaucratism and one of the major impediments to such goals as genuine equality and social and economic improvement of society.

It is here that the link is made to the second position arguing that the campaigns are of limited utility—limited to noneconomic goals. Chicago political scientist Tang Tsou has tied the two positions together. Tsou argues that from 1935 to 1958 rapid socioeconomic transformation via mass mobilization strategies engendered high popular support. But beginning with the GLF and culminating with the GPCR, Mao's mass mobilization strategy produced a crisis of legitimacy in the basic institutions, leading to their breakdown:

> Thus, just as the thought of Mao and his policies in the Great Leap Forward produced an economic disaster, the thought of Mao and his policies in the GPCR seem likely to have serious consequences in the next few years not only for cultural

and academic life but also for the political system as a whole. What we have witnessed is the tragedy of a once impressive political system which has outlived its usefulness [Ho and Tsou, 1968: 347].

Simply put, Tsou is arguing that after the initial transitional period the effort to fulfill economic goals is where the limitations of Mao's strategy can first be seen, but by the time of the GPCR the inadequacies of this mobilization strategy are spread throughout the society. (See also Lewis, 1963: 99–100; Pye, 1968: passim, and 1972: 209–292.)

MacFarquhar has made the most succinct statement of the position that Mao's strategy is unable to fulfill economic goals: With the GLF, "mass mobilization . . . had proved inadequate . . . [as a] sure-fire method of economic development [1969: 55]." (See Schwartz, 1968a: 205–227, for a similar view.)

Not surprisingly, economists who accept Western, capitalist theories of economic management appear most committed to arguing that mobilization strategies have limited utility in economic situations:

> In its early stages a mobilization phase may proceed without substantial losses in incentives or efficiency. However, beyond a certain point [undefined] disincentive effects and inefficiencies are likely to cancel out some of the gain due to increased mobilization of inputs. . . . If in spite of this slowdown, mobilization measures continue to be enforced, a point may be reached when the negative incentive and efficiency effects outweigh the positive [Eckstein, 1968: 704].

Economist Barry Richman takes a similar position on this issue, although he states the case somewhat more positively:

> Where ideology has not been pushed too far, to the detriment of economic, technical and managerial rationality, the environmental changes have tended to have a beneficial effect on management and development [1969: 340].

Some of the Chinese leaders opposed to Mao in the wake of the GLF apparently concurred with the views of these Western analysts. They are reported to have argued that although mass campaigns might be utilitarian for struggle goals ("revolutionary struggles") or ideological ends ("political reforms"), campaigns should not be used for promoting economic goals ("socialist construction"):

> There has been quite a bit of argument within our Party over the question of launching large-scale mass movements in socialist construction and, above all, on the industrial front. Some say that "mass movements are all right for revolutionary struggles but not for construction." Others say that it is a rather complex thing to run modern industry and in this respect, instead of organizing mass movements, we should establish a "regular regime." Still others say that mass movements may be all very well in carrying out political reforms in factories and businesses, but that in carrying out technical reforms we should rely on systematic "scientific methods" instead of mass movements, and so on and so forth. The basic standpoint is that the Party's mass line in socialist construction should be replaced by a set of "regular"

methods, and lively and vigorous movements by bare administrative orders. They even call their methods "normal," "scientific," truly Marxist–Leninist methods and call mass movements "abnormal," "unscientific" methods which, according to them, run counter to Marxism–Leninism [Ko, 1960; 192].

Many of the views cited in this section are marked by some vagueness as to their precise meaning—undoubtedly because most of the comments and positions are taken in passing, rather than in a systematic effort to understand the dynamics and impact of the campaign mobilization strategy. The one major exception is the work of William Skinner and Edwin Winckler. Although they do not systematically introduce data to test their positions fully, they are sufficiently thorough in their examination of the dynamics of the campaigns to permit the extraction of testable hypotheses. Thus, their analysis warrants our attention.

THE SKINNER–WINCKLER MODEL

The analysis of Skinner and Winckler is based on Columbia sociologist Amitai Etzioni's compliance model (Etzioni, 1961). Etzioni sees a three-tiered relationship between societal goals, the application of power, and the character of the subordinates' involvement (see Table 1.1).

TABLE 1.1
Etzioni's Compliance Model (Simplified)

	Stage set		
	1	2	3
Goals	Ideological[a]	Order	Economic
Power	Normative	Coercive	Remunerative
Involvement	Commitment	Alienation	Indifference

[a]Etzioni uses the term *culture*. Skinner and Winckler's adaptation to *ideological* will be used here.

Although Etzioni's model is far more complex, it is sufficient here to note the importance given to congruence of the stage sets. "Congruent types are more effective than incongruent types [Etzioni, 1961: 14]." For example, if ideological goals are sought, Etzioni argues that it is more effective to use normative means or power and to expect commitment in response. Conversely, it is unrealistic or ineffective to use, for example, normative means to achieve order or economic goals.

It is this notion of congruence that becomes the point of departure for Skinner and Winckler:

When goals, power and involvement are not congruent, the theory predicts that there
will be a decline in performance, creating costs for superordinates and thus a
tendency for change toward congruence [1969: 411].

Using the patterns of change evident in rural Chinese society after 1949,
Skinner and Winckler attempt to apply the compliance theory to China. Essentially they argue that the Maoist Chinese leadership has emphasized ideological
goals at the cost of economic and particularly order goals. "This tendency to
sacrifice economics to ideology has led repeatedly to a crisis in the order and
economic sectors [1969: 415]." How does this occur? According to Skinner and
Winckler, the leadership favors the use of normative power, most commonly
used in China as the central element of the mass mobilization campaign. This
leads to a breakdown in the economic and order sectors, thereby forcing the
normally dominant leadership "to accede to the proponents of remunerative
power at those phases of the cycle in which economic performance and social
order are dangerously impaired [1969: 416]."[29]

There is a parallel breakdown in the character of participant involvement.
Although some lower-level participants do increase their commitment as normative power or mass mobilization is increasingly applied during campaigns, many
increasingly move to alienation and ambivalence.

As the campaign comes to seem more and more shrill in its threats and promises and
less and less substantial in its accomplishments, an increasing number of lower
participants move over into alienation [1969: 418].

This alienation and negative outcome of the campaign is indicated by the
phases contained in each of several cycles Skinner and Winckler see as occurring
in rural China (1969: 424–425), shown in Table 1.2.

Why does each cycle seem to deteriorate, to degenerate into a crisis situation
with high alienation? According to Skinner and Winckler this deterioration due
to the incongruence of goals and power:

The major point here is that for the greater part of the compliance cycle the effective
power mix does not match the goals being pursued very exactly [1969: 420].

In essence, the model argues that when there is congruence in the first phase
the dominant leadership consciously decides to throw the system into a state of
incongruence. The consequences of this decision propel the system through a
series of phases, which, with the intrusion of opposing policy leadership, leads
the system back to a stage of normalcy or congruence:

These features reflect our impression of what has occurred repeatedly in Communist
China. The discrepancy between power and goals which develops during the radical

---

[29] In the rhetoric of the GPCR, it was Liu Shao-chi and other "capitalist roaders" who
were accused of being "proponents of remunerative power," whereas Mao and his supporters advocated greater use of normative power or mass mobilization.

TABLE 1.2
Phases of Compliance Cycles in Rural Chinese Society

Phase	Title	Summary of content
1	Normalcy	State of equilibrium; congruence of set 3: economic goals, remunerative power, and indifference.
2	Mobilization	Normative power proponents seize the initiative at end of phase 1, pushing involvement to high levels and the stage set to incongruence and the beginning of the campaign.
3	High tide	Peak of campaign and normative power—power becomes more radical than goals, producing increasing disaffection and alienation by peasantry, requiring check on mobilization and movement to coercive power.
4	Deterioration	Involvement has moved to alienation, and there is an increasing stress on order over ideological goals. But power is still mixed between normative and coercive. This incongruence opens the door for remunerative power proponents.
5	Retrenchment	Alienation peaks, remunerative power is increased. "The crisis is past."
6	Demobilization	A continuation of phase 5 in which alienation is reduced with the increasing application of remunerative power leading the way to congruence of set 3 and phase 1 again.

phases rests on an ideological tenet of the [normative power] proponents which holds that the proper kind of normative power properly administered is more efficacious than remunerative power in achieving economic as well as ideological ends. In affirming the power of socialist thinking to achieve production victories, the regime propagates policies and encourages procedures which are unrealistically related to goals [1969: 422].

Are these procedures really unrealistically related to goals? Is crossing the congruence boundaries to use normative means to achieve economic or order goals unrealistic at least in China's socialist society? It is this notion of the utility of incongruence that will be tested here.[30] First, however, what of the proponents of the third position?

[30] The total Skinner–Winckler model is not of central concern here. It is, however, possible to identify this one important area of congruence where my data can be used as a partial test of Skinner and Winckler's and indirectly Etzioni's models.

In private communication with me, Skinner and Winckler have noted that they also mention accomplishments stemming from the campaign. My presentation of their views does not dispute this point. I don't think they are against the use of campaigns in China. The logic of their argument inescapably suggests that campaigns might be *more* useful in fulfilling some goals than others (e.g., ideological versus economic). This is precisely why I see them as arguing that campaigns have limited utility—more accomplishments in some areas, more diminishing returns in others.

Campaign Mobilization Strategies: Positive Utility

Some argue that the campaign mobilization strategy has been very effective in China's attempt to achieve the goals of a socialist society. They believe it has been effective not only in the early period, the 1950s, but in the 1960s and 1970s as well, and not only for ideological goals but for economic ones as well. They accept the position that, at least in China, normative power is at least as efficacious as remunerative power (to use Skinner and Winckler's terms) if not more so in achieving economic goals. This effectiveness is based not merely on the ability of the leadership to control, but also on the strong positive relationship between leaders and masses and the genuine positive content of the Communist programs and their enactment via the mass mobilization campaign strategy.

Underlying their arguments is their rejection or at least questioning of the assumptions that the capitalist West is a model that must be followed by all societies, that liberal "democratic" institutions must prevail, that stability and order along with an independent bureaucracy are essential to achieve the goals of participation, prosperity, and equality.

These adherents accept the fundamental Maoist and Chinese Communist belief that, at least for Chinese society (if not all societies), the primary goal is to ensure the greatest level of equality; that is, to maximize the distribution of power and resources throughout the society. From this perspective, they all come to the conclusion that mass participation, decentralization, and emphasis on human resources—part and parcel of mass mobilization strategies and the implementation of Maoist mass line politics—have been the central most important ingredients in fulfilling this goal of greater equality.

In terms of historical analysis, the most noted proponent of this view is Washington University historian, Mark Selden. Selden eloquently argues that the social and economic programs of the Yenan period (see Chapter 2 for a brief summary), which emphasized mass mobilization tactics, were critical in beginning the process of social and economic equalization. For the first time, the peasant was mobilized out of his passive role into willing, positive, active participation based not merely on broad, diffuse notions of nationalism, but on a strong commitment to the total social and economic transformation of society:

> the Chinese leadership, from village cadres up to the Central Committee, enjoyed a mandate based on a bitter common struggle involving an entire people. The result was a vivid awareness of the possibilities of dedication and innovation inherent in China's peasant society. . . . The deep commitment to patterns of development predicated on the elimination of distinctions between town and country, prosperous and poor, dynamic and stagnant, eloquently attests to the continued allegiance to the highest ideals of the Yenan Way in revolutionary China [1971: 278].

In short, Selden is arguing that the commitment to eliminate these inequalities evolved from the development of mass line techniques. The most important of these techniques is the mass mobilization campaign. Moreover, this commitment and pattern has continued to the present time:

> The history of the Chinese Communist movement since the Yenan period, particularly its extraordinary record in carrying forward China's economic development and social transformation, has been shaped in large measure by the enduring commitment to the mass line [Selden, 1971: 276].

Johns Hopkins University political scientist, Richard Pfeffer is less impressed with the campaign mobilization strategy, but not because its utility is limited; rather, because, as he argues, many of the campaigns were muted by "growing bureaucracies" (1972: 625). In sharp contrast to MacFarquhar, Tsou, and others, Pfeffer argues that it is precisely the campaigns they reject as utilitarian—the GLF and the GPCR—that were able to return to the Yenan strategy, giving full play to popular mass participation, decentralization, and mass mobilization.[31] Pfeffer's basic position is clear: The Maoist strategies, when they have been given full reign, have had a marked positive effect in achieving China's socialist goals.

On the specific issue of the utility of the campaign strategy in achieving economic versus ideological goals, University of Texas political scientist, Gordon Bennett has perhaps made the most precise statement to date. Although somewhat cautious, he concludes that campaigns "in balance . . . contribute more to *economic growth* than they take away [1976: 15]." He notes the role of campaigns in overcoming managerial and resource bottlenecks. Even more important, he notes that the campaign strategy might well be more beneficial for developing societies that have greater human than capital resources. Stanford University economist, John Gurley continues this line of reasoning:

> Perhaps the most striking difference between the capitalist and Maoist views is in regard to goals. Maoists believe that while the principal aim of nations should be to raise the level of material welfare of the population, this should be done only within the context of the development of human beings and of encouraging them to realize fully their manifold creative powers. And it should be done only on an equalitarian basis—that is, on the basis that development is not worth much unless everyone rises together; no one is to be left behind—either economically or culturally. Indeed,

---

[31] The Great Leap Forward has probably been the most maligned of all the campaigns. In fact, my own data suggest that at least in terms of immediate, short-run consequences, its outcome was more negative than beneficial. However, more recent work has suggested that the long-term benefits of the GLF may substantially outweigh the short-run negative consequences (Lippit, 1975) and further that some of the economic policies stemming from the GLF, such as rural industrialization, may have very high economic utility (Riskin, 1971).

Maoists believe that rapid economic development is not likely to occur *unless* everyone rises together. Development as a trickle down process is therefore rejected by Maoists, and so they reject any strong emphasis on profit motives and efficiency criteria that lead to lopsided growth. Their emphasis, in short, is on man rather than on"things" [1970: 38].

This emphasis on human potential grew from the Yenan experience. It has solidified in practical institutional terms as the mass mobilization campaign strategy.

To this relatively young, recent, and ever-increasing chorus of new thinking in the West about the overall and long-term positive utility of the mass mobilization campaign strategy in the Maoist era, I would add my own support, support that will become clearer in the explication of hypotheses generated in opposition to those extracted primarily from Skinner and Winckler's work.

HYPOTHESIS CONSTRUCTION

It is now possible to formulate hypotheses that can be used to test whether the campaigns are of a more positive or more limited utility, especially with respect to the three campaign types: ideological, struggle, and economic. In evaluating the campaigns' utility, this research holds problematic not only the number of negative outcomes, or shortcomings, but to what extent there are also achievements or positive outcomes.[32] In contrast to Skinner and Winckler, I am specifically interested in testing whether shortcomings and achievements vary in a systematic fashion between different types of campaigns at different levels of mobilization.

Hypotheses Based on the Skinner–Winckler Model

To provide a sufficient test of Skinner and Winckler's ideas it is necessary to use a greater number of cases than they use. In their discussion, only eight rural campaigns are used for illustration, five of which are economic, and three, struggle. To confine their discussion, they of necessity limited their examples to rural campaigns. Yet the implications of their argument suggest they would see similar patterns for other areas of society. Thus it is reasonable to test their model from a sample of campaigns from all sectors of society.[33] On the question of goals there is a basic congruence between their economic, order, and

[32] The terms *achievements* and *shortcomings* are those used by the Chinese. Along with *mobilization*, they constitute the major variables of this study. Their meanings and the process of measurement are the subjects of Chapters 4, 5, and 6.

[33] For a detailed explanation of the process used to select the campaigns see Chapter 3.

ideological goals and the three posited by Yu (1967): economic, struggle, and ideological.[34]

The basis for departure is the notion of congruence. Since campaigns primarily use normative power,[35] the congruence model implies that the outcome should be more favorable or less negative for ideological campaigns than for struggle and certainly economic campaigns since remunerative means are most prevalent during noncampaign periods. Although this inference is primary to the ability to extract testable hypotheses, the influence is not large, given Skinner and Winckler's own statement:

> Intense or prolonged application of normative power is effective in changing attitudes and is therefore fundamental to the achievement of ideological goals [1969: 412].

If ideological goals are most effectively pursued during campaigns, then it is reasonable to expect that campaigns emphasizing ideological goals should be better able to generate achievements and consequently have fewer shortcomings. Hence the first hypothesis:

Hypothesis 1: Campaigns having predominantly ideological goals produce higher levels of achievements relative to shortcomings.[36]

Skinner and Winckler also argue that

> remunerative power is particularly suited to maintaining the performance of activities over a long period of time, and is therefore particularly fundamental to the achievement of economic goals]1969: 412].

Remunerative power is most likely to occur in the absence of campaigns. Moreover, Skinner and Winckler argue that Maoist leadership, by emphasizing the campaign mobilization process, has shown a tendency to sacrifice economic to ideological goals (1969: 415). To Skinner and Winckler, the pursuit of

[34] The one exception might be the correspondence between order goals and struggle goals. Struggle goals include breaking the political, economic, and/or social power of an enemy group or class (e.g., landlords, capitalists, or capitalist roaders), and reducing the potential for disruption or sabotage by these or other groups (e.g., counterrevolutionaries). But the latter is also an order goal. Even the former involves indirect efforts to protect the social order, by eliminating the power of enemies deemed harmful to the state and society.

[35] I am not saying that there are *no* coercive or remunerative inputs, but that the primary inputs are normative. To argue otherwise one would have to produce evidence that power inputs for economic campaigns are primarily remunerative and those for struggle campaigns are primarily coercive. But even Skinner and Winckler argue that the peak or high tide of every campaign cycle is strictly normative, although as campaigns "degenerate" they all go through a coercive power phase. However, according to their diagram (1969: 419) clearly the most predominant type of power in the total campaign cycle is normative.

[36] Although it involves a major inference to extract from Skinner and Winckler's model the idea that positive outcomes may also be present, the logic of both the presence and relative levels of achievements is inescapable, given their own statements and the Etzioni model

economic goals through the use of normative power appears to be of low utility. Thus, one would expect them to conclude that there is a low utility in using economic campaigns that emphasize the realization of economic goals. If this is the case, then one would expect the shortcomings of economic campaigns to exceed levels of achievements:

Hypothesis 2:   Campaigns having predominantly economic goals produce lower levels of achievements relative to shortcomings.

For coercive power, Skinner and Winckler argue that it

is relatively effective in deterring people from undesired activities, and is therefore particularly fundamental to the achievement of order goals [1969: 412].

This type of power is most likely to occur in the latter stages of a campaign, but since it is not the predominant form of power input, shortcomings by their logic should prevail over achievements, although the difference might not be as great as with economic campaigns.

Hypothesis 3:   Struggle campaigns having predominantly order goals produce higher levels of shortcomings relative to achievements.

Following Skinner and Winckler's logic it is also possible to contrast the three types of campaigns along each of two variables, shortcomings and achievements.

Higher levels of achievements should be expected for campaigns having predominantly ideological goals, since during the campaign with its high levels of mobilization or normative inputs congruence would be greatest. Conversely, lower levels of achievements should be found for struggle campaigns having predominantly order goals and especially for campaigns having predominantly economic goals since congruence would be greatest in the absence of campaigns:

Hypothesis 4:   Levels of achievements are higher for campaigns having predominantly ideological goals than for campaigns having predominantly struggle or especially economic goals.

The same logic applies for shortcomings. Shortcomings should be least likely for ideological campaigns. They should be higher for struggle and especially economic campaigns since congruence is lacking. Skinner and Winckler have clearly indicated their belief that the Communist leaders have erroneously attempted to use normative power to achieve economic goals. Hence the following hypothesis:

Hypothesis 5:   Levels of shortcomings are lower for campaigns having predominantly ideological goals than for campaigns having predominantly struggle or especially economic goals.

Although these hypotheses are stated in terms of and drawn directly from Skinner and Winckler's work, they are all clearly compatible with the positions of others who hold the campaign to have limited utility. All these hypotheses may, however, suffer from improper generalizability.

In making statements about the utility of campaigns, there is an unfortunate tendency to concentrate on the HAPC (Higher-Level Agricultural Producers' Cooperative), the GPCR, and particularly the GLF (Bennett, 1976: 76). Using such a narrow base runs the risk of selecting examples unrepresentative of campaigns as a whole.

Indeed, a cursory survey of a list of campaigns does suggest that these three campaigns may in fact be among those with the most difficulties, the most shortcomings. If this is true, many who question the utility of campaigns, if they have based their opinions on these three campaigns, may be inaccurately generalizing from them to campaigns in China as a whole.

Hypotheses Based on the Positive View of the Campaign

We can now formulate hypotheses to test the alternative position—in essence, that the mass line and mobilization strategies developed in the Yenan period have, on balance, been utilitarian in achieving socialist transformation in the post-liberation period.

Campaigns confront major problems, conflicts, or contradictions in the society, both ideologically and structurally. Rather than serving as the source of conflict, campaigns endeavor to open up conflict or contradiction and resolve it.[37] In University of California sociologist Franz Schurmann's terms, campaigns are the unity of ideology and organization to resolve existing contradictions (1968). Thus, depending on the magnitude of the contradiction, it is reasonable to expect an equivalent level of mobilization to resolve it:

> The conviction that social mobilization could motivate men through organization arose from the belief that men in a truly solidary group can work better than in a team which is only an aggregate of individuals. That belief is similar to what American sociologists call "group dynamics." Moreover, since the Chinese communists believe that group participation is essential to processes of political indoctrination, it should follow that work group functioning by "mechanical" principles of social cohesion will be susceptible to ideological appeals. Lin Piao's famous statement that men are more important than weapons has its counterpart in the Great Leap Forward policy on motivation and incentives; men must be appealed to, not through material

---

[37] Solomon, however, believes campaigns to be a source of conflict (1971: passim, e.g., 254).

rewards or techniques, but through spiritual values transmitted by ideology [Schurmann, 1968: 101].[38]

Mobilization, therefore, is a critical intervening factor in the outcomes of the campaign process. If this view is correct, motivation and commitment should not change with changing goals whether ideological, struggle, or economic. At the same time it is necessary to recognize the existence of shortcomings. As mobilization increases and pressures begin to mount, excesses are more easily spawned. This suggests that there is a direct relationship between mobilization and shortcomings:

> *Hypothesis 6:*   Levels of campaign mobilization are directly correlated with levels of shortcomings.

By the same reasoning achievements should also increase as greater levels of mobilization are reached and more and more effort is invested in the campaign:

> *Hypothesis 7:*   Levels of campaign mobilization are directly correlated with levels of achievements.

By implication it should also be the case that achievements and shortcomings should be directly correlated (although one may rise consistently faster than the other):

> *Hypothesis 8:*   Levels of shortcomings and achievements are directly correlated.

However, none of the three preceding hypotheses takes into account potential differences between types of campaigns.[39] What might they be?

STRUGGLE CAMPAIGNS

As previously indicated, struggle campaigns are the working out of antagonistic contradictions, that is, conflicts between the enemy and the people. The problems to be solved, the emotions aroused, are much stronger in this type of campaign. Excesses, errors, and shortcomings are much more easily spawned, for example, when a peasant, face to face with a landlord, feels protected by a more powerful force on his side and is tempted to seek immediate retribution for the abuses he, his family, and his friends have suffered. The same peasant should be considerably less prone to commit excesses when, in the course of an ideological

---

[38] This and subsequent quotes cited to Schurmann, 1968 are from Franz Schurmann, *Ideology and Organization in Communist China*, rev. ed. Copyright © 1966 and 1968 by the Regents of the University of California. Reprinted by permission of the University of California Press.

[39] Hypotheses 6–8 were developed in the course of research, before any data had been processed.

campaign, he is trying to persuade a friend who may be thinking the wrong thoughts but who has done this peasant no injustice. So too, should peasants be less prone to react negatively when they join together, for example, in an effort to seek greater collective production and ultimately increased personal benefits. They may still be dissatisfied about some aspects and there most certainly will be shortcomings in most campaigns. The point is that for struggle campaigns the excesses are likely to be greater given the level of mobilization:[40]

Hypothesis 9:   For struggle campaigns, the level of shortcomings exceeds the level of mobilization and is higher for struggle campaigns than for other types at equivalent levels of mobilization.

Struggle campaigns have as their goal eliminating the power and position of the enemy. They are aimed, therefore, more at eliminating what is bad than building what is good. One should expect lower levels of achievements relative to mobilization:

Hypothesis 10:   For struggle campaigns, the level of achievements is lower than the level of mobilization, and is lower for struggle campaigns than for other types at equivalent levels of mobilization.

ECONOMIC CAMPAIGNS

Economic campaigns confront nonantagonistic contradictions (e.g., city and country, industry and agriculture, mechanization and cooperation, leaders and masses). Many Western analysts have argued that campaigns are not utilitarian in achieving economic goals. Some Chinese leaders, opposed to Mao, apparently have agreed. However, there is a growing group of Western observers, some of whom I have mentioned earlier, who essentially agree with Mao that mobilization could forge the commitment to Schurmann's notion of a "truly solidary group," enhancing work relationships rather than mitigating against them. Normative means would actually enhance economic goals. Thus, given the economic campaigns' emphasis on the positive—i.e., socialist construction (compared with struggle campaigns) higher levels of achievements should be expected.

Moreover, during economic campaigns, for the average worker or peasant, there is a much clearer relationship between mobilization inputs and achievements, especially remunerative rewards. Hence it should be relatively easy to

---

[40] Hypotheses 9–14 were developed after the preliminary results showed distinctive differences between the three types of campaigns. They represent predictions as of that time, predictions that are not in the final analysis (see Chapter 7) sustained for each hypothesis. They are presented at this point and in this manner to focus, at an early stage, on the differences between types of campaigns.

convince peasants to join Mutual Aid Teams by arguing, for example, that the harvest will increase and, as a consequence, so will their income.

The same level of mobilization in an ideological or, especially, a struggle campaign may produce noticeably fewer achievements because it is considerably harder to convince a peasant of the utility of criticizing someone acused of bad thinking (especially if the accused works hard in the fields), or to struggle a capitalist roader who has never apparently harmed the peasants' ability to improve their livelihood. Hence, achievements should be higher for economic campaigns:

> *Hypothesis 11:* For economic campaigns, the level of achievements exceeds the level of mobilization and is higher for economic campaigns than for other types at equivalent levels of mobilization.

Although shortcomings occur in economic campaigns, it is expected that the level will be lower than for other types of campaigns at an equivalent level of mobilization. Economic campaigns do not deal with enemy groups or classes; the contradictions are not antagonistic. Class enemies (e.g., landlords, capitalist roaders), who would be likely to cause difficulties as targets during struggle campaigns, are not present. There is greater emphasis on the positive, even when compared to ideological campaigns, as the latter are directed more toward correcting erroneous thinking and actions.

> *Hypothesis 12:* For economic campaigns, the level of shortcomings is lower than the level of mobilization and is lower for economic campaigns than for other types at equivalent levels of mobilization.

IDEOLOGICAL CAMPAIGNS

For ideological campaigns there is a more direct relationship between levels of mobilization and levels of achievements and shortcomings. As in economic campaigns, the contradictions are not antagonistic, but neither are the rewards so obvious. There is no reason to argue, therefore, that levels of achievements should be higher or lower than levels of mobilization.

> *Hypothesis 13:* For ideological campaigns, levels of achievements are directly related to levels of mobilization.

Nor is there any reason to argue that shortcomings should deviate from similar levels of mobilization:

> Hypothesis 14: For ideological campaigns, levels of shortcomings are directly related to levels of mobilization.

THE TASK AHEAD

No one has yet compared all types of campaigns systematically. There is no body of literature to call upon for assistance in the methodological task ahead, there is no data bank to tap. There are no established and acceptable measures of the three major variables (mobilization, shortcomings, and achievement). Thus, it is necessary to proceed slowly, to describe how the sample was selected, the data gathered, and the measures used were constructed. This is the task of Chapters 4, 5, and 6. The results are reserved for Chapter 7. First, however, it is important to gain a better sense of the unit of analysis, the campaign; the relation of various campaigns to one other and other crucial events; and the cyclical patterns of campaigns that may have developed over time.[41]

---

[41] Those who are well acquainted with this material may wish to turn to Chapter 3, or perhaps to the end of Chapter 2, which contains a discussion of the causality of campaigns and whether they occur in cycles.

2

The View from
Tien An Men:
The Pattern of
Campaign Mobilization

To win countrywide victory is only the first step in a long march of ten
thousand *li*. . . . The Chinese revolution is great, but the road after the revolution will be longer, the work greater and more arduous. . . . We are not only
good at destroying the old world, we are also good at building the new.
—Mao, 1967: Vol. 4, 347

On October 1, 1949, standing atop the majestic Gate of Heavenly Peace—*Tien
An Men*—in the historic center of Peking, Mao Tse-tung proclaimed the founding
of the People's Republic of China. To the millions who had fought and struggled
for the Communist cause over the preceding 30 years, this was a day of
liberation from oppression, from the slavery of a landlord system, from the
horror of 100 years of war, from the ravages of hunger, poverty, and disease, and
from the degradation of imperialism.

For many this liberation was more symbolic than real. The deprivations of
the past century in particular were still very real on that historic October day.
Landlords in many areas of the country were still extracting usurious rents,
bendits still roamed some areas of the countryside at will, and much of the
industrial and commercial sectors of the economy lay in shambles. The Communists were committed not only to putting their society back together, but also to
constructing a totally new society, forging new institutions and new modes of
thinking—or, as some have put It, creating a new Communist person. To Mao and

the new leaders of China, the revolution was not behind them; it lay ahead, a challenge and task of immense magnitude. Mao made this quite clear in his report to the Party Central Committee in March 1949, quoted at the beginning of this chapter.

Mao in 1949, as before, remained convinced of the need for continuous revolution (Schram, 1971; Starr, 1971). If China were to be transformed there would have to be a continuing mobilization effort guided by mass line politics, politics that would come to fruition in a stream of virtually unending mobilization campaigns.

Had Mao, in 1949, conceptualized a master plan of specific campaigns for the transformation of society? I do not think so. There is no evidence that Mao knew of specific campaigns that were to be undertaken 5, 10, or 20 years hence, except for a few campaigns, such as those involving the transformation of agriculture. Even in regard to many of the agricultural campaigns, which he believed necessary in 1949, their timing was not at all predictable. Often it was not possible to determine before the end of one campaign what the next would be, let alone when it would begin.

I do believe, however, that Mao, among others, was all along convinced of the utility of the campaign mobilization process in the socialist transformation of Chinese society. In this context, virtually all major campaigns are related. Since 1949, campaign has followed upon campaign, not because there was a master plan of specific campaigns in 1949 but because the outcome of one campaign produces new social and political conditions, giving rise to new contradictions and the belief that new campaigns could resolve these contradictions.

I will in this chapter briefly describe some 50 campaigns, including all the larger ones and all those in the research sample. (These campaigns are listed in Appendices 1 and 2.) My aim is twofold: to set forth the specific purposes of the campaigns in the research sample, and to trace the sequence of these campaigns so that we may see whether they were the result of a long-term plan and to what extent one flows from, or is interrelated with, others.

FORGING THE CAMPAIGN STRATEGY: THE YENAN PERIOD

Chapter 1 has stressed Mao's reliance on the mobilization campaign as the central means for carrying out the mass line. As indicated in Chapter 1, this reliance is rooted in the concrete historical experience of the Yenan period. It was then that the mobilization campaigns began in earnest.[1]

[1] Some mobilization efforts, such as Agrarian Reform, were undertaken in the earlier Kiangsi period, but the full pattern of policy implementation through mass mobilization campaigns was not completely developed until the Yenan period.

The most famous campaign of the period was the *Cheng-feng* campaign of 1942–1944, launched on February 1, 1942, with two speeches by Mao. It was essentially a rectification campaign aimed at correcting various errors of cadres. The problems, stemming from the diversity of cadre background and experience, necessitated a broad effort of ideological education to build "a unified party with common ideals, ideology and goals [Selden, 1969b: 104]." It is not surprising that Mao attacked most strongly the error of failing to relate theoretical study to concrete practice—the heart of his approach to mass line politics developed in his essays in 1937 (1971: 65–133). The time had come to be certain that Mao's theories of leadership would be understood and implemented by the cadres.

Six other campaigns were developed in the Yenan period, affecting all walks of life in the liberated areas. Heavy constraints on resources existed because of Japanese and KMT blockades. To reduce costs to the taxpayer and strengthen local government, personnel cuts as high as 20% in the army and the government bureaucracy were made during 1941–1943 in the campaign for Crack Troops and Simple Administration. In 1941–1942 the first To the Village campaign gave many of the intellectual cadres who had come from the cities and areas outside the liberated zones a concrete understanding of the peasant–masses emphasis of the Communist revolution. This movement, a precursor to *xia fang*, the sending down of cadres and intellectuals in the 1950s and 1960s, had as its goal the destruction of "barriers between outside and local cadres, between bureaucrats and village cadres, and between administration and production, while strengthening the lower levels of government [Selden, 1969b: 104]."

Between 1942 and 1944, the campaign for the Reduction of Rent and Interest sought to ease the burden on the peasantry. A precursor to Agrarian Reform, this campaign allowed landlords and rich peasants to maintain their positions of power while it restricted their exploitation of the peasantry. This was viewed at the time as a necessary compromise between the goal of ending exploitation by landlords and the need to carry on a united front in the war against Japan. Even this partial limitation of the power of the landlords increased the enthusiasm and support of the peasantry for the Communist party.

By 1943, there was a strong drive to increase production on both the agricultural and industrial fronts. Tied directly to the *Cheng-feng* campaign, the rural cooperative effort was part of a fundamental process to restructure life "in all its social, economic, political, and military configurations, at the village level [Selden, 1969b: 104]." The first Mutual Aid Teams were formed at this time by Party cadres for the purpose of increasing production by sharing human and animal labor power along with available implements.[2] The Production campaign

---

[2] Here the Communists were capitalizing on a traditional institution; peasants have long exchanged tools and labor during busy seasons.

was developed not only to increase the scope and pace of industrial production through cottage industries, but even more to require all cadres to take part in labor, not just as leaders but as participants, thus tying the campaign directly to the rectification effort. Finally, there was an educational effort to increase literacy and spread health and hygiene to remote villages. The vehicle was the *min ban* ("people-operated") school. The authority and responsibility given to the peasants to run these schools was likewise tied in with the emphasis on working with and learning from the masses.

The Yenan campaigns were the first concrete expression, affecting all walks of life, of the mobilization campaign based on mass line politics. The major elements of each of these campaigns would be repeated in other campaigns in the years to come, during the continuing transformation of Chinese society. In fact, in 1943 Mao called for continuing campaigns to increase production, support the army and the government, and "cherish the people."

> From now on, such campaigns should be launched everywhere in the first month of every lunar year, and in the course of them the pledges to "support the government and cherish the people" and "support the army and give preferential treatment to the families of the soldiers who are fighting the Japanese" should be read out time and time again, and there should be repeated self-criticism before the masses of any high handed behaviour of the troops in the base areas towards the Party or government personnel or towards civilians, or of any lack of concern for the troops shown by the Party or government personnel or the civilians (each side criticizing itself and not the other) in order that these shortcomings and mistakes may be thoroughly corrected [1967: Vol. 3, 134].

THE FLOW OF CAMPAIGNS: 1949–1975

By 1949, it was clear that a new stage had arrived. The future tasks were obviously a part of Mao's thinking as he wrote "On the People's Democratic Dictatorship" to commemorate the twenty-eighth anniversary of the Communist party of China:

> The serious problem is that the education of the peasantry. The peasant economy is scattered, and the socialization of agriculture, judging by the Soviet Union's experience, will require a *long time* and painstaking work [emphasis added; 7 years later this process was basically completed]. Without socialization of agriculture, there can be no complete, consolidated socialism. The steps to socialize agriculture must be coordinated with the development of a powerful industry having state enterprise as its backbone [1969: Vol. 4, 419].

Mao also foresaw the time when at least one of the marginal classes, the national bourgeoisie, would become the target for remolding. "When the time comes to realize socialism, that is, to nationalize private enterprise, we shall carry the work of educating and remoulding them a step further [1967: Vol. 4, 419]."

By 1949, the first step in the agricultural transformation process, Agrarian Reform, was well under way. For several years prior to 1949, as areas were liberated from the Japanese or the KMT, a Rent Reduction campaign was undertaken. These campaigns, similar to those of the Yenan period, were followed by Agrarian Reform if the area seemed sufficiently secure and the peasants politically prepared.[3]

Although the Agrarian Reform campaign had in fact been in operation for some time, it was given new impetus in June 1950 with the enactment of the Agrarian Reform Law and the interpretive directives set forth by Liu Shao-chi. The hallmark of these directives was the stress placed on moderation. Investigation was to be carefully carried out to prevent improper expropriation. Moreover, for the time being, "the rich peasant economy should not be destroyed [Liu Shao-chi, 1950: 8]."[4]

> Only when the conditions mature for the wide use of mechanical farming, for the organization of collective farms and for the socialist reform of the rural areas can the need for a rich peasant economy cease, and *this will take a somewhat lengthy time to achieve.* [Liu, Shao-chi, 1950: 28–29; emphasis added].

The central need at that time was to consolidate Communist control in the villages with the support of the peasantry, without alienating the richer productive forces (i.e., the rich peasants). The Agrarian Reform process was therefore to be limited strictly to the landlords (Chi, 1963: 41–45; Liu Shao-chi, 1950: 5–9, 28–32).

In spite of this limitation, the struggle that ensued with the landlords encompassed a broadside attack on the age-old system of rural social stratifica-

---

[3] One of the best accounts of Agrarian Reform to date is William Hinton's *Fanshen* (1968). It is an intricate account centered in a single village of the setbacks, the struggle, the achievements of the early campaigns in that village after its liberation, including Agrarian Reform and particularly the rectification campaign that followed it.

[4] Agrarian Reform was carried out over the better part of a decade or more, from the time it was implemented in Yenan until its completion in all parts of the country in the early 1950s. [Agrarian Reform was also attempted in the Kiangsi soviets of the early 1930s (Kim, 1969).] Over this period of time the policy regarding the treatment of rich peasants oscillated, depending on the political situation. One policy deemed them to be class enemies facing the same guidelines for expropriation as the landlords. Another policy ordered that their land, or at least part of it, be protected from expropriation, that the "rich peasant economy" be protected so they could continue to contribute to the productive process. The latter policy was followed more in the early years after 1949, since the responsibilities of governing all of China kept the Communists from being able to deal with any but the worst problems (principal contradictions) at that time.

This meant, of course, that areas liberated earlier would have more time to resolve local problems after Agrarian Reform before moving to the stages of agricultural cooperation, and that they would be rid of the pernicious influence of rich peasants (J. Chen, 1957: 68–71). These two factors would work to the disadvantage of areas liberated later—areas predominantly in southern China.

tion (Schurmann, 1968: 4; Townsend, 1967: 90). In this respect Agrarian Reform was more a political struggle to eliminate the landlords as the most powerful rural class than a struggle to increase productive power (*NFRB*, December 2, 1950; *PC*, February 1952: Vol. II, No. 2: 10).

> China's vast population alone made land reform one of the greatest social revolutions of modern times. . . . Land reform did not lead to an economic revolution, for production patterns in the village did not change fundamentally. But as a social revolution, land reform succeeded in destroying the traditional system of social stratification in the rural areas [Schurmann, 1968: 437].

Yet, even before Agrarian Reform was basically completed in the end of 1952 (Schurmann, 1968: 437), additional steps in the agricultural transformation process had been indicated. The first, Mutual Aid Teams (MAT), had been promoted by the Party back in 1943, during the Yenan period (*PC*, November 1, 1951: 8). Others were to come. The issuing of the Party decisions on mutual aid and cooperation on December 15, 1951, seems to have been a signal to move forward with the organization of MATs, at least in some areas where Agrarian Reform had been completed (J. Chen, 1957: 97). Even by the end of 1951, it was indicated that Agricultural Producers' Cooperatives and collectivization, "as in the Soviet Union," would follow (*PC*, November 1, 1951: 8). The "Decisions on Mutual Aid and Cooperation in Agricultural Production," adopted by the Party Central Committee on February 15, 1953, further indicated that the "ultimate goal in the countryside [is to lead] the whole peasantry to Socialism and Communism [*PC*, July 1, 1953: 8, supplement]."

In the meantime, in other areas of life during 1950 and 1951, campaigns were under way to consolidate Communist power and eliminate or neutralize opposition elements. The most important of these campaigns was the Suppression of Counterrevolutionaries, carried out for the purpose of rounding up remaining KMT spies and those who had committed crimes. It lasted throughout much of 1951 and in the countryside was tied to Agrarian Reform (see, for example, *NFRB*, April 15 and September 5, 1951; *CZRB*, May 19, 1951 and January 1, 1952). Counterrevolutionaries, like landlords, were enemies of the people, and if they did not admit to their mistakes and reform they would be forced to do so. Most of those executed during this period were among this group, particularly those who had committed murder, rape, exploitation, and other serious crimes.[5]

---

[5] Some have called this period a "reign of terror." (See Mu, 1962: 142.) The campaign of Ideological Remolding that followed has been described in similar terms. It "built up into a frantic, violent, and almost hysterical 'struggle' [Barnett, 1964: 128–129]." In the emotion of the campaigns' "high tides," some people were wrongly apprehended or improperly punished. What of the large majority of these targets? They probably represented no more than 1% of the population. Should they not have been apprehended? Informants who lived in China during this period speak less of terror and violence and more of careful efforts to register, investigate, and even assist potential criminal elements before they were arrested

The Ideological Remolding campaign followed by the end of 1951 and continued into 1952.[6] Less severe than the Suppression of Counterrevolutionaries campaign, this campaign was aimed at the elimination of incorrect thinking among intellectuals through criticism and reeducation rather than through struggle and suppression.

Still another major campaign during this early period was the Resist America–Aid Korea campaign. Begun in October 1950, with China's entry into the Korean War, it consisted of several subcampaigns directly aimed at supporting the war effort (*JFRB*, October 22, 1952). Some were ideological, such as the Comfort of Korean People's Army and Chinese Volunteers, launched in Peking in November 1950 (*SCMP*, No. 15, November 22–23, 1950: 8). Although undertaken between April and July 1950 in an effort to support the Stockholm Peace Conference (in the summer of 1950), the campaign for Peace Signatures was later tied to the Resist America–Aid Korea campaign. Moreover, the same organizational structure (e.g., committees, institutions of government) seems in many areas to have been used for both campaigns.

Other subcampaigns were economic in their orientation, such as the effort to collect money for arms donations, which began in November 1950 (*SCMP*, No. 19, November 25, 1950: 25). Tied into this effort was the Victory Bond campaign. Although actually begun in January 1950 to celebrate the founding of the People's Republic of China (PRC), much of the money collected during the year and a half the campaign lasted was used to increase production for the war effort. There was also the drive by both individuals and whole factories to sign hundreds of "patriotic pacts" to increase production. These efforts, of course, served to increase production not only for the war, but for the economy as a whole (see *RMRB*, April 30 and October 21, 1951; *NFRB*, April 29 and May 14, 1952).

The Resist America–Aid Korea campaign was also tied to the Three-Self Movement, a campaign for the reform of Christian churches. The specific purpose of the campaign was to break ties with missionaries and Western

---

and sent to labor camps or to jail. Curiously these authors make no mention of the process, which is long standing communist policy. "We should have fewer arrests and executions, wanton arrests and executions can cause widespread fear and silence everybody. Under such an atmosphere, there would be very little democracy [Mao in Joint Publications Research Service, No. 50792: 56]." In short, the retributions implied in the notion of a "reign of terror" are completely antithetical to the communists' commitment to the mass line and mass mobilization campaigns. Thus it is only reasonable to conclude that improper investigation, summary punishment, terror, hysteria, etc., were more the exceptions than the rule.

[6] According to Barnett (1964: 129), it began in September at Peking University. In Canton it appears not to have begun until May 1952, after the Three- and Five-Anti campaigns were basically completed (Vogel, 1969: 84). The later starting dates for many campaigns in the south is quite common during the early 1950s since liberation in the south came later than in many areas in the north.

religious organizations, from the Vatican down (*RMRB*, October 1, 1951; National Council of Churches, 1963). Christians were exhorted to sign statements affirming their independence from Western religious institutions. This step and the more public test of support for Korea and the Chinese troops and opposition to American imperialism were considered to be essential steps affirming correct ideological thinking.

By the end of 1951, basic order had been restored throughout much of China. Agrarian Reform was well on its way in most areas. But within the bureaucracy and industry major problems remained. Some who opposed the Aid Korea–Resist America campaign committed acts of sabotage such as purposely sending bad medicine to the troops. These individuals were to be struggled at the time of the Three- and Five-Anti campaigns.

The Three-Anti campaign began in December 1951 (*PC*, March 16, 1952: 7). It focused on the elimination of corruption, waste, and bureaucracy in the government and in the Party. Corruption was seen to be the most serious of the three evils since it was the most obvious betrayal of support. Those found to be corrupt were usually struggled. Those accused of waste and bureaucratic excess generally faced only criticism and self-criticism. (For an explanation of the distinction between *struggle* and *criticism/self-criticism* see Chapter 4.) The problems were often caused by the need to recruit new cadres rapidly into the government and the Party to help run the cities. In cities like Shanghai and Canton, foreign influence was greatest. Many cadres, especially newcomers, were poorly steeled in the ways of Communist mass line politics and were susceptible to traditional ways of coping: corruption, waste, and bureaucracy. In this respect the problems were somewhat similar to those occasioned by the influx of intellectuals to the liberated areas in the early 1940s.

The Five-Anti campaign began shortly afterward.[7] The immediate goals were the elimination of the five bad ways of bribery, tax evasion, theft of state property, cheating, and speculation. In a larger sense, however, the campaign was aimed at placing controls on industry and commerce. It is well to remember that from 1949 to 1952 the capitalist sector in China was given relatively free rein. For example, one old worker at the Kailan coal mines in Tangshan told us that up until 1952 and the Five-Anti campaign, the workers still had to "beg" the capitalist owners for the more obvious institutions of a socialist society such as child care and a medical clinic. The question of the socialization of industry and commerce was not even to be considered. At the time even the prediction was lacking of when this might happen. Certainly no one knew it would take another 4 years to be completed. In the meantime, capitalists were allowed to maintain their positions although their authority would be taken over by Party and government cadres as industry was gradually socialized.

[7] For an account of the Five-Anti campaign in Shanghai, see Gardner, 1969.

With the completion of these two campaigns toward the end of 1952 (in some places as early as mid-1952), the Communists had carried out campaigns affecting all major sectors of society (e.g., intellectuals, the countryside, industry–commerce, leadership). All of the campaigns were at least in part aimed at establishing the authority of the Communists by controlling or eliminating the power of the remaining opposition.

In a sense, the promulgation of the National Constitution in 1954 represented the consolidation of Communist authority, although in fact this had been basically accomplished by the end of 1952. The campaign to discuss the draft constitution occurred during the summer of 1954. The draft constitution was ratified in September 1954 at the First National People's Congress. In his summary report to the Congress, Liu Shao-chi looked back on success, confident and pleased:

> We Chinese people have won complete victory in our long drawn-out revolutionary struggles against imperialism, feudalism and bureaucratic-capitalism [PC, October 1, 1954, No. 19: 6].

Although Mao too was confident in 1955, he was reported to be cautious and vigilant over the tasks still to be done:

> It is no easy task to complete our socialist revolution, and no easy task to fulfill the programme we have set outselves for the period of transition. And we cannot shut our eyes to the fact that we shall meet with many more difficulties en route. . . .
>
> Foreign imperialists without and lurking reactionaries within our borders are working by every means to undermine and even destroy our socialist construction. We must be vigilant [PC, May 16, 1955: 11–12].

Among the difficulties were the attitudes of intellectuals. Many intellectuals continued to believe that they should be free of Party control in their interpretations of Marxist truth—a position considered to be an unacceptable breach of Party discipline. In July 1954 the Central Committee of the Party received a report from Hu Feng, a literary figure closely associated with these views. He reiterated views expressed before for fewer controls over intellectuals (Goldman, 1962: 122–124). By the end of 1954 Hu Feng had been singled out for criticism as the focus of a new campaign.

Hu Feng was not anti-Communist. The question here was therefore not how to deal with those who opposed Communism, but rather how to handle those who disagreed on the role of the mass line and the Party in the literary world (Goldman, 1962: 105, 111–125). In fact, Hu Feng and others who agreed with him had been criticized during the Ideological Remolding campaign in 1951 (Goldman, 1962: 118). At the time their disagreements with the Party were not considered as serious as the disagreements of others. The conflict, the contradiction, had been allowed to remain, but now Hu Feng had prompted the move to resolve it.

By the middle of 1955 the campaign had been broadened and given a new name, *Su Fan*, or the Elimination of Counterrevolutionaries. It was aimed at particular cadres whom the Party felt to be counterrevolutionary, those who had not been struggled in earlier campaigns either because their position was not evident at the time or because their prior actions had not appeared to be so serious.

However, one high-level cadre has told me that no one knew the *Su Fan* campaign would follow the struggle against Hu Feng. This cadre believed that even the national leaders did not know. Likewise he felt that the campaign that followed *Su Fan* was not planned in advance. This was the *Shen Gan*, or Investigation of Cadres. This was an extremely thoroughgoing investigation of every cadre, aimed at revealing everything about the cadre's past and present associations. Wherever possible their associations were checked for any bad affiliations or acts they might have committed. The mere hint of any problem would require a cadre, especially a Party cadre, to step aside, to suspend responsibilities temporarily while a thorough investigation was made.

Concurrent with these campaigns was increased activity in the arena of socialist transformation in the countryside. The development of cooperative forms of agriculture had not proceeded very rapidly after Agrarian Reform had been basically completed in 1952. At least one researcher had argued that in mid-1955 the emphasis was still on the development of Mutual Aid Teams (Grossman, in Schurmann, 1968: 447).

The forming of cooperatives for the permanent investment of labor and material resources had begun as a program much earlier. By autumn 1951 there were some 400 cooperatives in the country (J. Chen, 1957: 61). In 1952 it was clear that cooperatives were to be a transitional form between mutual aid and collectivization (*PC*, July 1, 1952: 16). However, it does not appear that the campaign for cooperatives really got under way until December 1953, with the promulgation of the Central Committee's "Decisions on the Development of Agricultural Producers' Cooperatives" (Crook and Crook, 1966: 9). Even by the end of 1954 only 2% of the peasants had been organized into cooperatives (Schurmann, 1968: 454).

Moreover, in late 1954 and early 1955, pressures were brought on the Agricultural Producers' Cooperatives (APCs) to release people who did not want to continue as members and to disband or divide many of the cooperatives. Similar efforts had been made in 1953, but this time it seemed more serious. In April 1955 the Central Committee warned, "Do not commit the 1953 mistake of mass dissolution of the cooperatives again [J. Chen, 1957: 228]." But the dissolution of cooperatives and sabotage by former landlords, rich peasants, and others continued (Schurmann, 1968: 442).[8]

---

[8] For an example of this problem, see the discussion of Sandstone Hollow, the production brigade I visited in March 1972, in Chapter 4; see also J. Chen, 1957: 209–220.

These attempts to sabotage the campaign for cooperatives undoubtedly influenced Mao's decision to act. For Mao the pace of socialist transformation in the countryside was much too slow. On July 31, 1955, Mao delivered a strong attack on cadres who felt that the transformation process was moving too fast. Mao called for an early completion of the Mutual Aid Teams in all areas. Where these teams had already been formed it was time to move to the formation of APCs. And where APCs were already formed they could be strengthened and enlarged. In short, he called for a new surge of campaign activity in all peasant villages.

Even though the July speech was not made public until October 1955, it is clear that there was a marked increase in the organization of cooperatives. Another half-million had been formed by the end of 1955 (Schurmann, 1968: 454). By late 1955 the rapid formation of cooperatives brought the decision to move to a still higher stage cooperative—the Higher-Level Agricultural Producers' Cooperative (HAPC).

The formation of HAPCs began in earnest in early 1956 and was virtually completed by the middle of 1957 (Schurmann, 1968: 454). No longer would peasants receive remuneration for their investments of land and implements. The rich peasant economy was to be eliminated fully, less than 6 years after Liu Shao-chi indicated it would be a "lengthy time." It was time for a fully socialist economy. In fact, the process of cooperativization had moved far faster than Mao had envisioned in his speech in mid-1955.

> We must here and now realize that there will soon be a nation-wide high tide of socialist transformation in the countryside. This is inevitable. By the spring of 1958 ... co operatives of a semi-socialist type will embrace some 250 million people, about 55 million peasant households (averaging four and a half persons each), which will mean half the rural population. By that time many counties and provinces will have basically completed the semi-socialist transformation of the agricultural economy, and in every part of the country a small number of semi-socialist co-operatives will have become fully socialist. By 1960 ... we shall in the main have achieved the semi-socialist transformation of the remainder of the agricultural economy involving the other half of the rural population.... from 1960 onwards the semi-socialist co-operatives will be gradually developing into fully socialist ones, group by group and stage by stage [Mao, 1971: 413].

In 2 years campaign mobilization had accomplished what Mao, perhaps on the basis of the poor mobilization performances of the 3 years prior to his speech, thought would take more than 5 years to complete. Why had the process moved so slowly from the end of 1952 to mid-1955 and then so fast for the next 2 years? In retrospect it is possible that the conflict between Mao and Liu over the pace of change (now apparent in the wake of the GPCR) may have played a role (Schram, 1972: 283). Liu Shao-chi seems to have felt during these years that the pace should not be faster. Moreover, he appears to have argued that mechanization should precede cooperativization (Schram, 1972: 283). On both these questions, Mao presented opposing positions in his July 1955 speech.

Meanwhile, on the industrial–commercial front, the stage had been set for the campaign for the Socialist Reform of Private Business. Bad elements among the government and Party cadres had been eliminated in the *Su Fan* and *Shen Gan* campaigns,[9] and, according to one cadre, a thorough investigation of private capitalist enterprises had been made. If the Socialist Reform of Private Business was to be completed, so too should the socialization of agriculture. To Mao the two were inextricably linked:

> industry and agriculture, socialist industrialization and the socialist transformation of agriculture, cannot be separated, cannot be dealt with in isolation from each other. Moreover, there must be no attempt to overestimate the one and underrate the other [*PC*, November 1, 1955: 10].

The socialist transformation of most commercial establishments and industry was completed within a relatively short period, as early as mid-January in Peking, and certainly by May 1956 elsewhere (*PC*, February 1, 1956: 12–14; May 1, 1956: 7; May 16, 1956: 14). The shortness of the campaign was in part due to the earlier (1952–1955) gradual socialization of larger industries and businesses. Thus in 1955 private industry accounted for only 16% of the industrial output, although in August 1955 there were still 850,000 private trading firms, many of which were run by a single family (*PC*, May 16, 1956: 7, 11). Although many would continue to operate on a "state–private" basis for some time to take advantage of management capabilities of the former owners, the former owners would continue to receive some return on their investments. The tide had clearly shifted to socialization.

One of the periodic health campaigns also occurred in the late spring of 1956.[10] Efforts were made to eliminate flies and mosquitos as carriers of disease, and rats and sparrows as destroyers of grain. (The elimination of sparrows was soon stopped when it was realized they also ate harmful insects.) The campaign appears basically unrelated to other campaigns of the time, although the increased efforts of collectivization provided a broader organizational framework in which to carry out the campaign.

The termination of the *Su Fan* and *Shen Gan* campaigns of 1955 brought a report by Chou En-lai on the status of intellectuals. New efforts were to be made to recruit them into the Party:

---

[9] A third campaign in the socialist transformation process of 1955–1956 is the Administrative Simplification campaign, an effort to decrease the size of bureaucracies. The cadres who had been removed in the *Su Fan* and *Shen Gan* campaigns and sent to production units became part of the first step in the simplification process.

[10] Other health campaigns have been periodically carried out, both before and after this one (see, for example, *PR*, March 25, 1958: 16–17; January 20, 1959: 12–14; April 29, 1959: 19). Only this one is specifically mentioned here because it is included in the research sample.

a new situation has arisen in which intellectuals, particularly those of high standing in learning and technical accomplishment, must make greater contributions to society [Chou, in *KMRB*, December 3, 1955].

The Hundred Flowers campaign, announced by Lu Ting-i in May 1956, was a genuine effort to draw intellectuals out, to get them to share their opinions on how society could be improved. However, the responses of many dissenting intellectuals did not consist of suggestions for improvement within the basic framework of the Communist political system; rather, they tended to attack the system itself.

Mao's response was a speech delivered in February 1957, "On the Correct Handling of Contradictions among the People." In a small but significant campaign, this speech was discussed during the next 2 months by virtually every group in the country.

The speech interpreted the criticisms of the Party and Marxism as well as some of the problems of the time, both internal and external. As I mentioned in Chapter 1, there are two kinds of contradictions: antagonistic and nonantagonistic. The latter exist among the people, whereas the former exist between the people and the enemy. Recalling his earlier theoretical essay "On Contradictions," Mao reiterated that antagonistic contradictions *could* be dealt with on the same noncoercive basis as nonantagonistic ones. Moreover, Mao stressed that criticism should not only be accepted, but welcomed. He believed that in learning to deal with criticism in the proper manner the Party and leadership cadre would be strengthened:

> In China, although in the main socialist transformation has been completed with respect to the system of ownership, and although the large-scale and turbulent class struggles of the masses characteristic of the previous revolutionary periods have in the main come to an end, there are still remnants of the overthrown landlord and comprador classes, there is still a bourgeoisie, and the remoulding of the petty bourgeoisie has only just started. The class struggle is by no means over. The class struggle between the proletariat and the bourgeoisie, the class struggle between the different political forces, and the class struggle in the ideological field between the proletariat and the bourgeoisie will continue to be long and tortuous and at times will even become very acute. The proletariat seeks to transform the world according to its own world outlook, and so does the bourgeoisie. In this respect, the question of which will win out, socialism or capitalism, is still not really settled. It will take a fairly long period of time to decide the issue in the ideological struggle between socialism and capitalism in our country.... The only method to be used in this struggle is that of painstaking reasoning and not crude coercion [Mao, 1971: 463–464].

Here, then, was a central theme of the speech, to once again remind cadres of the essence of mass line politics and democratic dictatorship, to steel them for the coming ideological struggle. At the same time Mao cautioned that counter-revolutionaries still existed within the society and must be rooted out and dealt with as enemies of the people (1971: 462–472). Whether this was a harbinger of the attack on rightists to begin later that year is questionable, given the suddenness with which the attack began in June 1957. However, there is certainly a direct link between the problems Mao outlined in his speech and the Rectification and Anti-Rightist campaigns to come.

A short lull followed the discussion of Mao's speech in May 1957. This preceded the beginning of the Rectification campaign, which informants say was planned to follow the study of Mao's speech. This campaign was to assist cadres in their rectification of attitudes in working with the masses. However, rather than offer constructive criticism, intellectuals and others who opposed the Party took the opportunity to attack it (see *RMRB*, July 24, 1957: 7). The extent of their attack had increased to the point where, by mid-June 1957, it was decided that they must be struggled. This developed into a broad-based Anti-Rightist campaign to remove all rightists in opposition to Party leadership.[11] By the time the campaign terminated in the spring and summer of 1958 (*PR*, August 26, 1958: 4), thousands of intellectuals, cadres, and others had been struggled. Many were sent down to rural units to mix mental and manual labor and thereby understand proletarian life and thinking better (Crook and Crook, 1966: 174).

Since many rightists were still in the countryside at the beginning of the GLF, they provided additional labor power for the GLF mobilization drive soon to get under way. As Mao and others had indicated on many previous occasions, the development of industry was inextricably linked to the concurrent development of agriculture (e.g., *HQ*, 1959: No. 16). The question was how this development was to take place. At the Third Plenum of the Eighth Central Committee, in September–October 1957, there was an apparent split over the process of transformation. One group felt "material incentives" should be emphasized. Mao and others "advocated a policy of *social mobilization* in order to achieve rapid economic growth [Schurmann, 1968: 196]."

In the "Sixty Articles on Work Methods," apparently written in January 1958 and distributed by the Central Committee in February, Mao summed up the preceding 10 years and set the tone for the GLF:

> Our revolutions follow each other, one after another. Beginning with the seizure of power on a nation-wide scale in 1949, there followed first the anti-feudal land reform; as soon as land reform was completed, agricultural co-operativization was begun. There also followed the socialist transformation of private industry, commerce and handicrafts. The three great socialist transformations, that is to say, the socialist revolution in the ownership of the means of production, were basically

[11] At the Third Plenum of the Eighth Central Committee, held in late September 1957, it was decided that a nationwide ideological campaign of Socialist Education should be developed to parallel the Anti-Rightist campaign (Solomon, 1971: 358). It was geared, at least in part, to checking up on the performance of the HAPCs. Five aspects were stressed for investigation: distribution, division of authority, check for thrift, involving peasants in administration, and overall planning and publicity (Crook and Crook, 1966: 22–23).

completed in 1956. Following this, we carried out last year the socialist revolution on the political and ideological fronts. This revolution can be basically concluded before July 1st of this year. But the problem is still not resolved, and for a fairly long period to come, the method of airing views and rectification must be used every year to solve the problems in this field. We must now have a technical revolution, in order to catch up with and overtake England [Schram, 1971: 226–227].

In December–January 1957–1958, at a meeting of the Politburo, plans were made for a mass water conservation campaign. It was to be one of several mass mobilization efforts designed to produce a "great leap" in production. In February 1958, Po I-po, chairman of the State Economic Commission, presented to the National People's Congress, the "Year of the Leap: China's Economic Plan for 1958." In retrospect, however, the GLF seemed to be more "the product of a vision rather than a plan [Schurmann, 1968: 74] ."

> One might try ... to visualize the situation in the summer of 1958. A wave of excitement was sweeping China, compounded of enthusiasm at the bountiful harvest and whipped by mass movements led by excited Party cadres. The millenium truly seemed not far off. Both the country's leaders and mass-level Party cadres began to speak of an imminent transition to communism. China, it seemed, had reached the "break-through" point; the great harvest was only the beginning of the real agricultural revolution. In the industrial areas production figures were rising by leaps and bounds. Differences between modern city and backward village, between superior mental and inferior physical labor, would soon be overcome. The commune would become the form of social organization from which communism would be developed. Total mobilization of the country's labor was to be the instrument by which the economic and technological revolution would be consummated. Liu Shao-chi exclaimed exultingly· "If everyone works, work hours can be shortened; all will have time to study, to rest. Half work, half study—half tilling, half study, thus education will be universalized and raised, and the difference between mental and physical labor will be overcome" [Schurmann, 1968: 383].

> As the Great Leap Forward grew in intensity, it began to spread to the entire society.... [It] quickly became a gigantic nation-wide mass movement which affected city and country alike [1968: 465].

> Mao Tse-tung's vision of Chinese society saw all major contradictions in it capable of resolution with a single grand program—The Great Leap Forward. The Great Leap Forward thus became a total program of action carried out simultaneously in the economic, political, and social realms. Its driving force was ideology [1968: 102].

The apparent key to success was to be the organization of all possible excess labor power. Cadres, housewives, students, from the youngest to the oldest, were drafted to work in continual shifts day after day, night after night on massive labor projects (including the Ming Tombs Reservoir outside Peking and the Great Hall of the People). In a symbolic gesture suggesting that all must participate, on Sunday afternoon, May 25, 1958, Mao, Chou En-lai, Liu Shao-chi, Teng Hsiao-ping, Peng Chen, and other national leaders joined those working at the Ming Tombs Reservoir (PR, June 3, 1958: 4).

To support the process in industrialization, at least 90 million people participated during the summer and fall of 1958 in the Backyard Furnaces campaign,
the massive effort to produce steel in small furnaces (*SCMM*, April 2, 1968: 31).
The goal was not only to surpass Britain in steel production, but to have these
furnaces produce the steel essential to agricultural and small industrial needs, so
that larger steelworks could concentrate on large-scale industrialization and
construction. Everyone, not just industrial workers, was to understand, through
practice, something of the industrial process (*PR*, November 4, 1958: 4).

The organizational efforts of the Backyard Furnaces campaign fed into the
organization of the Communes campaign (*RMRB*, December 31, 1958). The
Communes campaign formally began with the promulgation of the August 29,
1958, "Resolution on Some Questions concerning the People's Communes"
(Crook and Crook, 1966: 32). There had been, of course, some earlier experimental communes to which Mao had given his support during his well-publicized
inspection of one of these in early August (*PR*, August 19, 1958: 4).

The communes were, of course, the direct descendents of the HAPCs. The
assumption linking the two was that larger organizational units would not only
provide for better circulation of scarce resources but release the labor power of
those previously needed as supervisors of small units. Allied to this was the
decision to establish communal dining halls and child care facilities to release the
labor power of women. The establishment of rural communes was followed in
the late summer and fall of 1958 with the attempt to form urban communes:

> [They] attempted to do in the cities what was done in the villages. . . . It was
> only during that time that the Chinese Communists had the utopian dream of
> transforming the nature of the city from one where people just live together to one
> where they would be members of a collective living and working together [Schur-
> mann, 1968: 387].

Concurrently in 1958, under the banner of the Cultural Revolution, campaigns were carried out in the fields of science, health, culture, and education to
effect ideological changes (*WHB*, December 30, 1958). In response to Mao's
speech on resolving contradictions and the National Propaganda Work Conference of March 1957, units were mobilized to change their ideological perspectives and work-style to reflect that of workers, peasants, and soldiers more fully
(Canton People's Publishing House, 1958). This work was centered in schools,
especially in the universities. It was intended to bring the intellectual and
cultural sectors of society in line with the newly changing social and economic
conditions in industry and agriculture.

Another aspect of the Cultural Revolution carried out earlier in the spring of
1958 involved the Anti-Illiteracy campaign (Crook and Crook, 1966: 178–179;
PR, February 24, 1959: 14), and "people-operated" spare-time schools (*PR*,
October 14, 1958: 21).

Both aspects of the Cultural Revolution were interrelated, aimed at decreasing the gap between those having formal education and the majority of the proletariat, who had little education (Crook and Crook, 1966: 174–175).

In short, the GLF grew out of Mao's belief in and the successes of mass line politics and the mass mobilization campaigns. Although there is no evidence before the end of 1957 predicting that the GLF would occur, it is clear that the GLF attempted to bring together the experience of all past campaigns. "The Great Leap Forward must be regarded as the most momentous instance of ideology in action in the brief history of Communist China [Schurmann, 1968: 74]."

Industry was to be decentralized. Power was to be shfted downward from Party and government bureaucrats and technical experts to the masses. The communes tried "to break through from the village to the *hsiang* (township) to the *hsien* (county) and link up with the larger world [Schurmann, 1968: 486]."

Perhaps the GLF tried to move too far too fast, beyond the prevailing objective social contradictions. The contradictions were simply too great to overcome in so short a period. For whatever reasons, reverses began to occur (see Chapter 7). The first came before the end of 1958 with the disbanding of communal dining halls and the Party Central Committee resolution of December 1958 to increase material incentives (Walker, 1968: 444; *PR*, September 1, 1959: 13–14). This resolution also returned the basic level of ownership from the commune to the production brigade (often the same as the former HAPC). By November 1960 land ownership (as well as accounting and payment) had been further decentralized in most communes to the production team (*PR*, September 1, 1959: 13–14). The essential ongoing functions of agricultural production had been removed from commune responsibility. Even though the communes were eventually divided to total some 74,000—tripling the original 24,000 of 1958 (Skinner, 1964–1965: 389, 397; *PR*, November, 1963, No. 44: 34)—their large size (average 1800 households per commune) seemed best suited to large construction and social overhead projects, such as communication, water conservation, the maintenance and sharing of machinery (e.g., tractor stations), and rural industrialization (Crook and Crook, 1966: 49).

The attacks on the GLF at the Lushan Plenum in August 1959 stemmed in large part from a critical speech made by the then defense minister, Peng Te-huai. That criticism not only cost Peng his job, it also was the apparent source of the *Fan You Qing* or Counter Rightist Sympathies campaign that surfaced in early 1960.[12] If Peng failed to understand the importance of the

[12] One former cadre told me that although the campaign did not really seem to have begun in earnest until January–February, it was a direct result of the Lushan Plenum. "Without the criticism of Peng Ten-huai, this campaign never would have happened." Before National Day (October 1, 1959), he saw a report in the office of a very high level cadre. He was then allowed to read the report, which he said included a call for a campaign against rightist sympathies.

GLF policies, certainly there were others who did also (*WHB*, October 20, 1959). This wrong thinking, particularly "bureaucracy, sectarianism and subjectivism," was to be criticized and eliminated so that the efforts to increase production could continue (Crook and Crook, 1966: 62–63). The campaign was short-lived and no one appears to have been struggled. It was concluded by the spring of 1960.

In May 1960 there was an effort to oppose the new United States–Japan security treaty. However, the effort was very short-lived, lasting only a few days. One informant compared it to "a single blast of wind." It appeared unrelated to other major events of the time. Given the almost total lack of mass participation, there is reason to question whether it was even a campaign.

In the meantime, in late 1959 and early 1960, a new effort was mounted in the cities. This was the effort to organize small street industries, many of which are still in existence today. Although the effort is sometimes referred to as phase 2 of the Urban Communes campaign, it appears to have been more of an effort at organization than mobilization (Schurmann, 1968: 384–386).

In March 1960, Li Fu-chun, vice-premier, delivered the "Report of the Draft 1960 National Economic Plan" to the second session of the Second National People's Congress. He called for emphasis on agriculture and technical innovation and technical revolution (*PR*, April 5, 1960: 9, 198–19). Clearly, because of organizational problems and natural disasters (which were to continue), agriculture needed assistance.

In fact, two of the next campaigns, beginning in 1961 and intertwining themselves for the next 5 years until the end of 1965, were the campaigns to Aid Agriculture and Return to the Village. Together, these campaigns had as their goals assisting agriculture while confronting the problem of population growth in the cities. The unemployed, often youth whose low grades prevented them from continuing to the next level of schooling, and, to a lesser extent, cadres who needed ideological rectification, were urged to go to the countryside. Moreover, every unit was expected to make a plan on how it could specifically aid agriculture.

By the Ninth Plenum in January 1961, it was clear that many of the key institutions originating in the GLF were not compatible with the present social conditions in the society. The reasons for this have, of course, been hotly debated. Was it basically due to bad policy or bad implementation? Mao, in his self-criticisms of June 1961 and January 1962, defended "the main thrust of the Great Leap policies, whatever errors of detail had been committed [Schram, 1972: 289]." Liu Shao-chi, in one of the first open breaks with Mao, suggested that the major hallmark of the GLF of "more–faster–better–more economically" was incomplete. The masses must be mobilized, but this must necessarily be done under the "centralized and united leadership of the Chinese Communist Party [Liu Shao-chi, in Schram, 1972: 289]."

> The Great Leap Forward was carried out somewhat too fast, for equilibrium was destroyed, so that after three years of leaping, it will take eight to ten years, starting from the present, to put things in order. This doesn't add up. . . .
>
> When the Chairman (Mao) says the situation is very good, he is refering to the excellence of the political situation. One can't say that the economic situation is very good; on the contrary it is very ungood [Liu Shao-chi, in Schram, 1972: 289].

The conflict, the contradiction, had emerged: "by 1962, the tension between Mao and Liu had clearly begun to reach a level where the contradictions were increasingly threatening to become antagonistic [Schram, 1972: 290]." The conflict worked itself out in a seesaw manner during the Socialist Education campaign and culminated in the GPCR. Mao told Edgar Snow in December 1970 that, in spite of his mounting disagreements with Liu, it was only in January 1965 that he concluded Liu had to be relieved of power (Schram, 1972: 292).

At the Tenth Plenum in September 1962, a new policy was announced to combat "capitalist tendencies in agriculture." Early efforts in the fall and winter of 1962–1963 began to reveal problems in the countryside (Chen, 1969). The central argument put forth at the time was the need for cadres to rely on poor and lower-middle-class peasants. By the end of March 1963 references began to appear in the media to the Socialist Education campaign.[13] The first major policy directive appeared in May in the form of the "Draft Resolution of the Central Committee on Some Problems in Current Rural Work." It became known as the "Former Ten Points" and is now assumed to have been authored by Mao. It stressed, again, mass line politics and the need to rely on the poor and lower-middle-class peasants. It introduced the term *Four Cleans*, referring to the need to "clean up" accounts, granaries, properties, and the earning of work points.

In September 1963 a second document was issued, entitled "Some Concrete Policy Formulations of the Central Committee of the Chinese Communist Party in the Rural Socialist Education Movement." It came to be known as the "Latter Ten Points" and is now said to have been authored by Teng Hsiao-ping (then Party secretary) and Liu Shao-chi. It stressed the need for work teams and consequent implementation of hierarchical Party control over the campaign. Upper-middle-class peasants and children of rich peasants and landlords who had not participated in exploitation of the peasantry were to be won over by patient, persuasive means. The campaign was to be mild in temperament and method, ideological in its thrust rather than devoted to class struggle. Little emphasis was placed on following the poor and lower-middle-class peasants.[14]

---

[13] Material in this section is drawn for the most part from the monograph by Baum and Teiwes (1968).

[14] Whyte (1970: 306) describes how relatively uninvolved the peasants were in this campaign.

With the lapse of a year, the situation seemed to have become more involved. A document entitled "The Revised Latter Ten Points" was issued, apparently also the work of Liu. Although it was similar in form to the document of the previous year, it showed a great deal more concern about the failures and errors of local-level cadres. But again the corrective device was to be, not reliance on poor and lower-middle-class peasants, but strengthened work teams.

Five months later, in mid-January 1965, a work conference of the Politburo, apparently acting under Mao's personal guidance, promulgated a 23-point directive, "Some Problems Currently Arising in the Course of the Rural Socialist Education Movement." The thrust of the directive was that not only basic-level cadres but also high-level cadres had erred, and some of the errors of the latter group were quite serious:

> The key point of this movement is to rectify those people in the positions of authority who take the capitalist road . . . some are out in the open and some are at higher levels. . . . Among those at higher levels, there are some people in the communes, districts, *hsien*, special districts, and even in the work of provincial and Central Committee departments, who oppose socialism [in Baum, 1968: 120].

Once again, emphasis for resolution of the problems was placed on mass line politics and the poor and lower-middle-class peasants. This stands in contrast to Liu's emphasis on an elitist approach to leadership:

> Liu [has placed a] continuing emphasis on organization, discipline, and the role of the elite in the political process. The whole difference between him and Mao in this respect is summed up in a remark which Liu is said to have made in September 1964, when he put forward his own, revised ten-point directive for the "Socialist Education Movement" which Mao had launched in May 1963. "To unite 95% of the cadres," he said, "is the precondition for uniting 95% of the masses." In other words, the success of our revolutionary work depends in essence on the quality of the Party organization. This corresponds exactly to Stalin's view, summed up in the slogan, "Cadres decide everything." It does not correspond to Mao's view [Schram, 1972: 292].

That the work teams and cadres supporting Liu Shao-chi's ideology did apparently try to disrupt Mao's approach to mobilization and mass line politics is apparent in this rather lengthy statement by Chen Yun-kuei on the problems incurred by the Tachai agricultural brigade:

> When the Socialist Education Movement started in 1964, Tachai Brigade itself was persecuted. We got a yield of 800 catties per *mu* that year. The "heavies" in the Socialist Education Movement said such a high yield was impossible. . . .
> Even flat land in this district, well supplied with water-conservation projects and electricity, could not reap 800 catties per *mu* at that time. So, in their minds, we had either exaggerated our harvest or not declared all our land.
> We were a model brigade. Chairman Mao had called on the whole country to follow our lead. So the Socialist Education cadres tried to discredit us by accusing us of making false statements. When the land was measured it turned out we actually

had slightly *less* than we had declared! This was a blow to them. So they decided to check our harvest. . . .

The big boys checked our granary. They totted up what we had distributed as surplus grain to our members and what we had sold to the state. The result tallied exactly with what we had said! . . .

They accused us of having too much unity among our cadres. Funny that. Too much unity. Our people asked them: "What's wrong with unity? Unity is strength, isn't it?" Useless. We were guilty of another "crime." . . .

Why did they attack us? We found out later that they were blindly following the pattern laid down by Liu Shao-chi's wife in her "Peach Garden Experiment." We represented the opposite line in agriculture. So we had to be crushed. Did you know how many cadres that went to this country in the Socialist Education Movement . . . ? They sent 3,800 people! Why so many? Why this gigantic campaign against us?

We couldn't understand it at the time, but we knew one thing: Those cadres did not follow Chairman Mao's line in their style of work. *They never applied the mass line, or anything approaching it. They and they alone had the final say!* [Emphasis added.]

So they called us a "Four Unclean" brigade. . . . When Premier Chou En-lai got to hear of this he sent a new Work Team. It stayed a month and, unlike the other, it relied in its work on the members of the Tachai Party branch and the broad masses of the poor and lower-middle peasants. Its conclusion: Tachai was declared a "Four Clean" brigade. . . .

This team followed Chairman Mao's revolutionary line for the Socialist Education Movement. . . .

The first Work Team, sent here by Liu Shao-chi . . . tried to doctor Tachai to death. Why? Because in June of the same year Chariman Mao had called on the whole country: "In agriculture, learn from Tachai."

Liu Shao-chi's Work Team wasn't sent to Tachai alone. . . .

This was the Work Team's method. They struck out at a huge number of cadres in order to protect a handful of their own people. In the process they protected landlords, rich peasants, counter-revolutionaries and bad elements, using such people to persecute our cadres.

The cadres were saved by the appearance of Chairman Mao's brilliant document entitled "Twenty-three Points on the Carrying out of the Socialist Education Movement in the Countryside." This directive made it possible for cadres who had been falsely labelled "counter-revolutionaries" to have their verdicts reversed. This not only liberated those cadres; through them, it safeguarded the interests of the poor and lower-middle peasants [Hunter and Hunter, 1972: 21–23].

In 1964 Tachai was selected as a National Model Production Brigade for Agriculture. Tachai had been selected because its production achievements were due to social mobilization efforts based on mass line politics resulting in strengthened cooperation rather than to financial, technical, or mechanical inputs from outside. First there was the slogan: "In Agriculture, Learn from Tachai." Then later a nationwide agricultural production campaign ensued to follow Tachai's pattern. A parallel campaign for industry, Learn from Taching, began at the same time. Taching is a huge industrial oil complex in northwest China. Like the Tachai campaign, this campaign was based on the principle of worker initiative. Both campaigns, although subsumed during the GPCR, appear destined to continue beyond Mao's death (see Epilogue).[15]

The reemphasis on mass line politics in the mid-1960s brought a resurgence of ideological campaigns as well. On February 1, 1963, a *People's Daily* editorial, "Learn from the Experience of the People's Liberation Army [PLA] in Political and Ideological Work," signaled the beginning of a campaign to Learn from the PLA. In particular, the editorial urged the emulation of two soldiers, Lei Feng and Wang Chieh, who had recently died while in the service of their country. Self-sacrifice and service to others were stressed. By 1963 the army had been remolded under the leadership of Lin Piao, who succeeded Peng Teh-huai as Defense Minister in 1959.

> In the PLA troops, everyone conducts ideological work, while [outisde the PLA] only a few cadres conduct ideological work [*NCNA*, February 1, 1964, in Gittings, 1964: 157].

The Party was hopefully to learn something of mass line politics from the army.

In 1964, the Train Revolutionary Successor Generation campaign was outwardly directed at the question of opposing Russian revisionism, but in fact it was an effort to implant Mao's mass line politics in youth. In many areas it took the form of heightened efforts to persuade youth to go to the countryside to aid agriculture and learn from the peasants (*NFRB*, August 15, 1964).

> The "Learn from the People's Liberation Army" and "cultivation of successors" movements, both of which focused on the guidance and training of cadres, suggest that the primary values of mass movements is that they provide a simulated revolutionary atmosphere for those who lack revolutionary experience [Townsend, 1967: 190–191].

The campaign to Study and Apply Chairman Mao's Thought had also begun in early 1964, in an effort to increase the political consciousness of the masses and prepare them for what became the greatest of all campaigns.

The stage had been set for the Great Proletarian Cultural Revolution. The first signs began as far back as December 1964 when Chou En-lai, in his report on the work of the government, put forward a criticism of the economic policies of the early 1960s—a criticism that emerged more forcefully during the GPCR (Schram, 1972: 292). In the fall of 1965, the Shanghai newspaper *Wen Hui Bao* published a criticism and repudiation of *Hai Jui Dismissed from Office*, a play by Wu Han, which was an allegorical attack on Mao for his opposition to Peng Te-huai in 1959. Publication had originally been refused in Peking by leaders of

---

[15] A special work conference was held in September 1975 for agricultural leaders, to emphasize the need to spread the Tachai model throughout the country. A second conference was held in December 1976. A national conference to Learn from Taching is planned for spring of 1977.

the Propaganda Ministry and the City Party Committee, including the mayor, Peng Chen, who was allied with Wu Han. Peng Chen attempted to protect Wu Han by issuing a mild criticism concentrating only on academic questions and avoiding political ones. Peng was repudiated in the May 16, 1966, "Circular of the Central Committee of the Communist Party," which was not published until a year later. By June 1966, the GPCR came into full view of the world with the posting of the first big character poster at Peking University.

No attempt shall be made here to document the struggle that ensued; that has already been done by several others.[16] Nor shall analysis be attempted of all the explanations offered for the GPCR; a summary is sufficient. The GPCR has been viewed as a

> power struggle within the Party [Newhauser, 1967]; as an effort to close China off from the world [Moravia, 1968, 1969]; or as a bigger and better Maoist purge [Chang, 1969]; or a revivalist movement against modernization [Baum, 1967]; or as a struggle between the "ins" and "outs" [Tsou, unpub.]; or as a quasi-religious search for ultimate values or "symbolic immorality" [Lifton, 1968]; or as a struggle between leaders and party [Schwartz, 1968a]; or as the extension of Maoist megalomania [Michael, 1967]; or as a response to America's Vietnam War [Schurmann, 1966]; or as a broad based assault on privilege and bueaucracy [Huberman and Sweezy, 1967]. There is some truth and much overlapping to all these interpretations [Pfeffer, 1971: 250–251].[17]

However, the thrust of the GPCR seems to have been a struggle over whom the Chinese revolution was to serve: an entrenched elite or the masses:

> Mao's policy . . . may be seen as an effort to secure the commitment particularly of the younger generation to the building of a more just society, a commitment that arises from participation in the revolutionary act of defying authority. Mao would rather delay China's industrialization than have its industrialization serve the purposes of an entrenched bureaucratic elite. In this respect, Mao continues to be true to his revolutionary heritage. At the same time, Mao shares with many the belief that bureaucracy and industrialization do not necessarily lead to an improved quality of life. To the extent that Mao's desire is to insure that industrialization serves the interests of his society, he is dealing with the central intellectual problem of our age [Oksenberg, 1968: 493].

There is nothing to suggest that Mao either carefully planned in advance or carefully manipulated the politics of the struggle that ensued:

> Mao probably had no detailed plan for developing the Cultural Revolution. But, based upon his ideology, his personality, his experience as a revolutionary and the

---

[16] For some concrete examples of the struggle see Bennett and Montaperto, 1971; Hinton, 1972; Hunter, 1969; Milton and Milton, 1976; and Nee, 1969.

[17] For still other interpretations see Lifton, 1968: 163–164; Wheelright and McFarlane, 1970; Robinson, 1969; Committee of Concerned Asian Scholars, 1972; and Nee and Peck, 1975.

developments of the Cultural Revolution, as seen in retrospect, it seems fair to conclude that Mao had a vision of what he sought to accomplish and an intuitive conception of the means appropriate to those ends [Pfeffer, 1971: 253].

At least one participant in the Red Guards saw this to be a source of many of the excesses that occurred. Dai Hsiao-ai, the Red Guard interviewed by Bennett and Monteperto (1971), argued that although the "Sixteen Point Decision" (August 8, 1966) and the "Eleventh Plenum Communique" (August 14, 1966) both called for heightened activism, neither gave details as to the concrete procedures for implementation.

> In the absence of specific instructions, students seemed free to act according to their own opinion of the conduct of individual local Party leaders. Most students of revolutionary class background, feeling a debt to the Party that had enabled them to improve their lot, continued to be reluctant to attack it. They became known as conservatives. Their opposite number, the progressives, seemed almost too eager to begin. This conservative—progressive split, born in the era of work teams, was now greatly intensified [Dai, in Bennett and Montaperto, 1971: 67].[18]

Whatever the sources of excesses during the GPCR, by February 1967 the army had been called in to restore order among many factionalized and even warring units (Bridgham, 1968: 12). This eventually led to a campaign entitled Support the Army and Cherish the People, which lasted throughout 1968 as an effort to gain cooperation from all diverse elements in the process to restore order.

Whatever added respect members of the army gained from this campaign was certainly of value in their role as leaders of the Rectification campaign, which began in 1969 following the Ninth Party Congress in April. The Ninth Congress confirmed the new Party leadership under Mao and Lin Piao and signaled the end of the GPCR. The Retification campaign was primarily directed at the Party to ensure that all who should have had undergone criticism or been removed.

Although partly an outgrowth of the GPCR, the Barefoot Doctors campaign dates back to a speech Mao made in 1965 criticizing the inadequate health care in the villages. In fact, there had been some efforts as early as 1960–1962 to get medical workers out to the countryside on a rotating basis. From 1962 to 1966 most medical school graduates were sent out to the countryside. The response in Shanghai to Mao's speech of 1965 was to send some 10,000 medical workers out to the countryside, some to be rotated back to the city as before and some to stay in the countryside on a permanent basis. Thus, although the Barefoot Doctors' campaign did not formally begin until September 1968, many of the institutional

----

[18] This and subsequent quotes cited to Bennett and Montaperto, 1971 are from *Red Guard!* by Gordon A. Bennett and Ronald Montaperto. Copyright © 1971 by Gordon A. Bennett and Ronald Montaperto. Reprinted by permission of Doubleday, Inc.

methods for equalizing the disparities between urban and rural medical services bagan as far back as 1960.

Some campaigns did not end with the GPCR. The Learn from Tachai and Taching campaigns are still underway as of December 1976. Also, since the GPCR there have been other national campaigns including the campaigns to Criticize Lin Piao and Confucius and to Study the "Dictatorship of the Proletariat."

In many sectors of Chinese life the GPCR was not a total departure from China's past, or even a return to the mass line politics of the Yenan days.[19] Rather, the GPCR should be seen more as a culmination of all the mass mobilization efforts before it. It did not bring to the fore radically new institutions never before attempted. Rather it brought into the central arena of Chinese life institutional forms, based on Mao's mass line politics in health, education, and the training of cadres, that had been tried but not thoroughly implemented because of opposition from Liuist policies and the backward and traditional character of social conditions. It is in this sense that "Chairman Mao's Revolutionary Line" won "still greater victories" during the GPCR and that the campaign mobilization strategy, including the GPCR, has been an unending process.

THE FLOW OF CAMPAIGNS: CAUSAL RELATIONSHIPS?

That the campaign mobilization effort has been continuous is beyond doubt. Even when campaigns of high mobilization have not been prominent, there have been many other campaigns under way with lower levels of mobilization.

I have in this chapter suggested how the campaigns have been related to each other and to other events. Although not every campaign necessary flows from another, especially in the case of smaller campaigns, the evidence suggests that most campaigns are interrelated with others. More specifically, the evidence suggests that the outcome of one campaign influences the timing and character of the following campaign, particularly within any given sector of the society (e.g., agriculture, industry, the Party, intellectuals). For example, there has been a clear development in the area of agriculture: first, Agrarian Reform, then Mutual Aid, Lower-Level Cooperatives, Higher-Level Cooperatives, Communes, and Aid Agriculture. The progression of campaigns aimed at intellectuals has also been clear: from Ideological Remolding, to the criticism of Hu Feng, to *Su Fan*,

[19] Pfeffer (1972: 623–628) makes the argument that only the GLF and the GPCR really qualify as a return to the mass line politics of Yenan. He has conceded, however, in a discussion I had with him, that he may have failed to consider sufficiently the impact on the GPCR of mass line politics and campaigns in the period from 1949 to 1966

to the Hundred Flowers campaign, to Mao's speech "On Handling Contradictions," to the Rectification campaign of 1957, to the Anti-Rightist campaign. Campaigns in other sectors also reflect these interrelationships, although their interrelationships may not be as strong as in campaigns relating to intellectuals and agriculture.

On the other hand, the understanding of this relationship has become possible only in retrospect. There appear to be no indicators able to predict the emergence of campaigns some years hence. Moreover, no evidence of any kind of master plan involving *specific* campaigns has yet been found. There are, however, indications that there was a degree of prior knowledge of agricultural campaigns—the evidence presented suggests that by 1949, or shortly thereafter, it was clear that there would be several steps in the transformation process, at least to the level of collectivization or a "fully socialist agricultural economy." However, the institutional forms each step would produce were not always clear. This is particularly the case with the communes, which seem to have been discussed in concrete terms only in late 1957, or perhaps early 1958. However, in the process of agricultural transformation the actual timing of the campaigns was not predictable.

In other areas there is even less evidence that any clear path was seen. For example, the criticism of Hu Feng and the *Su Fan* campaign that followed it seem to be a reaction to Hu Feng's own report, rather than a planned progression from the Ideological Remolding campaign of 1951. During the following 2 years, each successive campaign was an outgrowth and a reaction to the problems produced by the prior campaign. Nowhere is this clearer than in the failure of the Rectification campaign of 1957 and its sudden transformation into an Anti-Rightist movement. The one exception in this period might be the campaign to study Mao's speech on contradictions and the rectification campaign that followed. However, even if the rectification campaign had been planned at the time Mao made his speech, the period of prior knowledge was less than 3 months.

In short, there appears to be no master campaign plan. Campaigns seem to flow from the problems or contradictions at hand and from the consequences of previous campaigns. Other writers have, howwever, commented on the overall ebb and flow of campaigns. This cyclical pattern is noted in a Central Committee report on the Socialist Education campaign:

> the class struggle is protracted, complex, repetitive, alternatively resurgent and recessive, and sometimes acute [Chen and Ridley, 1969: 99].

Edgar Snow has suggested that Mao carried out campaign strategy "by alternating surprise, tension, and easement [1972: 187]." In his 1959 essay "On Dialectics," Mao himself alluded to the importance of mixing both tension and relaxation:

Where there is tension, there is relaxation. It is no good to have tension all the time and there should be tension as well as relaxation. Becoming too tired is no good either. It was a very good thing for the people in Honan and Hopei to concentrate on setting up red and expert schools. But they overtaxed themselves and fell asleep in classrooms. We must have both tension and relaxation. We just cannot work under tension all the time without relaxation, nor can we relax without doing work whether we are engaged in manual labor or mental work [Joint Publications Research Service, 1970: 33; see also Mao, 1967: Vol. 4, 244–245].

Liu Shao-chi, at least at the time of the GLF, appears to have agreed with Mao on the presence of some type of cycle:

The development is U-shaped, i.e. high at the beginning and the end, but low in the middle. Didn't we see very clearly how things developed on the production front in 1956–1958 in the form of an upsurge, then ebb, and then an even bigger upsurge or, on other words, a leap forward, then a conservative phase and then another big leap forward [in Ho and Tsou, 1968: 711–712].

Liu, however, apparently placed much more stress on the need for equilibrium, for stability (Schram, 1972: 289).

Richard Solomon appears to agree with Liu Shao-chi, but goes further, suggesting that the "radical" cycles seem to come after periods of poor economic performance.

First there is a phase of conflict between radical and conservative groups ("reds" and "experts") within the Party leadership over proper policies for social advance—a debate in which several years of poor economic performance enable the radicals to build support for a basic institutional restructuring of society. The radical claim is that they will "liberate the productive forces" (popular energies) through a rearrangement of the "relations of production" (the pattern of property ownership and work organization).

This change in policy line within the leading councils of the Party is followed by an inner Party rectification campaign in which lower level opponents of a more radical line are criticized or purged, and the new Party organization is mobilized for the leadership tasks of a new mass campaign. A period of public "study" and discussion ensues, in which the objectives of the campaign are propagated to "the masses" and objections are refuted. On the basis of these preparations, a period of intense institutional change or labor mobilization then takes place.

In the period of "upsurge" in organizational change or work activity, excesses are committed by over-zealous Party cadres. These excesses produce economic or organizational difficulties which more conservative leaders invoke in order to shift opinion within the Party "center" toward a period of consolidation. The radicals thus begin to lose their influence in policy-making. "Expert" considerations reemerge and a more moderate orientation persists until further economic or social problems once again enable the "reds" to reassert their influence over Party policy. Then another round of the pattern or cycle begins [Solomon, 1971: 347–348].

Solomon's characterization of campaign cycles may or may not be valid; however it fails to specify the missing link—the source of economic or social problems giving the "reds" or "radicals" the change to assert their power and push for a campaign.

Economists Barry Richman (1969) and Alexander Eckstein (1968) both hold that it is the campaigns themselves that create the problems. However, in contrast to Solomon they argue that campaigns, at least economic ones, follow periods of good rather than poor economic conditions. According to Richman,

> The Red Chinese regime [sic] seems to follow an oscillation theory of industrial and general economic management, with ideology implemented most intensively when economic conditions are relatively good, and relaxed when the reverse is true. For the regime has seen from the Soviet experience in particular that economic progress and relative affluence can lead to revisionism and softness with regard to pure Communist ideology. This may explain much about the current Chinese political and civil crisis; the regime's growing fanatical emphasis on ideology at all levels of society follows several years of substantial economic progress—or economic recovery. Hence a type of vicious circle is in operation where economic progress results in extreme stress on ideology, which in turn leads to economic crisis, and then to relaxation of ideology [Richman, 1959: 3–4].

Eckstein, essentially in agreement with Richman, cites the good harvests of 1955 and 1958 to support this perspective (1968: 708). However, in 1958 at least, the GLF was already well under way early in the year, long before the size of the harvest was known. Only the full implementation of communization was delayed until after the harvest, although the decision to communize was apparently made at the Peitaho meetings in August 1958, before the harvest was in.

Solomon, Richman, and Eckstein have all concentrated on the GPCR, the GLF, and, to an extent, the HAPC. As suggested in Chapter 1, cursory evidence suggests that these campaigns are among the few that had very high negative results. Certainly it is widely held that the GLF is to date the economic campaign with the greatest number of short-term problems. If this is indeed so, then their generalizations are built on examples unrepresentative of the campaigns as a whole. (See Chapter 7 for further discussion of this point.)

Skinner and Winckler may also have overemphasized negative examples, although they have included other campaigns in their discussion of cycles.

They cite eight cycles dating from 1949 to 1965. Are there really just eight cycles in the rural sector? In an earlier draft of an article published in 1969 Skinner identifies only five cycles (1965: 13). There is nothing said in the second version (1969) to explain on what basis the number has been increased to eight. Moreover, in the discussion of the seventh cycle Skinner and Winckler say nothing about the Learn from Tachai campaign, which got under way during that period. They mention instead only the Socialist Education campaign, which seems to have been directed more at cadres than the masses. Perhaps the Tachai campaign should be an additional cycle. If so, it would overlap with the GPCR since the Tachai campaign still continues. This might well create some confusion in their model. And here is precisely the point. To make sense, the cycles must be tied to campaigns rather than dates. Skinner and Winckler imply as much when they indicate that, particularly in the early years, cycles and their phases begin at different times in different parts of the country (1969: 428).[20] Thus, in the agricultural sector, one must see not just eight cycles, but many, including other national campaigns like Learn from Tachai or the Water Conservation campaign of late 1957—1958 (Oksenberg, 1969) and many, many regional and local campaigns, too numerous to list. Each constitutes a cycle. By the same token, so do all the campaigns in other sectors, a point to which Skinner and Winckler also allude (1969: 426). Again these would include many smaller campaigns whose "high tide" is not very high and whose negative outcomes (e.g., crisis and alienation) are not very negative. (See Chapter 1 for an extended discussion of the views of Skinner and Winckler.)

Here is where Skinner and Winckler's model breaks down. Nowhere in the model is there any built-in structure to suggest that some positive results, achievements, may accompany the difficulties. Positive results are considered to be apart from campaigns, occurring during the phase of "normalcy" and as the return of remunerative benefits. Any model that has not built in both shortcomings and achievements as direct outcomes of campaigns, no matter how useful it may be in illuminating the overall policy cycle process, must ultimately be rejected as unusable in understanding the full meaning and utility of the campaign process.

What is one left with, then, to explain the flow of campaigns? Not much beyond basic agreement that there is a cyclical process alternating between low and high tides, for whatever reason. But I do have one further suggestion along this line.[21]

There is some evidence to suggest that—whether or not the total pattern was planned in advance—economic campaigns are generally preceded by ideological rectification campaigns. Rectification campaigns may also follow larger campaigns, especially those with higher levels of shortcomings.

The pattern seems to have started as far back as the Yenan period, when the *Cheng-feng* (rectification) campaign preceded several others, in production, agricultural cooperation, and other areas discussed at the beginning of this chapter. In late 1955, the thoroughgoing *Shen Gan* movement to investigate all cadres for "bad" backgrounds undoubtedly produced a more ideologically responsive cadre, more capable of carrying through the Socialist Reform of

---

[20] For example, Rent Reduction began in 1942 in Yenan, but in Sinkiang along the Russian border in 1952 landlords and "local tyrants" were still collecting usurious rents; the Rent Reduction campaign had yet to be carried out, not to mention Agrarian Reform (*XQRB*, January 31, 1952).

[21] I am indebted to Richard Barrett for the following insight.

Private Business and the move to HAPCs. Again in 1957 it is clear that the impact of the Rectification and Anti-Rightist campaigns was to solidify a more unitary ideological view among cadres. This undoubtedly reduced opposition to GLF policies:

> Mao . . . believes that consciousness . . . can be a powerful motive for action and can help to drive development forward. The rationale of the Great Leap Forward expressed this idea in the assertion that the rectification campaign of 1957 and the Leap were one continuous process in which, beginning from criticism of the bureaucracy and the bourgeoisie, the masses achieved a level of consciousness which both prepared them and motivated them to "seize power" and to create their own alternative, non-elite, society with its characteristic economy, and drag urban modern industry into its orbit. Thus, political consciousness becomes a pre-condition of economic development or, as Mao would put it, "a great spiritual force becomes a great material force" [Gray, 1973: 116].

It has also been noted how the ideological efforts of the Socialist Education movement tied into increasing production:

> Production plans were drawn up during the stage, toward the end of which mass meetings were held to announce the conclusion of the movement and to "inspire the masses to attain a high tide of production." In other words, at this conclusion, the Socialist Education movement was usually transformed into a movement for the promotion of agricultural production for the coming year [Chen and Ridley, 1969: 46].

Finally, after the GPCR, there is an example of an apparently stillborn production campaign with parallels to the GLF—stillborn, apparently because of the Sino–Russian border clashes.

Then, in at least one or two cases, there appear to be rectification campaigns aimed at correcting problems of preceding campaigns. In 1947 and 1948 rectification campaigns were carried out where there was Agrarian Reform (Teiwes, 1971: 49). Hinton describes at length the rectification campaign carried out to correct the abuses of Agrarian Reform in Long Bow village (1968: 318–364, 417–475). After the first stage of the GLF came the Counter Rightist Sympathies campaign. A rectification campaign followed the GPCR.

The first pattern, of a rectification campaign preceding an economic one, seems more common. However, in both cases, it would appear unwise to attempt too much generalization and particularly to assert the presence of a causal explanation. A pattern appears to be present only for a very few sets of campaigns. Moreover, there is no evidence to suggest that in every case there is some predetermined plan to move from a rectification campaign to an economic one, followed, if necessary, by a second rectification campaign. On the other hand, it is quite possible that having passed through a rectification campaign the leadership often sees the potential for the successful completion of an economic campaign. Po I-po, vice-premier and chairman of the National Economic Commission in 1958, stressed this link in his report to the National People's Congress on February 3, 1958:

> Is it possible to [leap forward]? Our answer is "yes." A favourable situation has been created by the nationwide rectification campaign, the anti-rightist struggle and the socialist education campaign. This means that our political system has been further consolidated; unity among the people has been further strengthened; the socialist consciousness of the entire poeple further enhanced. There can be no doubt that the unprecedented enthusiasm for socialism which has arisen out of the rectification campaign will exert a far reaching influence on the development of our national economy [PR, March 4, 1958: 11].

It would appear that Mao and his supporters were convinced of a link between the use of normative—ideological—inputs, in addition to just remunerative ones, and the achievement of economic goals—a pattern that cuts across the congruence of stage sets suggested by Etzioni and applied by Skinner and Winckler.

If there is any validity in the pattern of rectification campaigns preceding economic ones, even for just some campaigns, it is merely illustrative of a more generalized phenomenon previously discussed. The Chinese leadership operates by recognizing contradictions in the society. Campaigns are aimed at resolving these contradictions, and their resolution produces further contradictions needing to be resolved. Although there appears to be a link between some ideological and economic campaigns, it is necessary to be cautious about the predictability of any model to explain the flow of all campaigns. Not only are many of the larger campaigns left unexplained, but literally hundreds of campaigns of rectification, health, literacy, production, planting and harvesting, which tend to be recurrent and far too numerous to mention, are also unexplained—see Appendix 2 for a partial listing. (Also see Crook and Crook, 1966: 124; Goldman, 1967: 89; Teiwes, 1971.) For any meaningful understanding of causality of campaigns, one simply must return to the theory of contradictions.

With the theory of contradictions and this brief glimpse of the flow of campaigns in mind, we can turn to an examination of the major dynamic of the campaign, mobilization, and then to the shortcomings and achievements. However, to lay the groundwork for this examination, it is important to first look at the methodology of the research process.

3

Methodological
Approaches

> The method of studying social sciences exclusively from the book is ... extremely dangerous. ... We need books, but we must overcome book worship, which is divorced from the actual situation. This study of books must be integrated with our country's actual situation.
>
> —Mao, 1971: 42–43

Social science research on China is normally characterized by its inability to move beyond the documentary, library research approach into field investigation and the use of quantitative data. Of course, this is largely due to the inaccessibility of both China and good quantitative data about it.

This research represents an early effort to begin combining these different approaches, based on the belief that the results combining multiple approaches will be more thoroughly grounded. Since it is an early effort, a more thorough explication of the methods process is necessary than would be required in other research situations where procedures of sample selection, data collection, and analysis are established and frequently used.

THE SAMPLE

To date, at least 100 national mass mobilization campaigns in China have been identified—national in the sense that the same campaign occurred concurrently in several geographical areas of the country. (See Appendices 1 and 2 for lists of these campaigns.)

Literally hundreds of more localized campaigns have focused on such matters as water conservation, elimination of bad elements or ways of thinking in specific institutions, and the building or improvement of the communications system, e.g., railroads and waterways. These localized campaigns are far too numerous to deal with in one short study; Appendix 3 lists a few of them. There are also periodic campaigns, such as those for planting and harvesting, for increasing industrial production, and for improving environmental health.

Out of all this field, ultimately 36 were selected for intensive study. Selection began before field research with a preliminary study. The initial list included all those campaigns given in Appendices 1 and 2. First, a survey was made of several major periodicals from China to obtain data on mobilization activities of the campaigns. (Section D of the Interview/Data Collection Schedule, Appendix 5, was used as a guide in the survey.) Selection of approximately one-third seemed to be reasonable; the resulting number would allow some statistical comparisons and still not be too large to cover in a year of field research. These campaigns were scaled according to the Guttman technique described later, and a purposive sample was selected. Some campaigns were dropped at this point because the general survey produced little or no information on them.[1]

Fifty-five campaigns remained. They were divided into four different sets of categories. They were divided (1) on the basis of F. T. C. Yu's types (1967: 201–202) of economic, struggle, and ideological campaigns; (2) on the basis of focus in institutional areas of life: agricultural, intellectual, the Party, factories, health, military and combinations of more than one area; (3) according to whether the focus was urban or rural or both; and (4) by periods: early (1950–1954), middle (1955–1960), and recent (1961–1972).[2]

The object was to get as equal a representation as possible between each category of each set, listing no campaign more than once in each set. Starting with the highest ranking campaign, campaigns were selected for inclusion. The process went on until 40 campaigns had been selected. This allowed every category in each set, except the second, to have about one-fourth or more of the campaigns in the sample. The idea, of course, was to make the selection as

---

[1] Although it would have been possible to obtain information about them in a more intensive study, it seemed that most of these campaigns would have been less important, and therefore would have yielded less information about the mobilization process. In other words, the cost of mining information about these campaigns was seen to be too high.

[2] Alan Liu (1971: 185–186) has developed categories along two dimensions: functional diffuseness versus specificity, and whether or not there were specific targets in the campaign. But the abstractness of the functional approach did not seem to be offset by heuristic benefits of explanation. So, even though the proportional representation of campaigns in each of these four categories works out reasonably well, specifying campaigns by this set did not seem to suggest any useful benefits (see Chapter 7 for a test of Liu's categories).

representative as possible in terms of rural–urban balance, temporal sequence, and categories of campaigns.

Forty campaigns were selected rather than 35 to allow for those that might have to be dropped because informants could not be found, because other data would be insufficient for scaling purposes, or because it would be difficult to distinguish them from other campaigns and they would be best combined with those campaigns. Three campaigns were dropped for lack of informants: Reform of Christian Churches (1950), Party Rectification (1953), and Socialist Education for the Peasants (1957). Three were combined with others because the data and the informants could not make meaningful distinctions: Industrial Production (1958) with the overall Great Leap Forward; Return to the Village (1962) with Aid Agriculture; and Bring Socialist Culture to the Villages (1963) with Socialist Education.

Finally, in the process of research, a pair was added to the remaining 34: Learn from Taching and Learn from Tachai. These campaigns began in 1964, and continue to the present time. They increase the number of campaigns still in progress used in the study. They are examples of campaigns to increase production, which were underrepresented in the set of 34.

In short, 36 campaigns were selected for study; included are all 23 of the highest scoring campaigns in the preliminary study along with 11 of the others from that study and 2 added during the course of research.

Some who lean toward quantification in the social sciences might argue that this sample is too small for meaningful analysis and comparison. Others, in Chinese studies, have argued that it is too large, necessitating the digesting of too much material.[3] There are, of course, reasonable arguments for both limiting and expanding the sample. This is not a study just of campaigns; it is also a study of mobilization. The campaigns are selected, in part, as a means to an end. If anything, one might wish to argue that fewer campaigns would allow more in-depth analysis of the mobilization process. But to narrow the selection too far risks precluding observations on meaningful and important variation in the mobilization process.

DATA COLLECTION

Four major types of sources were available: secondary sources, such as monographs and books; primary source materials, such as newspapers, policy documents, radio broadcasts; personal experience during 5 weeks in China; and

[3] One sinologist in history and government, upon reading the research proposal, even suggested that I concentrate on just one campaign.

interviews with informants who had personal knowledge of the campaigns in China. Each type of source has its own limitations and merits.

Secondary Sources

Most of the secondary sources are monographs and books written by Western, usually American, writers. Many are useful in pointing to general and often key issues in the mobilization process from which it is possible to gather data on how the campaigns have ebbed and flowed (Chapter 2). These sources tend, however, to be poor providers of information on the mobilization process, such as the indicators needed for measurement and detailed qualitative descriptions of mobilization. There are notable exceptions. These tend to be narratives based on the experiences of people who have lived in a total community for a period of time. William Hinton's *Fanshen* (1968), the best example, is a graphic primary source on the details of the mobilization process.

Primary Sources

The primary sources used include numerous runs of newspapers, periodicals, pamphlets, and monitored accounts of radio broadcasts, as well as specific policy documents, which surfaced from time to time during the research. Because of the limited time available and the large quantity of material, I had to be selective. The most parsimonious method was to rely on the preliminary efforts of others. The Union Research Institute (URI) in Hong Kong maintains the most extensive collection of topically arranged newspaper clippings on China. Although that collection is less complete for the 1960s than for the 1950s, it is nonetheless a valuable answer to what might otherwise be insurmountable problems of selectivity. Where the collection was weak on any given campaign, or where it seemed useful to do so, other sources were used.

The amount of URI materials on these campaigns alone can be indicated by the fact that one research assistant was used 4 hours a day for 10 months just to cull information in sections C, D, E, and F of the Interview/Data Collection Schedule for 39 campaigns and to select materials important enough for further study. When it became apparent that one assistant could not complete the task, a second was added for the last 2½ months of the research time. This addition permitted a check on reliability. Each assistant was asked to redo the coding of campaign indicators for two campaigns the other had done, a total of four replicated codings. Given the large amount of material, and the opportunity for differences in interpretation, any lack of agreement in coding was insignificant.

The primary source materials provided a wealth of data on indicators of campaign activity, both for mobilization and for achievements and short-comings. There was also a good deal of material on the overall pattern of campaigns. However, in the area of detailed qualitative descriptions of the campaign process, these sources were predictably disappointing. They tend to lack the graphic portrayal of interactions, the tug and pull between reluctance and enthusiasm that one can find in narratives by those who have observed events firsthand over a period of time in a single locality.[4]

Personal Experience

In March and April of 1972 I visited China as a member of a 30-person Committee of Concerned Asian Scholars Friendship II delegation. For the most part we spent only a half-day to a day in each production brigade, factory, health, school, or other unit visited. There was little time to gain much in the way of insights. However, a few exceptions did produce some useful information, often by happenstance where a comment or question here or there would open a very useful discussion. By far the most valuable experience was our 5-day stay at a rural production brigade, Sandstone Hollow. At Sandstone Hollow, where we lived, and once or twice even worked, with the peasant families, there were many opportunities to probe, at some length, into the mobilization process. Included in the study is material from some 15 hours of recorded tapes, of which 6 are devoted to a protracted discussion of the socialist transformation process in the village.

Of course, it was not an easy process to separate the chaff from useful material. During the trip, the group I traveled with worked out a system of questioning that allowed each of us to take up the same line of questioning, in turn, to ensure maximum clarity and consistency. Of course, we were able to compare notes as we went from meeting to meeting, unit to unit, and experience to experience. There were three basic types of presentations. Sometimes we felt blanketed by a great public relations "snow job" that would do credit to the information office of most any government or any well-organized Western corporation. Often there would be a generalized presentation of revolutionary development over the past years in a given unit, with specific references to the enthusiasm of the masses at various points, all developed within the framework of Mao's thought. And then, on occasion, there would be a really frank discussion of who did what, when, and why; of who was opposed to this or that, why and what was done about it, and how the struggle came out in the end—i.e.,

---

[4] Two reasons might be noted for this. Some materials are often couched in generalized analytical terms, precluding long narratives of localized situations. On the other hand, there is also a good deal of material describing local case examples. Much of this portrays situations of enthusiasm and success. Often the description is of a "model" situation that people will hopefully look up to as an ideal example or goal. This material has its own positive value in the actual mobilization process, but it is less than adequate in describing the full dynamics of that process.

whether the forces of Mao's side won or lost the particular struggle at hand. In general, this third type of presentation was more likely when we talked with peasants and workers instead of cadres. Perhaps they were just more down to earth in presenting their thoughts. Of course, in any one day we tended to get some of all three types. But on occasion we would receive a really heavy dose of the third type. And here, for the most part, we found the graphic description, the emotional portrayal far too real and far too alive to be disbelieved. As one of the leading skeptics of the delegation admitted, "While there was a lot that was very difficult to believe, there was much that was impossible not to believe."

Here then was a rich source of information about group interaction dynamics of the mobilization process that was impossible to overlook. Here in the setting of the mobilization drama were the actors recounting their own stories. In one case, there is the vivid picture of how one worker pointed across the table to another and said with a smile, "He opposed our way of thinking at the outset, he was on the side of the counterrevolutionary forces." And then the two began to tell us their story of mobilization. Placed up against what we know from other sources, both sympathetic and critical, these parts of our experience produce a compelling story too real to reject, too graphic to be disbelieved.

Interviews with Informants

Informants were people who had lived in China and were living in Hong Kong at the time of the study (1971–1972). I interviewed each person in a formalized investigative situation. These people provided much information on the activities of the campaign mobilization process. Unlike using primary sources, interviewing was a parsimonious method because the specific responses desired could be obtained with a few short, simple questions. Informants were also a source for some discussion of the detailed interaction of the mobilization process, although on this more subjective level one had to be skeptical since informants represented a very skewed cross section of the Chinese population.

Since a great deal of time was spent in this interview process, it is important to deal at some length with the informants' numbers, availability, types, and reliability, as well as the bias introduced.

The primary reason for going to Hong Kong for research was the availability of informants. I refer here to informants rather than refugees because not all left China without the permission of the government and because the word *refugee* sometimes has the all too simple connotation of someone who left because he or she rejected the Communist system. Although a few expressed a total rejection, many, if not most, of those I interviewed left China in a real state of conflict: proud of their country, basically accepting and agreeing with the system and its values, but feeling that they had been dealt an injustice that forced them to leave. (Such was especially the case of many urban youth sent to the countryside to live when they wanted to remain in the city.)

NUMBERS

Approximately 205 hours were spent in 105 sessions obtaining information on the 36 campaigns in this research. Although a great deal of time was spent in this process, the number of informants interviewed was small (13). Most were interviewed about a number of different campaigns. In 9 cases each person discussed from 1 to 4 campaigns. Three discussed 6, 7, and 8, respectively. And one was interviewed on the rather large number of 21 campaigns, nearly 60% of all the campaigns.[5]

Where possible, at least two interviews were obtained for every campaign. For 6 campaigns there were 3 interviews apiece, but in 10 cases it was not possible to locate a second person who was at least a teenager at the time of the campaign and who had been a direct participant in it—both essential criteria for interviewing an informant on any given campaign.

AVAILABILITY

With the exception of urban youth who had been students and were then sent down to the countryside, there were limited numbers of people willing to be interviewed. There were drawbacks to interviewing these students in that most were so young that they really remembered only the GPCR.

Thousands of former residents of China now live in Hong Kong, but most prefer not to talk about their past, at least to a total stranger. Many are sufficiently secure economically that they are not interested in the marginal economic incentive that is customary in the interviewing process (about $3.50 per 2-hour session). It is possible that some fear the interviewers are either agents of the right (the United States government—in particular, the CIA) or the left (working for or reporting to Communist representatives in Hong Kong). They may think retribution will be exacted on their relatives still in China, even though there is little evidence to substantiate this.

[5] This person was interviewed so frequently because he is, as every scholar who has come in contact with him knows, one of the most informed and reliable of former residents of China. In addition, he was a middle-level cadre in several different posts in China for 12 years, from 1954 to 1966. Since coming to Hong Kong he has been engaged in continuing research on China. Although the additional knowledge gained since he left China would have interfered if he were to be treated as a single case, as an informant he was invaluable. He is a source to whom one could turn to check out minor facts and details and even to check on the reliability of statements made by others. When one would occasionally find the rare oversight in his encyclopedic knowledge of facts and figures, his good-tempered nature was always quick to admit it.

Although each of my informants was told that he or she need not answer personal questions that would identify a village or relatives, only one person took advantage of this option. At least in one case, a KMT (Nationalist government) relief agency in Hong Kong refused to cooperate because it said Communists had appeared at the Universities Service Center—at the invitation of the director and/or his assistant.

I was, therefore, primarily dependent on people working at the center who had either lived in China or who were willing to introduce acquaintances who had. All the informants were obtained in this way.[6]

TYPES

The following classification distribution is based on each informant's principal status, when in China:

student	5
teacher	2
peasant	2
cadre	1
member of "bad classes"[7]	3

Alternatively, if one looks at the total number of classifications the informants occupied during a campaign that they discussed, there is a greater spread.[8]

student	10
teacher	2
peasant	2
cadre	2
military	2

[6] Another alternative was to use a paid go-between. But on the basis of reports of others who tried this, the risks of uneven quality, poor reliability, and just plain fraud seemed high enough to offset the advantage of obtaining a few other useful people. Thus this alternative was eliminated at the outset.

[7] There are five "bad classes" in China: counter-revolutionary, landlord, capitalist, rightist, and rich peasant. All three of these informants were labeled as rightists and were struggled during the Anti-Rightist campaign of 1957.

[8] In spite of this greater spread, it was hoped that another one or two cadres could be located. Since cadres provide leadership in most campaigns it is likely they would be more aware of the content and process of most campaigns. It was also hoped that another peasant or two could be located since neither of the two interviewed had actually been peasants prior to the GLF. One had been a small merchant in a town near his village and knew of the transformation process; the other went from school to a collective farm only shortly before the GLF.

There is also the problem of geographical limitation. Only five of the informants discussed experienced outside of Kwangtung province and only one was actually from North China. (See Appendix 4 for a more detailed analysis of the informants' backgrounds.)

medical worker	1
worker	2
member of "bad classes"	1
small merchant	1
youth sent to countryside	3

INTERVIEW SETTING AND PROCESS

All the interviews were conducted at the Universities Service Center in Hong Kong in an office purposely devoid of political slogans or pictures. (The only exceptions were a few interviews with my language tutor.)

I conducted all the interviews alone, except for two where my assistant was present for the first half-hour or so to be sure that the informants' poor Mandarin and their heavy Kwangtung rural accents would not interfere with my understanding their comments.

Although some interviewers use a tape recorder and/or an assistant, after discussion with my assistant and others it was decided that neither was necessary. Since the questions in the interview called for simple, straightforward responses, it would be easy to record the responses manually on an interview schedule. Also, my assistant was known to nearly all my informants, and they might have been unwilling to discuss some things in his presence. However, I was always able to check with my assistant later about an informant's reliability.

Prior to the first interview date the informant was given a general introduction to the topic and to my background. This, plus the fact that all except one of the informants knew me and/or my assistant, seemed to eliminate any suspicion or hostility. Upon their arrival for the interview I attempted to put them at ease and expressed interest in their comfort.[9] Once at ease, informants began to ask questions about me. Those of a personal nature I readily answered (e.g., how old I was, whether I was married, whether I had children, where I had gone to school). However, I attempted to delay questions about China, either by changing the subject or, in the face of persistence, by suggesting that since time was short and their questions required a long answer I would save some time at the very last interview to respond. Their persistence increased, of course, after I came back from China as all were most interested and had many questions to ask. The result was rather long sessions at least with two informants after all the interviewing with them was complete. I felt this was a rather low cost when placed against the risk that my opinions voiced during the process of interviewing might have interfered with the character of informants' comments.

[9] They were offered tea and asked, for example, if the room was too cold or hot or did they have a rough time getting to the center on the bus. At least one break was taken during each session, at which time they were encouraged to "look around"—go read a newspaper, help themselves to refreshments, etc. As they reappeared for additional sessions, they were also encouraged to chat about their own lives and opinions regardless of the relation to the research topic.

The possibility that persons who have left the People's Republic of China might be less willing to talk with people like myself with sympathetic views toward China seems unfounded. The informants most critical of Chinese society (the three "bad elements") seemed to make an extra effort to educate me about the "realities" of China. At least one, when I told him that I would have to halt interviewing temporarily because I was going to China, made a very impassioned plea not to believe what I was told in China. On the other hand, most of the others I interviewed, when they finally learned of my attitudes, seemed to be impressed by the respect I had for China and what it was trying to do, although I was critical of certain aspects. Although life in China had simply become too hard for most informants as individuals and they were unhappy about certain policies, they were far from rejecting of the total society. After they came to Hong Kong they were faced with that society's crime, pollution, corruption, and neglect, and its crass and alienating character, all of which are virtually absent in China. One could see a certain nostalgia in their comments, such as "If I had only been able to work in a factory in the city instead of having to work on a commune, I would have stayed in China." These were typical of the student informants as well as other youth with whom I spoke informally.

The interviews were conducted around a schedule of questions (Appendix 5). I skipped around a great deal, using the questions to prompt informants and letting informants go where their thoughts would take them. If it seemed promising, I encouraged them to talk about topics only marginally related to the topic at hand. However, when a long-winded oration on the general failure of Communism or other similar topics seemed to be forthcoming, I tried to move on to other subjects.

It took an average of 3 hours to cover all the questions. The range was from 1 to 12 hours. The first time an informant was interviewed on a campaign there was more ground to be covered. Sections A, H, and sometimes B were not repeated if the informant was interviewed about more than one campaign. At the beginning of the interviewing process minor uncertainties in terminology needed to be resolved and questions clarified. Also, some informants had more information or were better at recalling it than others. Finally, there was the character of the campaign itself. A short, small, and relatively unimportant campaign, like the Peace Signatures campaign of 1950, just did not require as much time to discuss as did larger ones like Agrarian Reform or the GPCR.

Since it took about 3 hours to cover all the questions but each session lasted only 2, informants were asked to return. In the interval, the results of the first interview were carefully gone over. Vagueness or incomplete responses were noted and checked, and, if necessary, questions were prepared for follow-up. Points of apparent conflict with other sources were noted and checked. Finally, a general evaluation of informants, including a specific look at their backgrounds, determined whether it would be useful to invite them back for discussions on other campaigns. In two cases this was not done. In one the informant had apparently not participated in any other campaigns. In the other the informant chose not to return apparently in part because she had just found a job and did not feel that the extra money was worth the cost in time and in potential psychological stress in the recall of her campaign activities. One person after two campaigns and a second after three campaigns were rejected for further interviews because they simply spent too much time trying to tell me how bad Communism was. Both were "bad elements." The other seven informants were invited back until there were no more campaigns they had participated in for which I needed additional interviews.

RELIABILITY

Using informants of this type had its risks. With one exception, they all left China without permission of the government and in some way were unhappy about some aspect of life there. Informants in Hong Kong simply do not represent a cross section of China's population. To what extent might their unrepresentative character affect the outcome of the research?

First, how would background and experience influence their attitudes toward China? These informants tended to be urban, from Kwangtung Province or its capital city, Kwangchow, and members of the bourgeoisie or even the "five bad elements." Would they not see things in a distorted manner? This did seem to be the case in discussing campaigns where the informants themselves had been targeted as the subject of attack or criticism. On the other hand, in situations where the campaign had not been directly aimed at the informant, the nature of their responses closely paralleled those from the few atypical informants interviewed who did not have "bad" backgrounds, or even written sources. For example, a person who in 1957 was struggled as a rightist tended to get lost in defending himself when talking about that campaign. However, on the Agrarian Reform campaign, in which he participated as a work team member, he was quite informative. The answer, then, was to interview informants about campaigns they were not the targets of; but if they were targets of a campaign they were interviewed on, I judged the results in that light.

Second, to what extent might informants lie? This could be a serious problem if one were engaged in specialized research. At least one researcher engaged in work on the legal system found many "instant" legal experts (Cohen, 1967). However, my assistant had been specifically instructed to make it very clear to each informant that they would have useful information no matter what their background and experience. Everyone who had lived in China experienced at least 1 campaign, if not 10, 20, or even 100, and could provide me with useful information. Moreover, for those who might have been worried about revealing personal information that might identify their home or family, I made very clear that this material was not essential to my research and they could decline to answer. Only one exercised this option, and that was apparently because she was embarrassed about talking to a young foreign male. Finally, since informants knew me and/or my assistant, a personal bond existed that encouraged the reporting of events as accurately as possible. Informants had positive incentives not to lie. They were assured of having useful information to share. To the extent they were willing to present a useful and coherent picture of events, they knew they would be invited back.

Third, how accurate would recall be? The potential for serious problems here seemed greater because people were being asked to recall events that occurred as long as 20 years earlier. Other researchers cautioned that I would face problems of informants placing events in different time frames. Some even felt that the resulting confusion would invalidate the usefulness of the interviewing technique for these earlier periods.

In terms of pinpointing the actual months and years of a campaign, this often proved to be the case. I asked informants to name a season if they were peasants; if they were teachers or students I asked them to recall at what point in the semester the campaign occurred. However, in terms of years, the process was more difficult. An informant might date a campaign in relation to another, but then there might be a year or two in between the two campaigns.[10] By and large, I avoided questions about dating beyond relating the events concerned to other events. One exception was the cadre interviewed, who was able to provide most of the important dates in question. Undoubtedly his current research role has helped to refresh his mind.

In terms of campaign indicators, the informants' recall capabilities proved to be far better than expected. Although campaigns occurred quite frequently, they were different enough from the pattern of everyday life to stand out in a person's memory. They were the most unordinary of the ordinary. For example, one informant described in vivid detail some of the mobilization activities of the Land Reform campaign. The informant then admitted that it was her first real trip to the countryside. Clearly the experience had left an indelible impression on her mind. This same informant also had very clear memories of work on the night shift for the construction of the Ming Tombs Reservoir during the GLF. Although the events of other campaigns were not always so dramatic, there still was enough that was different or unusual about them to etch them into a person's memory. This is not to say there were no problems of recall, but the problems were far less than other people may have encountered on other topics.

Fourth, how often did informants respond to questions with a thoughtless yes or no? On the whole, most questions required only simple, direct replies, in

---

[10] One of the peasants I interviewed dated the move to HAPCs as 1954–1955, while arguing that his cooperative was among the last 15% to be formed. Despite persistent questioning on four different occasions, he would neither concede that it was actually lower level cooperatives that he was speaking of or that he had mistaken the dates.

order to avoid long, subjective, and possibly unreliable replies. Unless the probability of an event was rather high (e.g., a newspaper article or radio broadcast), I asked for a concrete example if informants returned a simple yes. If they failed to produce an example, the coding was changed unless they strongly insisted that the event occurred but they could not remember a concrete example at the time. In that case a question mark was added. (The coding system will be explained in the next section.) Even when an example was given, it was often important to inquire beyond the example to be sure that the event described was directly related to the campaign and not just historical happenstance. When simple negative answers were given, particularly those that seemed unlikely given the campaign, the question would be rephrased or repeated later in the interview.

Fifth, when the response to a question varied from informant to informant, how much of the variation could be ascribed to unreliability, and how much to legitimate variation (participation in different units, different geographical location)? Written material sometimes helped to weight the balance in favor of one informant or another, but at other times it caused further problems. Occasionally two informants agreed but the written source differed.

The analytic process necessitated the examination of all sources with respect to their relative reliability. In the absence of a uniform pattern, it seems reasonable to assume that the divergence was due primarily to genuine variation rather than to unreliability. In short, in spite of the complications inherent in combining informant and written sources, this is ultimately the best way to counter problems of informant unreliability.

DATA ANALYSIS

All responses of informants to questions on mobilization, achievements, and shortcomings were coded on the interview schedule. The frequency with which events occurred and any doubt an informant had whether an event occurred were noted. A similar coding process was completed for all written sources—mainly Chinese newspapers examined by my assistants but also other primary documents examined by them as well as by me. The frequency of any given event in each campaign was weighted as follows:

0—Not present (usually found in the interview only).

1—Recorded once or responded yes.

2—Recorded two or three times.

3—Recorded more than three times.

4—Occurred too often to record all occurrences (usually five or more).

?—No data available.

Occasionally informants indicated a moderately high or very high frequency for an event and their response would be coded 2, 3, or 4, as appropriate.

In order to obtain dichotomous categories of "present" or "absent," the weighted results were analyzed. In most cases all sources agreed. When there was disagreement, if one source was scored as 2 or more, the event was assumed to have occurred in at least one place and it was coded "present." When a given event was coded only 1 or 0, the presence of uncertainty was noted along with the general evaluation of the source. For example, the cadre interviewed was evaluated as the most reliable and his responses were preferred when there was no clear-cut choice.

As I have said, disagreements were not frequent. Nonetheless, a system of scoring was devised to find out whether any one campaign or any one indicator across all campaigns had a high level of disagreement or unreliability. Four types of disagreements were isolated. They have been scored by increasing level of disagreement.

1—One informant disagrees, but the other(s) is in agreement with the written source; or where there are three informants but no written source there is a 2—1 split.

2—No written sources consulted have recorded the indicator and the two informants disagree.

4—The written sources and the informant(s) disagree but in neither case has the indicator been recorded as occurring more than once.

8—The written sources and the informant(s) disagree to the extent that one or the other records the indicator as having occurred more than once.

Each indicator for each campaign has the potential disagreement score of 8. A single indicator across all campaigns produces a denominator of 288 (8 X 36 campaigns). The observed score of disagreement/unreliability is the numerator. The result is the disagreement/unreliability ratio.

One might have expected that this disagreement/unreliability ratio would be especially marked in the areas of achievements and shortcomings, as official written sources might emphasize achievements whereas informants might emphasize shortcomings. In fact, there was less divergence here than for campaign mobilization (range, .00—.38). The range for shortcomings is .01—.11, and for achievements it is .01—.24. To understand this, it is important to note that the Chinese tend to discuss their problems in the press, often in order to encourage discussion and resolution of the problems at basic levels in the society. Also, as mentioned earlier, most of the informants recognized much that was good in the system and the society. They had no desire to cover up achievements in China. These factors, along with the more public or obvious character of the activities in question, serve to produce the relatively low levels of disagreement/unreliability.

It was noted whether the length of the campaign or the time of occurrence was related to the disagreement ratio. A correlation of tau_b −.09 suggests little relationship between campaign length and disagreement. The same is true for the order of occurrence from 1950 to 1968 where the correlation with disagreement is only tau_b −.05.

The range of disagreement on any given indicator across all campaigns is from .00 to .38. However, no potential indicator with a disagreement ratio of over .15 was used. Nine potential indicators, otherwise statistically acceptable for inclusion in the final scales, were rejected for having unacceptably high levels of disagreement/unreliability.

The coded responses were then analyzed on a Guttman scaling program. [11] Guttman-type scaling is uniquely suited for analyzing these data since its analytic properties do not test the assumption that all indicators occur at the same time. [12] Rather, it tests the extent to which there is a building effect such that when one indicator is present all indicators preceding it in the scale should also occur. Statistically acceptable scales produce a stair-step pattern. The expectation is that the pattern of events will stop at different points on the "stairs" for different cases (i.e., campaigns). It is on this basis that one can make statements about which campaigns have greater levels of mobilization, shortcomings, and achievements than others.

Yet, even with this technique in one's analytic kitbag, there is much still to be said for qualitative analysis, since many elements of the mobilization process are best portrayed by narratives of concrete examples. Above all, there is the subtle interplay of forces that can be fully characterized by neither a statistical analysis of indicators on the one hand nor the narration of human dynamics on the

---

[11] This program was written by Nancy Moxley for the Department of Rural Sociology, Cornell University, generalized by me for Cornell, and adapted for use on the Michigan Terminal System by Dan Ayres. It is slightly revised from the original Guttman method (1947), as it allows for missing data and permits one to sort out events that do not seem common to a single universe. For a similar example using this process see Cell (1974). In this respect it is similar to Lingoes' Multiple Scalogram Analysis (1963), except that where Lingoes restricts selection of indicators to rigid statistical criteria, this program allows a combination of conceptual and statistical factors in the selection process. The results, however, tend to be similar, except this method permits an indicator with a somewhat higher error score in a scale, but a strong conceptual basis to be included in the scale because it can be compensated for by other indicators with lower error ratios. Error ratio is defined as "errors/lowest column nonmodals" in scale. See Guttman scalograms in Chapters 4, 5, and 6 for examples of error ratios. Errors in these scalograms are ◊ or \.

[12] More rigorous social science analysis disparages such ordinal nonparametric techniques as Guttman scaling. No claim is intended here as to its singularly compelling capabilities. One must be candid about this. In social science research on China, the alternative, however, is usually not more robust parametric techniques; rather it is case study analysis. Although this approach is not rejected either, the point is to use the best alternatives possible, not to revere the possible alternatives.

other. Each of these considerations is met from examining a wide variety of sources. As such, there is no single one best way to proceed, no single type of source that is best suited for the complex task at hand. In short, we must move slowly and carefully to describe the construction of measures for mobilization, achievements, and shortcomings—the task of the next three chapters.

4

Mobilization

> Our central task at present is to mobilize the broad masses to ... spread revolution throughout the country.
>
> —Mao, 1971: 51

The first rays of the early light began to flicker through the trees surrounding the dormitories of Peking University.[1] As the students emerged from the dormitories, they carried not their books for classes, but small bundles containing a change of clothes or two, a *mian bei* (a sort of quilt stuffed with cotton), and perhaps a toothbrush and towel. As more and more students emerged, one could sense a ground swell of excitement as the breaths from many conversations merged into small white puffs of "smoke" in the crisp cold winter air.

It was the winter vacation of 1951, but the students were not going home. Exams had been cut short. The resumption of classes had been delayed for several days. This had not happened since the Communists had come to Peking in 1949. The students were being mobilized to *xia xiang*, or go out to the countryside to participate in the campaign to Resist America–Aid Korea. More than 90% of the 1000 students then enrolled in Peking University had been organized according to "small groups" (formalized study groups) to spend the next few days living, working, and talking with the peasants of Chang Ping county, just north of the city.

Xiao Long was among them.[2] A second-year student in the Department of

---

[1] At that time it was known as Yen Ching University. The name was changed in 1952.

[2] A pseudonym for one of my informants. She left China in 1964, on an authorized exit visa as her husband is Hong Kong Chinese. She remains sympathetic toward the socialist system in China. The description by her was given in an interview. It is edited for clarity and grammar.

Chinese, she had grown up in Peking. She was the daughter of a machine inspector in a cotton mill.

> I was excited, but also very unsure about going to the countryside. Sure, I had taken trips out into the surrounding countryside, but I had never really talked with a peasant family before, let alone lived with one! My classmates weren't any more certain. You know, most of the students at the university at that time were from the upper classes, better off than my family. Most could even speak English before they enrolled. None of us had any feeling of what it was like to be a peasant. Looking back, I suppose none of the peasants we were to meet knew much about university students.

At the time, most students thought they were just going for a few days to help in the campaign. They were planning to visit homes during the day and to stage plays and other cultural activities in the evening to promote the Resist America—Aid Korea campaign as well as other campaigns under way at the time. One of the plays they staged depicted the power of the landlords and how it was broken by the peasants and the cadres of the Communist party culminating in the Agrarian Reform campaign.

> You know, I never knew just how much the peasants hated the landlords until that night. As the "landlord" was being attacked on the stage by the "peasants," the peasants in the audience got so caught up in their hatred for the old system that some of them rushed the stage to attack the "landlord." And the poor student who was playing the landlord was so scared that he ran off the stage in fright! And the acting was pretty bad at that. So I guess they must have really hated them.

Thus, the students who had gone to the countryside to assist in the mobilization of the peasants had also come to understand better, through graphic experience, the peasantry and their livelihood. The students themselves had been mobilized to reduce the barriers of ignorance between classes and groups that the old society left behind.

Going to the countryside, staging dramas, and working and living with the peasants are only a few of many activities that are often part of a mobilization campaign. I shall in this chapter discuss many of the major activities that occur during campaigns, in order to see which ones form a pattern that can be used to measure the relative levels of mobilization among campaigns. After viewing the overall process of mobilization, I shall examine in depth one major phase of the process: the role of criticism/self-criticism and struggle. Finally, I shall consider the emphasis the Chinese have placed on persuasion rather than coercion as a key to the mobilization process.

MOBILIZATION INDICATORS

Although it is not his explicit intention to do so, J. P. Nettl (1967) has come very close to characterizing in theoretical terms the process of mobilization in

China. He considers mobilization to be a process that is induced, rather than a state that "can be worked out either from 'hard' objective indices, or simply abstracted from subjective notions like participation, levels of cognition, etc. These latter are treated as second order consequences [Nettl, 1967: 32]."

Nettl sees mobilization as essentially (1) attitudinal in that it is a commitment to action, and (2) a means of translating such commitment into action. Several stages are involved:

1. The presence of values and goals that require mobilization.
2. Action by leaders, elites, or institutions that seek to mobilize the people.
3. Means of achieving the mobilization, both institutional and collective.
4. Those symbols and references through which values, goals, and norms are communicated to, and comprehended and internalized by, the people to be mobilized.
5. The process through which "mobilization takes place in terms of individual interaction, the creation and change of collectivities and structures, the crystallization of roles, the effect of subsystems and their boundaries [1967: 33]."
6. Estimated figures for the numbers mobilized (or the proportion of the population mobilized) also estimates on the degree of mobilization among various sectors of the population.

In translating Nettl's formulation into the specifics of the Chinese process, five of the six parts will be used.[3]

1. The values are those briefly characterized at the outset of Chapter 1 as those of *socialist transformation*. The goals in this case are the specific aims of the individual campaigns described in Chapter 2. Since the concern here is the process of mobilization, these values and goals will not be examined at greater length.
2. The building of commitment among individuals and groups through leadership communication takes place through informational activities, including the media and special information meetings.
3. The institutional means of achieving mobilization include the use of Party and mass organizations and the guidance of leadership cadres.
4. The process by which mobilization becomes human interaction, i.e., the translation of commitment into action, is inherent in mass participation activities of the campaign, including meetings of criticism and struggle, and in the special work of the necessary activity at hand.

[3] It would be difficult to obtain accurate estimates of the proportion of population mobilized for any given campaign. The attempt, however, has been made to determine whether one or more sectors of the population (e.g., peasants, workers, intellectuals) have been mobilized and what effects, if any, the mobilization of multiple sectors has had on the outcomes of the campaigns. See Chapter 7.

5. The three preceding aspects of the mobilization process each produce symbols and references used to communicate and concentrate action during the mobilization process. These include speeches, statements, and slogans.

The importance of symbols in the mobilization process has been noted by others:

> A significant tool of government is that of ceremonialism and symbolism in their myriad forms. . . . They may, of course, be weapons of revolution and revolt as well as authority. . . .
> Impressive situations, either historical or hoped for, are presented in a desirable light, with life, warmth, and color; and vigor and vitality are developed in the otherwise abstract of group unity. Flags, music, festivals, and holidays; . . . demonstrations, monuments, buildings, and public ways—all play their part in the ritualism which envelops social life in a network of observances intimately associated with movements in the lives of the great masses of individuals [Merriam, 1945: 81–82].

Relating Merriam's observations to political participation in China, Townsend notes,

> the enormous importance of public symbols and rituals, . . . though frequently denigrated as lacking substantive political content, nonetheless hold great political meaning for at least some participants [1967: 7].

Many such symbols have been identified in order to use them as indicators of mobilization. In accordance with Nettl's definition (1967: 33) they are divided into three groups: informational (building of commitment by leaders), organizational (institutional means of achieving mobilization), and mass participation (means of translating commitment into action). Informational activities are those that tend merely to impart information to the masses involved in the campaign. The masses receive the information in a passive rather than active manner (e.g., attending meetings to listen to speeches and reports rather than participating through discussion). Organizational activities involve the institutional structures used to facilitate the campaign. These two groups of indicators are consequently more likely to relate to leaders or cadres rather than the masses. Mass participation indicators, on the other hand, involve the active participation of the population in the campaign. Because of the greater number of indicators in the first and third groups, these groups are further divided into subgroups on the basis of apparent similarities. Although there is no explicit supportive evidence, it appears that informational activities occur earlier in the campaigns and activities of mass participation occur later. Organizational activities seem to be scattered throughout the campaign. The point here is obvious: It takes informational and, to some extent, organizational inputs to turn commitment into mass action.

In the sections of this chapter that follow, I shall first list and then discuss the indicators of mobilization according to the categories just described. In discussing each of these indicators, I shall not attempt to cite all occurrences recorded for every campaign. In many cases this would consume half a page. Rather, references will, for the most part, be limited to sources that discuss the indicators as recurring phenomena in the campaign mobilization process.

One final caveat before we plunge into a long list: The indicators of campaign mobilization discussed here are by no means the only ones. The list is rather a gathering in of indicators that surfaced during the preliminary stages of research. There are unquestionably many more, although hopefully the most important are included. (Certain indicators were not included in the scale for statistical reasons although data were collected on them. These are listed in footnotes appended to each section.)

Informational Indicators: Media

Newspaper articles

Newspaper editorials

Slogans

Short stories

Stories of people sacrificing their lives in carrying out the campaign

Pamphlets

Books

"Campaigns usually begin with a series of articles and editorials in newspapers [Mills, 1959: 74]." All cadres are expected to keep abreast of information in newspapers and communicate it to the masses. Hence, newspapers are among the most common means used by the leadership to send information about a campaign to the masses. Slogans are always used in campaigns. Perhaps the most active use of slogans was during the GPCR, when every day in the upper right-hand corner of the *People's Daily* a slogan or single-sentence "directive" of the day from Chairman Mao would appear to guide the people in the work of the campaign.

Short stories are used to emphasize the work of the campaign. Also common are stories of people who sacrificed their lives in the implementation of the campaign. During the GPCR this was seen as the highest fulfillment of the slogan, to "fear neither hardship nor death."

Major speeches, directives, articles, and the like may be combined into pamphlets and occasionally into books. These are published for mass distribution and study during the campaign. They are often compiled by provincial propaganda departments so that they include not only material from the national level but also articles describing local conditions. Articles frequently center around the description of "model" groups that have done an especially good job of carrying out the campaign.[4]

Informational Indicators: Display

> *Dui lian*
> Banners
> Photographs
> Exhibits
> Handicrafts

Display indicators are directed at bringing the messages of campaigns before the eyes of the people and, hopefully, to the forefront of their thinking. I have already spoken of slogans. Slogans are displayed in all manner of ways. They are written on sets of paper and hung on either side of doorways (*dui lian*). They may become banners, which are used during parades, hung over the entrances to production and institutional units, and hung on stages as a backdrop for meetings and rallies.

Photographs, sometimes combined with other materials, are used in public exhibits. Such exhibits are likely to occur at a later stage of a campaign. During Agrarian Reform, for example, it was common to display weapons the landlords used to punish peasants who could not pay their rent. Sometimes these exhibits include handicrafts such as wood carvings or clay figures.[5] Repeated efforts have been made to encourage handicrafts to be political in character, promoting campaigns or other important events of the time.[6]

---

[4] Seven potential media-related informational indicators were rejected: Two, radio broadcasts and statements or directives from national leaders, failed to differentiate any campaigns yet had one and two errors respectively. One indicator at the other end of the scale, quotation signboards, differentiated only two campaigns and seems to have been used only after the GPCR began, thus violating the guideline of potential applicability to all campaigns. Finally, four indicators, songs, poems, statements from the organizations supporting the campaign, and labor heros emerging from the campaign, were rejected because of unacceptably high error ratios (errors/lowest column nonmodals in scale). For a discussion of errors and error ratios, see note 11, Chapter 3. For illustrations, see the scalogram in this chapter. Two of these also had high disagreement ratios.

[5] It would also be reasonable to argue that handicrafts ought to be an indicator of mass participation. However, in China handicraft production has for centuries been something of a regularized process involving only a small percentage of the population. Moreover, since 1955 most of the hitherto individual operations and small workshops have been centralized into small factories. This means that the vast majority of the population does not participate in the manufacture but sees the handicraft only as a finished product imparting political content.

[6] Five potential display-oriented informational indicators were statistically rejected: Two, slogan posters and propaganda posters, failed to differentiate any campaigns, yet had

Informational Indicators: Gatherings and Meetings

Film shows

Slide shows

Mobilization meetings

Group targets

Ideological targets

Propaganda units may go to local villages to show films or slides (originally known in China as "magic lantern shows") to promote the campaign. At the outset of virtually every campaign there is a mobilization meeting (Chen and Ridley, 1969: 124):

> [Mobilization meetings], an essential part of the process of putting politics in command, [are] for the cadres to make clear to the people the whys and wherefores of proposals to put forward and what must be done to implement them. . . .
> First a mobilization speech would be made [Crook and Crook, 1966: 223].

For most campaigns, targets are identified and often announced at the mobilization meetings. They may be a group or class of people or a way of thinking or acting (Mills, 1959: 75; Yu, 1967: 204). Group targets have included landlords, capitalists, bureaucrats, intellectuals, or cadres, depending on the campaign. The targets can either be considered "enemies" of the people, or people thought to be basically good but in need of some reform—depending on whether the principal contradiction to be resolved in the campaign is antagonistic or nonantagonistic. Paralleling these targets are ideological targets; that is, erroneous ways of thinking or acting. These erroneous ways can range from the exploitation of peasants to the evils of bureaucracy, corruption, and waste (attacked during the Three-Anti campaign) to more diffuse, "go slow" attitudes toward various campaigns, such as those for cooperatives or communization. Although the masses do participate in all these gatherings and meetings, they are for the most part passive rather than active participants, receivers rather than givers of information.[7]

---

three and four errors, respectively. Three indicators, postage stamps, cartoons (*man hua*), and blackboard bulletins (including big character posters—*dazibao*), had unacceptably high error ratios. Perhaps if *dazibao* had been separated from blackboard bulletins as an essentially mass participation activity, it might have been includable. One of these indicators, cartoons, also had a high disagreement ratio.

[7] Four potential meeting-related informational indicators were rejected: Two—large general unit meetings and drama troupes—failed to differentiate any campaigns yet had one and nine errors respectively. Two others, propaganda teams and dances to promote the campaign, had unacceptably high error ratios. Two of these four indicators, drama troups and propaganda teams, also had high disagreement ratios.

It should be recognized that the informational indicators listed here and in the two preceding sections are used to promote events and activities other than campaigns. In fact, newspaper articles, editorials, and radio broadcasts are perhaps as common apart from campaigns as during them. Others, however, such as mobilization meetings and stories of the sacrifice of life, are more prevalent during campaigns. On balance, it is quite likely that most of these indicators are used more intensively, involving more people, during campaigns than during noncampaign periods.

Organizational Indicators

The sending in of cadres from the outside

Work teams

Unit plan change

Unit reorganization

Reallocation of resources

Curtailment of programs

Cadres may be sent into the villages or into urban units to assist in a campaign on a temporary basis (Whyte, 1970: 297). Cadres are often sent in groups called work teams (A. Liu, 1971: 88—90).

Sometimes, in order to participate more fully in the mobilization efforts of the campaign, units suspend or alter their work and/or study schedules. The length of time varies, from several days, in many campaigns, to 2—3 years for schools during the GPCR. In the course of a campaign there may even be a basic alteration of the structure of the unit. For example, during the GLF, dining halls were established in part to release women for work outside the home.

Finally, but in the case of only a few campaigns, financial resources play a role. Occasionally, when existing sources of money (e.g., Party funds) are insufficient, there is a reallocation of financial resources to support the campaign. And, of course, during the GPCR it was even necessary for financial reasons to curtail or suspend some ongoing programs in order to promote the campaign.

Unlike most of the informational indicators, the organizational indicators presented here[8] tend to occur more during campaigns than at other times. There are exceptions, such as work teams, or visits from outside cadres, but even with

---

[8] Six potential organizational indicators were rejected. Three—conferences or policy meetings, local cadre meetings to prepare for the campaign, and the establishment of a special organizational office to direct the campaign—failed to differentiate any campaigns, yet had 4, 6, and 10 errors respectively. Three indicators—physical participation of national leaders, special training centers for cadres, and the establishment of special schools to educate the targets—had unacceptably high error ratios. All but two, local cadre meetings and special schools for targets, had high disagreement ratios.

these indicators there is an increase in occurrence during campaigns. This pattern also seems to prevail for indicators of mass participation.

Mass Participation Indicators: General

Letter writing
Essay writing
Ad hoc newspapers
Badges
Special mention of minority groups' participation
Special mention of youth groups' participation
Participation in campaign after working hours
Xia fang

The people are constantly encouraged to express their views. The writing of letters or essays during a campaign is very common. Sometimes these will appear in newspapers; sometimes they are circulated, read, and examined by cadres in the writer's group or by the members themselves.

The use of ad hoc newspapers to promote mass sentiment was most pronounced during the GPCR, when differing factions put out their own papers. In several other campaigns such newspapers were put out by units to promote mass participation. Although one might classify these newspapers as informational, their mass production character, including ad hoc organizational structures and distribution methods, suggests that they are in fact more an indicator of mass participation.

In some campaigns Mao badges or similar types of pins or badges are worn to promote the campaign. In fact, during the GPCR there was something of a competitive spirit in producing the most creative or biggest pin. One of the largest was a handmade effort worn by a kindergarten girl. Measuring nearly 6 inches in diameter, it covered at least a quarter of her chest.

Sometimes special mention is made of the participation of youth groups or minority groups in the mobilization process. Minority areas are often considered more backward, and the campaigns are in part designed to remove the differences that create this backwardness. Thus the special mention of a minority group's participation in the campaign is suggestive of a greater mobilization effort. For example, one informant who spent some time in Yunnan tribal areas during the GLF felt that if the "leap" or changes wrought in most of China were equal to 20 years of steady change, they were equal to a century in that "backward" minority area.

In many campaigns, people not only attended meetings after working hours, but contributed their efforts in many ways, such as helping to make banners or posters for rallies or meetings.

In terms of the participation of a large number of people in the mobilization process, there is probably no activity so great in effect as the efforts "to send people down to lower levels" (*RMRB* editorial, June 2, 1963). Two aspects of this effort, the leadership cadres going down to local levels to investigate, and work teams going out to promote the campaign, have already been discussed.

The aspect considered here, however, is that of sending down, mainly to the countryside (*xia fang*), large numbers of individuals as a part of the campaign mobilization process. The distinctive character of this activity is that, unlike the leadership cadres sent down to investigate (*xia xiang*) or work teams sent to assume leadership roles, these people are sent down primarily to work with the peasants or workers, to learn from them for a period of time ranging from a few weeks to several months or years.

This process is generally believed to have begun with the Rectification and Anti-Rightist campaigns of 1957 (Lee, 1966: 43). This may be true in terms of large numbers being sent down. However, the antecedents can be found in the Yenan period (Lee, 1966: 43; Selden, 1969b; Teiwes, 1971). Although the early 1950s did not see huge numbers of people being sent down, as a part of the Ideological Remolding campaign of 1951–1952, for example, many writers and intellectuals went to live and work in villages and factories in order to understand the lives of the masses (Goldman, 1967: 95, 99). Also, "as a result of the cooperativization campaign . . . many cadres moved directly down into the production brigades of the APCs [Schurmann, 1968: 451]."

These efforts in the early 1950s were slightly different from later periods in that those who went out to assist in the transformation process in the countryside were expected not only to learn from the peasants, but also to provide leadership:

> It is necessary to send large groups of cadres with short-term training into the countryside to guide and assist the agricultural co-operative movement; but the cadres sent down from above will also have to learn how to work from the movement itself. Going in for training courses and hearing dozens of rules explained in lectures does not necessarily mean one knows how to work [Mao, in *PC*, November 1, 1955: 34].

Later, especially in the late 1950s, the stigma of punishment became attached to having to *xia fang*. In 1957–1958, thousands of cadres and intellectuals were sent down to the countryside, many with no assurances that they would soon return. During the next 2 years in only one of China's 26 provinces, 20,000 cadres had been sent down (*HQ*, 1960, No. 15: 4). By mid-1965, before the start of the GPCR, millions of educated youth had been sent down to the countryside (*PR*, July 16, 1965). During the GPCR this process was, of course, greatly accelerated for both cadres and youth.[9]

---

[9] Eight mass participation indicators were rejected. All of them has unacceptably high error ratios: written pledges to promote the campaign, visits to model areas, special mention

Mass Participation Indicators: Meetings

Study group

Criticism/self-criticism

Struggle

Accusation/public trial

Condemnation

Criticism

"Recall bitterness, think sweetness"

Individual work models

Group work models

Village rallies

Regional rallies

National rallies

Until now, there has been no extended discussion of the role of meetings in the mobilization of the masses. The meetings under Informational Indicators involved passive rather than active participation by the masses. In this section a dozen different types of meetings that directly promote mass participation in the campaign mobilization process will be examined.

There is probably nothing more pervasive than the Communist use of meetings to foster mobilization (Mu, 1962: 153). Even by 1948, peasants seemed to be aware of this. In the 20 or so years preceding the arrival of the Communists in Long Bow village, there had not been a single village meeting. The landlords used the tactic of "divide and rule." In the new months after the Communists arrived meetings had become so common that the peasants began to complain:

> "Your mother's ... "[10] said Yuan-lung (an old peasant). "Another meeting! Will there ever be an end to meetings?" And he hummed a little jingle that he had heard that day from the disgruntled Li Ho-jen, "Under the Nationalists too many taxes; under the Communists too many meetings" [Hinton, 1968: 222].[11]

---

of the participation of women's groups, individual and collective competitions, personal material donations to support the campaign, homes visited to investigate, and the ceasing of regular occupational activities to participate in the campaign. Three of these eight indicators, written pledges, special mention of women's groups, and collective competitions, also had high disagreement ratios.

[10] A most graphic swear word in Chinese: *ta ma da.* It begins with a short, sharp *ta* followed by a long, strung out *ma* concluded by a quick *da.*

[11] Hopefully Yuan-lung has grown to like meetings. Obviously there has been no end to them nor is there likely to be one under the collective orientation of Communism. This and subsequent quotes cited to Hinton, 1968 are from William Hinton, *Fanshen: A Documentary of Revolution in a Chinese Village.* Copyright © 1966 by William Hinton. Reprinted by permission of Monthly Review Press.

"Study meetings . . . are by far the most prevalent and frequent [type of meetings] [Mu, 1962: 154]." "Study" and discussions tend to be organized around formalized study groups, "small groups" of 10–20 people each. They are usually based on one's primary unit of activity during the day (e.g., factory, agricultural work group, government office, school, or neighborhood if one is retired or a housewife). Each group has one or more leaders who often have special meetings with other small group leaders in the larger unit to report on past sessions and to plan for future ones.

Study meetings are constantly occurring, sometimes even on a regularized schedule (Mu, 1962: 154–155). It would appear, however, that they occur more frequently during a campaign (Whyte, 1970: 298), when they usually begin soon after a mobilization meeting. Discussion is concentrated on the information presented at the larger meeting. The idea is to increase mass understanding and commitment to the campaign mobilization effort about to begin (e.g., "to raise political consciousness"). Meetings tend to continue throughout a campaign both as a means to obtain feedback on the participants' attitudes toward the campaign and as a channel for the introduction and promotion of new policies developed during the course of the campaign.

Perhaps the most common type of meeting is one of criticism/self-criticism. Although these meetings may occur in larger group settings, they are as likely to be a part of the small group meeting. During campaigns they generally occur in relationship to a target who is among the masses, that is, who has not been classified as an enemy or a bad element. During rectification campaigns, for example, the focus is usually on cadres and how they can improve their work-style. Cadres are expected to criticize themselves first, but if their criticism seems unsatisfactory to the people attending the meeting, those people will offer their own criticism.

This process can become relatively intense, to the point where a unit's ordinary work is eclipsed. In fact, those who do not give satisfactory self-criticisms are usually asked to "step aside" (temporary suspension from duties) while they undergo further thought and examination.

A struggle meeting, on the other hand, involves more serious errors, usually committed by targets labeled as the enemy—e.g., landlords, rightists, and people with capitalist tendencies. Although these targets may be redeemable, and can later join the ranks of the masses, their errors are of sufficient magnitude that they must undergo an extended period of thorough criticism, self-examination, and denunciation that may even culminate in forms of physical abuse, usually unsanctioned by the campaign guidelines. Mass participation is relatively high.

If, however, a target's errors are so great that an early return to the ranks of the masses is not foreseen, there may be an accusation meeting. This is essentially a denunciation of the target through a portrayal of the target's crimes by the victims themselves. Sometimes, in the most serious cases, this is done in preparation for a public trial where the masses are again asked to present evidence of the target's crimes (Mu, 1962: 153, 160–161). These types of gatherings, almost always involving the whole village or factory, were relatively common during Agrarian Reform in the effort to expose and eliminate the most brutal landlords. Clearly, the sufferings the peasants received at the hands of these people contributed greatly to the level of emotional involvement at the gatherings.

A special type of meeting is held when the target or enemy is not present. Condemnation meetings are held to denounce bad forces such as "American imperialism" in Korea and Japanese "militarism" during the effort to oppose the American–Japanese security treaty in 1960. These meetings may also be used to denounce important persons who have become enemies, such as Liu Shao-chi. The masses are mobilized to condemn these targets in absentia. When the targets are considered to be less bad (i.e., not in the enemy category) but not immediately present in the unit, there is a criticism meeting.

In general, the various types of meetings are seen as distinct on a continuum of escalation depending on the severity of the error—i.e., criticism, criticism/self-criticism, struggle, condemnation, accusation, public trial. However, in reality the distinctions are not crystal clear. The masses sometimes get struggled, the enemies are occasionally just criticized. Although this may occur because of improper care guidance, it may also occur because in reality it is often rather hard to determine just what constitutes acts of criticism as distinct from acts of struggle. Peasants who feel a fellow peasant or cadre has committed a rather serious error may offer rather harsh criticisms, but the same peasants may not put much emotion into struggling a landlord who has been relatively lenient toward them.

Other types of meetings may combine both the negative and the positive. The "recall bitterness, think sweetness" meeting encourages the masses to think of the hard times before liberation and compare them with the present, improved conditions (Mu, 1962: 153; Whyte, 1970: 298). These meetings may be used at times when extra sacrifices are called for. Thus, though the sacrifices may seem difficult at the time, they may seem less so compared with the trials prior to liberation.

Still other meetings are called during campaigns to select work "models," people who have made exemplary contributions to work. During campaigns they are often selected because of their high activist commitment to the campaign. Mao spoke of their importance as far back as 1945:

> You possess three good qualities and play three roles. First, the role of initiator. That is, you have made surprising efforts and many innovations and your work has become an example for people in general, raised the standard of workmanship and inspired others to learn from you. Secondly, the role of the backbone. Most of you are not cadres yet, but you have formed the backbone, the nucleus of the masses;

with you it is easier to push forward our work. . . . Thirdly, the role of a link. You
are a link between the leadership above and the masses below, and it is through you
that the opinions of the masses are transmitted upwards and those of the leadership
downwards [*PR*, January 12, 1962: 17].

, For the most part they are veteran [workers], men and women highly skilled in
one or another branch of . . . work, politically advanced, popular and trusted by the
people [*PR*, January 12, 1962: 16; see also J. Chen, 1957: 125].

Models can be collective as well as individual in character. For example, an
entire brigade or factory might nominate one small work group as a model
group. These selections are reported to higher levels along with leadership
recommendations. At various points additional selections may be made for
country, provincial, or national models:

The election of model workers or teams was a spur to production. . . . There was
. . . a "mobile red flag" awarded every month to one of the [model] companies. As
to the model workers, their photos—taken by the commune photographer—were
posted up at the foot of the Tower of Heroic Ambition, with a brief account of their
accomplishments in work, study and physical training; and all were called on to
follow their example [Crook and Crook, 1966: 84].

Among the most symbolic of events are rallies, demonstrations, and parades.
They occur at all levels of society, although three distinct levels are considered
here: local (village to district or commune), regional (county to major city or
provincial capital), and national (in Peking, usually in Tien An Men square, and
given national publicity). These events may be aimed primarily at recognizing
achievements. For example, during Agrarian Reform land deeds were burned at
rallies symbolizing the end of exploitation by landlords. However, rallies are
more likely to be used to mobilize people for the effort ahead. For example,
many rallies were held in Peking at the outset of the GPCR to encourage the Red
Guards.

Again, although all the activities listed in this section occur apart from
campaigns, most of them are more likely to occur during campaigns. Certainly
the intensity and frequency of occurrence increases during campaigns.[12]

A MEASURE OF MOBILIZATION

Forty-three indicators have been reviewed. At the outset of this chapter, I
cited Nettl's definition of mobilization as essentially the effort to activate and

---

[12] Three potential meeting-related mass participation indicators were rejected. All had
unacceptably high error ratios: current events goups studying the campaign, meetings to
"pass judgment" (*pi pan*), and formalized (required) family discussions on the campaign.
One of these indicators also had a high disagreement ratio.

involve a population in pursuit of certain ends or goals. In the present study these ends or goals become those of specific campaigns, and the efforts to involve and activate are measured by indicators aimed at providing information, organizing, and fostering mass participation in the campaign. In describing each of the indicators I have tried to show, especially where it is not completely obvious, how it contributes to the mobilization process.

We can now proceed to an important question: Can the relative mobilization efforts of the campaigns studied here be measured by analyzing the indicators and particularly by ascertaining whether the indicators were present or absent for a given campaign?[13]

In doing this no assumptions are made about how much each indicator contributes to the mobilization process. Obviously, however, a photograph display to promote the campaign is a relatively minor contribution to the mobilization effort when compared to the process of criticism/self-criticism and other similar meetings or to the mobilization involved in large groups of people going down to the lower levels. Since the precise amount of mobilization each indicator contributes to the mobilization process is not known, an interval model of measurement is inadmissible.

However, ordinal techniques can be used: namely, Guttman scaling. Analysis shows that these 43 indicators form an acceptable scale.[14] (See Figure 4.1.) It

[13] One could, theoretically, develop alternative measures for most of the indicators. For example, one could obtain estimates of the number of people "sent down to the country-side" for each campaign. For informational indicators, such as newspaper articles, one could do a content analysis scoring the number of articles on any given campaign, or, alternatively, the number of times a campaign is mentioned in newspaper articles during the course of the campaign. The efforts required to complete such measurement accurately would, however, be much greater. Moreover, these measures, if obtained and used to order campaigns, would presumably be directly correlated with the present ranking of campaigns. Although there is no necessary assumption in the scaling process that campaigns at a higher rank in the scale will also have a higher incidence of any given indicator than campaigns at lower ranks for that same indicator, there is no reason to assume it would be otherwise. Thus, given the likelihood of similar outcomes, the advantage of the present method is the relative parsimony of data collection.

[14] Menzel (1953) states that the minimum acceptable level of scalability is .65. Since ties may inflate levels of scalability, for the purposes of testing the hypotheses (see Chapter 7), all ties along with all indicators with high disagreement ratios (above .15—see Chapter 3) have been eliminated. This produced the same ordering of campaigns and the scalability actually increased from .655 to .665. Although a higher scalability could easily be obtained by eliminating several indicators from the scale, more heuristic value was attached to including as many indicators as possible in this measure of mobilization.

The fact that 33 indicators did not fit the scale pattern within acceptable statistical limits may seem to be an unreasonably high percentage of the total number of indicators (see notes 4, 5, 6, 7, 8, 9). However, this high proportion is somewhat offset since no research of this kind on the topic has yet been done. Also, it was decided prior to data collection to include all indicators regardless of the source or of any a priori arguments about ability to

Campaign List No. (see Appendix 1)	Campaign Type	Campaigns	Scale step	editorials (I, 29)	articles (I, 33)	study groups* (M, 49)	essays (M, 39)	letters* (M, 47)	slogans* (I, 22)	mobilization meetings* (I, 74)	pamphlets* (I, 24)	individual work models (M, 4)	group work models (M, 6)	criticism self-criticism* (M, 52)	criticism (M, 71)	group target (O, 1)	ideology target (O, 2)	cadres from outside assist local unit* (O, 57)	photo display* (I, 37)	exhibits (I, 43)
		High																		
33	S	GPCR	29	1	1	1	1	1	1	1	1	1	1	1	1	1	1	1	1	1
19	E	Great Leap Forward	28	1	1	1	1	1	1	1	1	1	1	1	1	1	1	1	1	1
4	I	Resist U.S.–Aid Korea	27	1	1	1	1	1	1	1	1	1	1	1	1	1	1	1	1	1
5	S	Suppress Counterrev.	26	1	1	1	1	1	1	1	1	1	1	1	1	1	1	1	1	1
7	I	Three-Anti	25	1	1	1	1	1	1	1	1	1	θ	1	1	1	1	1	1	1
8	S	Five-Anti	25	1	1	1	1	1	1	1	1	1	1	1	1	1	1	1	1	1
18	S	Anti-Rightist	24	1	1	1	1	1	1	1	1	1	1	1	1	1	1	1	1	1
13	E	Higher Level Coops	23	1	1	1	1	1	1	1	1	1	1	1	1	1	1	1	1	1
20	E	Communes	22	1	1	1	1	1	1	1	1	1	1	1	1	θ	θ	1	1	1
21	E	Backyard Furnaces	21	1	1	1	1	1	1	1	1	1	1	1	1	1	1	1	1	1
36	E	Barefoot Doctors	20	1	1	1	1	1	1	θ	1	1	1	θ	1	1	θ	1	1	1
2	S	Agrarian Reform	19	1	1	1	1	1	1	1	1	1	1	1	1	1	1	1	1	1
26	E	Aid Agriculture	18	1	1	1	1	1	1	1	θ	1	1	1	1	1	1	1	θ	1
28	S	Socialist Education	18	1	1	1	1	1	1	1	1	1	1	1	1	1	1	1	θ	1
29	I	Successor Generation	18	1	1	1	1	1	1	1	1	1	1	1	1	1	1	1	1	1
		Medium																		
27	I	Learn from the PLA	17	1	1	1	1	1	1	1	1	1	1	1	θ	1	1	1	1	1
32	I	Study Mao Thought	16	1	1	1	1	1	1	1	1	1	1	1	1	1	1	1	1	1
22	I	Cultural Revolution, '58	15	1	1	1	1	1	1	1	θ	1	1	1	1	1	1	1	1	1
23	E	Urban Communes	14	1	1	1	1	1	1	1	1	1	1	1	1	1	1	1	1	1
24	I	Rightist Sympathies	13	1	1	1	1	θ	1	1	1	1	θ	1	1	1	1	θ	1	1
30	E	Learn from Tachai	13	1	1	1	1	1	1	1	1	1	1	1	1	1	1	θ	1	1
31	E	Learn from Taching	13	1	1	1	1	1	1	1	1	1	1	1	1	1	1	θ	1	1
14	E	Combat Four Evils	12	1	1	1	1	1	1	1	1	1	1	θ	θ	θ	θ	1	1	1
19	E	Cooperatives	11	1	1	1	1	1	1	1	1	θ	1	1	θ	1	1	1	θ	θ
6	E	Mutual Aid	10	1	1	1	1	1	1	1	θ	1	1	1	θ	1	1	1	1	θ
12	S	Eliminate Counterrev.	9	1	1	1	1	1	1	1	θ	θ	θ	1	1	1	1	1	1	1
15	I	100 Flowers	9	1	1	1	1	1	1	1	1	1	1	1	1	1	1	1	1	1
34	I	Rectification, '68	9	1	1	1	1	1	1	1	1	1	1	1	1	1	1	1	1	0
11	E	Business Reform	8	1	1	1	1	1	1	1	1	θ	1	1	1	1	1	1	0	0
17	I	Rectification, '57	7	1	1	1	1	1	1	1	θ	1	1	1	1	1	1	0	0	0
		Low																		
35	I	Support the Army	6	1	1	1	1	1	1	1	1	1		0	0	0	0	0	0	0
25	I	Anti Japan–U.S. Treaty	5	1	1	1	1	1	1	1	0	0	0	0	0	0	0	0	0	0
3	I	Peace Signatures	4	1	1	1	1	1	1	0	0	0	0	0	0	0	0	0	0	0
10	I	Study Constitution	3	1	1	1	1	1	0	0	+	0	0	0	0	0	0	0	0	0
16	I	Study Mao "On Contra. . . ."	2	1	1	1	1	0	0	0	0	0	0	0	0	0	0	0	0	0
1	E	Buy Victory Bonds	1	1	1	0	0	0	+	0	0	0	0	0	0	0	0	0	0	0
		Errors		0	0	0	0	1	1	2	6	1	4	1	4	4	3	4	3	2
		Nonmodals Down		0	0	1	1	3	2	6	9	6	9	7	10	9	9	11	11	11

Figure 4.1 Guttman scalogram of mobilization (scalability = .665).

Indicators

M 53	I 35	I 17	I 31	I 44	I 45	I 75	M 61	M 9	I 21	I 27	M 3	M 51	O 65	M 38	O 66	M 19	M 20	M 69	M 50	I 72	I 16	M 48	O 67	O 68
special mention youth participation	slide shows*	films	door scrolls (dui lian)*	short stories*	handicrafts	banners*	special mention of minorities participation	during leisure time work in campaign*	rallies in villages*	books*	go to lower levels (xia fang)*	recall bitterness meetings	unit re-organized*	ad-hoc papers published*	unit changes plans*	rallies in Peking*	rallies in provinces*	struggle meetings*	public trials	concemnation meetings*	sacrifice life*	wear badges*	reallocate money to support campaign*	non-campaign programs curtailed*
1	1	1	1	1	1	1	1	1	1	1	1	1	1	1	1	1	1	1	1	1	1	1	1	1
1	1	1	1	1	1	1	1	1	1	1	1	1	1	1	1	1	1	1	θ	θ	θ	1	1	0
1	1	1	1	1	1	1	1	1	1	1	1	1	θ	1	1	1	1	1	1	1	1	1	0	0
1	1	1	1	1	θ	1	1	1	1	1	θ	1	1	1	1	1	1	1	1	1	1	0	0	0
1	1	1	1	1	1	1	1	1	1	1	θ	θ	1	1	1	1	1	1	1	0	0	0	0	0
1	1	1	1	1	1	1	1	1	1	1	θ	1	1	1	1	1	1	1	0	0	0	0	0	0
1	1	1	1	θ	θ	1	θ	1	1	1	θ	1	1	θ	1	1	1	0	0	0	0	0	0	0
1	θ	θ	1	1	1	1	1	1	1	1	1	θ	1	1	1	1	0	0	0	0	0	+	0	+	8
1	1	1	1	1	1	1	1	1	1	1	1	1	1	1	0	0	0	0	0	0	+	0	+	8
1	1	1	1	1	1	1	1	1	1	1	θ	1	1	0	0	0	0	+	+	+	0	0	0	0
1	1	1	1	1	1	1	1	1	1	1	1	1	0	0	0	0	0	+	0	0	0	0	0	0
1	1	θ	1	θ	θ	1	1	1	1	1	1	1	0	0	0	0	0	+	+	0	0	0	0	0
1	θ	1	1	1	1	1	θ	1	1	1	1	1	0	0	0	0	0	0	0	0	0	0	0	0

1	1	1	1	1	1	1	θ	1	1	1	0	0	0	0	0	0	0	0	0	0	0	+	0	0
1	1	1	1	1	θ	1	1	1	1	0	0	0	0	0	0	0	0	0	0	0	0	+	0	0
1	θ	θ	1	1	1	1	1	1	0	0	0	0	0	+	0	0	0	0	0	0	0	0	0	0
θ	1	θ	1	θ	1	1	0	0	0	0	0	0	+	0	0	0	+	0	0	0	0	0	0	0
θ	1	1	θ	1	0	0	0	0	0	0	0	+	0	0	+	0	0	+	0	0	0	0	0	0
1	1	1	1	1	1	0	0	0	0	0	0	0	0	0	0	0	0	0	0	0	0	0	0	0
1	1	θ	1	1	0	0	0	0	0	0	+	0	0	+	0	0	0	0	0	0	0	+	0	0
1	1	1	1	0	0	0	0	0	+	0	+	+	+	0	0	+	0	0	0	0	0	0	0	0
1	1	0	0	0	0	0	0	0	0	0	0	0	0	0	+	0	0	0	0	0	0	0	0	0
0	0	0	0	0	0	0	0	0	0	0	0	0	0	0	0	0	+	+	+	0	0	0	0	0
0	0	0	0	0	0	0	0	0	+	0	0	0	+	0	0	+	+	0	0	0	0	0	0	0
0	0	+	0	0	0	+	0	0	+	0	+	+	0	+	0	0	0	+	0	0	0	+	0	0
0	0	0	0	0	0	0	0	+	0	0	0	0	+	0	0	+	+	0	0	0	0	0	8	8

0	0	0	0	0	0	8	0	0	0	0	0	0	0	0	0	0	0	0	0	+	0	0	0	0
0	+	0	0	0	0	+	0	0	+	0	0	0	0	0	0	+	+	0	+	+	0	0	0	0
0	+	0	+	+	0	+	0	0	+	0	0	0	0	0	0	+	+	0	0	0	0	0	0	0
0	+	0	0	0	0	0	+	0	0	0	0	+	0	0	0	0	0	0	0	0	0	0	0	0

| 0 | 0 | 0 | 0 | 0 | 0 | 0 | 0 | + | 0 | 0 | 0 | 0 | 0 | 0 | 0 | 0 | 0 | 0 | 0 | 0 | 0 | 0 | 0 | 0 |
| + | 0 | 0 | 0 | 0 | 0 | 0 | 0 | 0 | 0 | 0 | 0 | 0 | 0 | 0 | 0 | 0 | 0 | 0 | 0 | 0 | 0 | 0 | 0 | 0 |

| 3 | 5 | 4 | 4 | 3 | 5 | 4 | 5 | 5 | 4 | 1 | 9 | 6 | 5 | 6 | 2 | 4 | 5 | 6 | 5 | 4 | 6 | 0 | 1 | 0 |
| 12 | 11 | 14 | 15 | 15 | 14 | 14 | 15 | 13 | 17 | 17 | 14 | 17 | 15 | 15 | 12 | 13 | 13 | 11 | 9 | 8 | 10 | 3 | 3 | 1 |

Code: 0 = absent 1 = present 8 = missing data θ or + = error
Campaigns Type: I = ideological E = economic S = struggle
Indicator Type: I = informational O = organizational M = mass participation
* = indicator used for calculating correlations

107

consists of 29 steps with no more than three campaigns at any one step. Each indicator represents some added increment of mobilization. Thus, the cumulative effect at each step represents a greater level of mobilization than at the previous step. At the same time, care must be taken against unwarranted assumptions about exactly how much mobilization is added with each step.

Rather than determine how much mobilization each indicator adds to the overall total, it seems reasonable to try cutting the scale into distinct levels of mobilization. Two obvious cutting points appear: criticism/self-criticism, which ranks about one-third of the way through the scale, and "sending down to the lower levels," or *xia fang*, ranking about two-thirds of the way through the scale. As indicated earlier, both indicators represent substantial increments in total amount of mobilization for any given campaign. It is reasonable to argue that the cutoffs occur at a point where a single indicator represents a substantial increment in the total amount of mobilization. It would also seem reasonable to assume that although there may be a small variation within these three levels of mobilization because of disagreement, unreliability, and the like, the marked increments at the cutting points selected mitigate against campaigns moving from one level to another.[15]

Emerging from this division is an interesting relationship between the three levels of mobilization (see Table 4.1). One notes a decrease of informational indicators from medium to high levels paralleled by an increase in mass participation indicators as mobilization increases. This suggests that informational indicators are more likely at lower levels of mobilization, and may in fact tend to occur more at the outset of campaigns. The converse is true of mass participa-

---

contribute to a measurement of mobilization. Fully a fourth (9) of the indicators that did not scale failed to do so because they did not differentiate any case although many had relatively few errors. Almost half (16) of the indicators that failed to fit the pattern were those with high disagreement ratios (7 with high disagreement did fit the pattern). Many of those that did not fit the pattern were organizational indicators, such as the presence of a special administration to run the campaign and the establishment of centers to train cadres for the campaign, indicators that did not impinge on the lives of the informants in a direct, memorable manner. These indicators also tended to be infrequently mentioned in the press.

These factors suggest that if more reliable data could be obtained, they might have produced a great percentage of indicators fitting the overall pattern. Still, the number that did scale, 43, is rather large. For a complete list of indicators, disagreement ratios, and indicator types, see Appendix 5, section D.

[15] In spite of careful efforts to eliminate disagreement and unreliability, some undoubtedly remain in the scale. This is particularly the case in the minority of situations where only one response was obtained for a particular indicator. This might cause slight variations in ranking. Also, it is possible that the addition of other indicators might lead to some variation. However, with the exception of three or four cases where there are more than two or three errors in a row near the cutting line, the possibility of variation of more than one or two steps is negligible.

TABLE 4.1
Mobilization Indicators and Levels of Mobilization

Type of indicator	Level of mobilization		
	Low	Medium	High
Informational	5	11	1
Organizational	0	2	4
Mass participation	5	6	9

tion indicators.[16] This would seem to offer the scale some face value validity since it is reasonable to assume that informational inputs are more likely to occur at the outset of the campaign, which then moves into more and more mass participation activities. Moreover, it would also seem reasonable to argue that mass participation activities on the average involve greater amounts of mobilization than do informational activities. This would also give further validity to the scale as a measurement of mobilization since there are more mass participation activities at higher levels of the mobilization scale.

A more important indication of face value validity is the general impression of which campaign may be more or less important.

Perhaps the two campaigns most frequently cited as the "biggest" and most significant are the GPCR and the GLF. They rank first and second, respectively, on the scale. As for the campaigns that occurred during the mid-1950s, the Chinese themselves cite Agrarian Reform, Resist America–Aid Korea, Suppression of Counterrevolutionaries, and the Three- and Five-Anti campaigns as the "five great campaigns" (see, e.g., *PC*, November 16, 1957: 4; Peng Chen, in *RMRB*, August 7, 1957). All these campaigns are found at high levels of mobilization.

The possibility that levels of mobilization might be just a function of the length of the campaign was considered. If so, the longer the campaign, the more activities would occur during it. It was difficult to isolate this effect since campaigns requiring higher levels of mobilization (with more activities) might obviously require more time to complete. The tau_b correlation is moderate, .39.

---

[16] There is no necessary assumption in the scaling process that indicators occurring in relatively few campaigns tend to occur in the latter stages of a campaign, or, conversely, that those indicators occurring in most campaigns tend to occur first in the early stages of the campaign: i.e., that there is a direct correlation between an indicator's temporal order of first appearance in a campaign and its order of appearance on the scale. However, in discussing the indicators several cases have been cited where it seems clear when in the campaign the indicator tends to appear. If one were to expend the rather substantial amount of resources necessary to measure this relationship accurately, it is expected that a positive correlation would emerge between the order of indicators on the scale and the point in time they first emerged in campaigns.

Although a large correlation would be disconcerting, a correlation of this size seems reasonable; one might expect campaigns requiring low levels of mobilization to be carried out in shorter periods of time, and those with higher levels of mobilization to require more time.

Finally, it was observed that mobilization levels were virtually uncorrelated with the year the campaign began (.02), eliminating the possibility that the observed mobilization levels are a function of having begun earlier or later in the history of the People's Republic of China.

Thus, it would appear that the scale represents a reasonably valid measure of campaign mobilization in China.

MOBILIZATION AT WORK

Yet, now that a valid scale has been constructed, how much more understandable is the mobilization process in China? In talking about the listed activities as indicators of mobilization, it should be clear that we are just at the surface of the mobilization process. What of the process below the surface?

Mobilization in China is not a simple process. People cannot be automatically mobilized just because a cause may be to their benefit. Hinton, in his portrayal of Long Bow village, for example, relates that when the Communists first came and began to prepare for Agrarian Reform, some peasants even argued that it was right for landlords to own the land and thus to engage the peasantry in tenancy arrangements (1968: 129).

Mobilization spreads like waves on the surface of a pond. A small group of activists who understand the campaign and its importance must be found to take the lead; in the case of Long Bow, to speak out first (Hinton, 1968: 115). Sometimes no one can be found to start the process. Even if they can see the potential benefit, people may hold back. On at least two occasions the peasants of Long Bow held back when the Communist leadership tried to persuade them to come forward, to speak out. At one point they feared the KMT's return. They would suffer from having said too much against the landlords. At still another point when four erring cadres who had been arrested by an outside work team for wrongdoings were released and allowed to return to the village unpunished for lack of evidence against them, the peasants backed off, feeling that cadres were protected but that they, the peasants, would suffer if they spoke out (Hinton, 1968: 419–421). The old system had not changed. At least their comments reflected those fears:

"What's the use of speaking out? The old cadres mount the horse as if nothing had happened." "Yu-lai has returned and he is the same as ever." "It is better to work hard at production and let those meet who want to meet." "We are gloomy because our opinions are no use at all" [Hinton, 1968: 423].

Getting people to set aside these basic, honest fears and to join the mobilization effort of a campaign is a complex process. It has required light-years of commitment, persuasion, and patience. Certainly one critical element in whatever success and achievements there have been is the constant exhortation of the cadre leadership to be "responsive" to the masses, to engage in, and openly accept, criticism/self-criticism. In a November 14, 1950 *People's Daily* editorial on the work of cadres to establish the power in urban areas, this approach was stressed:

> When conducting a . . . campaign . . . attention should be given to the gathering of opinion of the masses on the work of the government and on the style of work of the cadres. During conferences, all attempts on the parts of the representatives at criticizing and examining the work of the government and the style of the work of the cadres, it should be accepted with the utmost modesty. It is up to all responsible personnel to carry out criticism and self-criticism in the most responsible, sincere and candid manner so as to increase the masses' confidence in the people's government, improve the relationship between the masses and the cadres, improve our work and conquer the obnoxious inclination for bureaucratism and orderism [*RMRB*, November 14, 1950, in *SCMP*, November 15, 1950: 8].

This could not be a forced process; cooperation was of the essence:

> The human consciousness may be compared to an artichoke. Its tender core is enclosed in layer upon layer of defenses, excuses, rationalizations, approximations. These must be peeled off if one is to discover the true complex of motives driving any individual. Such a process would hardly be possible if an individual's acts, as distinct from his words, did not reveal in a multitude of unconscious ways something of the core of his thought. Even then, with acts serving as guides to motivation, *no progress can be made unless the individual is willing to co-operate*. What made self-revelation possible . . . was the deep commitment . . . to the success of the movement. They freely examined themselves and their comrades . . . in order to remove obstacles in the way of more effective work. . . . this, not coercion, not curiosity, not some narcissistic self-torture made self-and-mutual criticism viable and grounded it in necessity [Hinton, 1968: 388; emphasis added].

For the Chinese population in 1949 China, this process was not easy to understand. Having come through two wars in the previous decade and the suffering that accompanied them, particularly at the hands of landlords and the Japanese, they were understandably more interested in food, clothing, and shelter than in the process of criticism/self-criticism.

In the midst of a Rectification campaign in 1948 in Long Bow village, an old woman peasant tried to extract more material goods from the suspended village head, Chun-hsi:

> "Two or three pieces of clothing! That's not enough," snorted Old Lady Wang, all primed for further battle.
> But Old Tui-Chin, the bachelor peasant, who was more and more emerging, by virtue of his extreme objectivity, as spokesman for the northern group, disagreed.

"We don't want the things, our aim is to get him to admit his mistakes and speak the truth."

At this, Old Lady Wang spat furiously on the ground. "Who can eat self-criticism?" she asked [Hinton, 1968: 338].

Some understood the meaning of criticism/self-criticism, others had yet to do so. Still, the peasants did not fully comprehend the intricacies of the mobilization process. The peasants became so worked up about the suspended village head that they urged he be sent to a people's court to be tried. Here the leading cadre stepped in; the peasants had gone too far:

The people's court is for serious cases that we cannot solve ourselves. As for Chun-hsi, his case is big, but not, in my opinion, big enough for that. Suppose you punish him severely? Are his crimes as big as those of others? Then what will you do with the others? Their punishment must be even more severe. I think it would be better to compare records. Let's balance his crimes against those of others. Let's consider his attitude. Did he speak frankly [Hinton, 1968: 339]?

Not an easy task, by any means. How to mobilize the peasants (and workers) to understand the significance of their actions so that they will be willing to participate yet not carry things to an extreme? The cadres of Long Bow often had to search for the intricately fine line separating success from failure in the mobilization process (Hinton, 1968: 335). They obviously did not always succeed.

If the process of correctly mobilizing through criticism/self-criticism was difficult, even more so was the difficulty of correctly carrying out "struggle" given the animosities and emotions the target of struggle often generated.

In the context of Maoist political behavior . . . "struggle" is a formally defined process in which the target, usually a political offender, is subjected to charge after charge with ever increasing emotional intensity until he admits his guilt. Yet the purpose of the struggle process is more than just punitive. Rather it is intended to provide the target with a starting point from which to begin actual political and ideological remoulding. Similarly, those who attack are also expected to learn as they do so and thereby to improve their own political and ideological competence. Struggle [is the] . . . acting upon a person or the environment in order to effect a basic change and realize a specific objective [Bennett and Montaperto, 1971: 36].

Thus, when the Communists speak of the "elimination" of a class such as the landlords, they do not necessarily mean physical elimination. Often they are referring to the transformation of people and whole groups such that the target person, class, or problem (i.e., contradiction) no longer exists (Liu Shao-chi, 1945: 7). Mao has related the essence of how he was transformed:

If you want the masses to understand you, if you want to be one with the masses, you must make up your mind to undergo a long and even painful process of tempering. Here I might mention the experience of how my own feelings changed. I began life as a student and at school acquired the ways of a student; I then used to feel it undignified to do even a little manual labor; such as carrying my own luggage in the presence of my fellow students, who were incapable of carrying anything, either on their shoulders or in their hands. At that time, I felt that intellectuals were the only clean people in the world, while in comparison workers and peasants were dirty. I did not mind wearing the clothes of other intellectuals, believing them clean, but I would not put on clothes belonging to a worker or peasant, believing them dirty. But after I became a revolutionary and lived with workers and peasants and with soldiers of the revolutionary army, I gradually came to know them well, and they gradually came to know me well too. It was then, and only then, that I fundamentally changed the bourgeois and petty-bourgeois feelings implanted in me in the bourgeois schools. I came to feel that compared with the workers and peasants the unremoulded intellectuals were not clean and that, in the last analysis, the workers and peasants were the cleanest people and, even though their hands were soiled and their feet smeared with cow-dung, they were really cleaner than the bourgeois and petty-bourgeois intellectuals. That is what is meant by a change in feelings, a change from one class to another [Mao, 1965: Vol. 3, 73].

The transformation process was not going to be easy whether for individuals or the social environment as a whole. The campaign was to be the vehicle, with mobilization the guiding strategy. Within this process two of the watchwords were to be *criticism/self-criticism* and *struggle* (Schurmann, 1968: xlii).

Mao was certainly aware that this process would fail if pushed too far too fast. Mao's exhortation was unmistakably clear that if one wanted to undergo transformation, "*you* must make up *your* mind" to do so. Hinton (1968: 388) has reinforced this by arguing that "no progress can be made unless the individual is willing to co-operate." Certainly the Party and others would do all they could to persuade, to channel, to provide the setting for a commitment to mobilization and change. But to use terror or coercion was to fail:

The Chinese communists leaders emphatically deny the utility of terror for long-range leadership purposes and recognize that its use, however guarded, must give way to methods of persuasion to induce support. In effect, the initiation of violence on any enlarged scale even to resolve agricultural crises and unrest is an admission of leadership failure and a retreat into reaction [Lewis, 1963: 5].

In marked contrast, the Russian Communist leaders seem to have all too often set aside the harder path of mobilization and fallen back on coercive measures to induce change (Whyte, 1970: 350). This should not obscure the fact that even in China, particularly during struggle campaigns, coercion is often improperly used due to pressure from the top to carry out the campaign rapidly, from errors of local cadres, and/or from emotions aroused in the "high tides" of some campaigns.

In specific terms, the commitment to persuasion often meant slowing the process of socialist transformation. For example, during the campaign to establish Mutual Aid Teams, cadres were admonished in a Party Central Committee directive not to push reluctant peasants too fast:

> Even in a village where the overwhelming majority of peasants have joined the Mutual-Aid teams or cooperatives and where only a very small minority of peasants remain individual farmers, the attitude of respecting and uniting such a minority should be adopted [in *PC*, July 1, 1953: 13].

What did this mean in practical terms? In Long Bow in 1948 it meant that for a number of weeks the peasants simply would not come to meetings. There were no more material goods to be divided (the "fruits of struggle"), only ideological matters to discuss. Besides, they had spring planting to do. Why should they go to meetings? As Hinton relates (1968: 431), one peasant said to his friend when he called for him for that evening's meeting after a hard day in the field, "I'm tired, I'm going to bed early. I don't want to go to any meeting. Can anyone arrest me for that?" Indeed, the peasants knew that, unlike in the old society, "coercion and beatings were absolutely forbidden [Hinton, 1968: 431]." Those who improperly used them on the masses would be called to account for their improper work-style.

And so to the process of persuasion yet another watchword was added: *patience.* As Edgar Snow has said of Mao, "although he distrusts long periods of stability and is never satisfied with the pace of change, . . . he is practical and capable of great patience in achieving a goal [1972: 187]."

A county Party secretary talked about patience in almost monotonous terms in describing the task of assigning class status, a task that could be easily generalized to the total mobilization process:

> We must explain, discuss, report, evaluate, classify, post results; explain, discuss, and report—again and again. This is very troublesome, very difficult, very time consuming [Hinton, 1968: 411].

It is easier to be impatient, as a work team cadre in Long Bow admitted one day in 1948:

> I am discouraged. Ten years ago when I began to work as a cadre people said, "When the Japanese are defeated, then the Revolution will succeed." But the Japanese have surrendered and war continued. Now ten years have passed. It is too slow. Where is the industry we dreamed about? [Hinton, 1968: 444].

In the village I visited in 1972, I was told that the use of persuasion and patience cost the village 3 long years in the effort to transform the land. The story, related to me by the Party secretary of the brigade, is worth retelling because, after all, it reflects his perception of how difficult the mobilization process is. The alternatives were stark: waiting 3 years or coercion:

> Before 1956, in the period of preliminary cooperatives, the work of transforming slopes into terraced fields could not earnestly begin. The ownership of the land was still private. It was most inconvenient to transform the land, to convert the slopes into terraced fields.

In the spring of 1953 we did attempt the transformation of slopes into terraced fields, but the class enemy made trouble. The class enemy incited some peasants. "Now you have transformed your land. If you withdraw from the cooperative and go alone, you will be better off." These people were taken in by the class enemy and withdrew from the cooperative. This caused difficulties on our part in transforming the slopes. Members of the cooperative said it was useless to transform the slopes. "If one slope is transformed into terraced fields, and that family withdraws from the cooperative, what is the use of doing that?"

So, actually, the work of transforming the slopes began only in 1956. In 1956 we established an advanced cooperative. The land was owned collectively, so it was very easy to decide which slopes should be transformed. . . . However, 3 years had passed in our 10 year plan [to transform the land].[17]

This certainly is *not* an isolated example. Participant–observer studies of villages in China since 1949 all observe at least one if not several instances of recalcitrant peasants who did not want to join a cooperative or participate in other aspects of the mobilization process (see, e.g., J. Chen, 1957: 107–111; Crook and Crook, 1966: 9–10; Myrdal, 1966: 145–149).

In summary, what can be said of the mobilization process? The least is that it is not easy. The most is that, given the social conditions of China in 1949 and the scope and breadth of the changes attempted since then through the campaigns, the effort to mobilize China's masses and to transform them and their conditions has unquestionably been one of the greatest social efforts in the history of humankind. However, hard reality is in between. Mass mobilization is a very intricate process. It is perhaps relatively easy to see, to capture, and to measure on the surface but relatively hard to capture and to share as it humps its way along, meeting this problem here, that roadblock over there, facing frustration around the corner, temporary setbacks at the next turn, all the while trying to keep moving with patience and persuasion, to avoid the breakdown into failure and coercion.

No system faced with problems and contradictions so massive could be without failures (or "shortcomings," as the Communists like to call them). It is time to turn to an analysis of these shortcomings.

[17] Transcribed from recorded tapes of the introductory session at Sandstone Hollow brigade, *Tsunhwa* County, *Hopei* Province, March 28, 1972. Edited for clarity and grammar.

5

Shortcomings

Achievements and shortcomings, difficulties and the bright future—these are the two aspects of a single process and are the unity of opposites. We would be blindly clinging to achievements and the bright future if we overlook our shortcomings and difficulties, and this would lead to complete failure in our work.

—*PR*, January 14, 1972: 9–10

The Chinese pay great attention to errors and difficulties, what they usually call *shortcomings*. In meetings large and small, cadres as well as the masses spend considerable time evaluating their work-styles, criticizing each other, and seeking ways to improve. Rectification campaigns, 4 of which number among the 36 campaigns studied here, are principally aimed at correcting shortcomings, primarily among cadres.

The Chinese quite clearly believe that lack of attention to shortcomings can lead to failure. Mao, for example, directly related the improper expropriation from middle peasant families in one village to the loss of support for the government:

> This is the most terrible thing! This is more dangerous by far than American imperialism. American imperialism is only a paper tiger, but if 27 middle peasants can be expropriated in one village, what would happen if this spread to the whole nation? This is forcing our friends to join our enemies [Hinton, 1968: 400].

In speeches and essays leaders continually discuss shortcomings and the need to correct them. Mao, for example, wrote several essays on this subject alone (e.g., 1965: Vol. 1, 105–137, 147–152, 295–310; Vol. 3, 35–52; 1967: Vol. 4, 197–200; 1971: 432–479).

Moreover, a great deal of time is spent classifying, codifying, and reporting errors committed. For example, for the period following the Rectification cam-

117

paign in Long Bow village in 1948, Hinton lists, on the basis of the summary reports, four different types of shortcomings along with the number of grievances for each type of shortcoming (1968: 361—363).

Such reports appear to be constant and widespread. As they appeared as part of the Rectification campaign in 1948, so too do they remain a part of the campaign process of recent years. The captured *Lien Chiang* documents clearly indicate the continual emphasis on the classification and reporting of shortcomings (Chen and Ridley, 1969).

The documents were obtained toward the end of the first year of the Socialist Education campaign in 1963, before the relatively more intense struggle of the Four Cleans period. Many of the documents were devoted to reporting campaign shortcomings. They are usually broken down into the three main categories of capitalism, feudalism, and extravagance—seen at that point in the campaign as three major errors or targets of the campaign. Separate lists were made for cadres and the masses. In one report, between the two lists there were more than 50 specific items (Chen and Ridley, 1969, 48—49, 186—187). The fact that incidents were never recorded for many categories suggests that such forms are prepared at higher levels and sent down for completion. This lends further support to the importance given to identifying and dealing with shortcomings.[1]

In this chapter I shall identify the indicators of shortcomings, construct a measure of shortcomings, and compare the results of this measure with the informants' subjective impressions of relative levels of shortcomings among campaigns.

THE INDICATORS OF SHORTCOMINGS

In the course of the research, a sufficiently large number of shortcomings potentially common to all campaigns were identified. It thus became possible to construct a measure of the relative level of shortcomings among the campaigns studied.

To identify potential indicators, a preliminary survey of both primary and secondary literature was made. The Chinese press reports many shortcomings because it is one vehicle used to encourage the correction of shortcomings. Informants seemed to do better, however, in the systematic reporting of shortcomings than the press, especially when compared to the press's reporting of achievements and particularly mobilization. But given the potential for high disagreement between these two sources, the actual amount of disparity was rather low. (See Chapter 3.)

---

[1] Not all the shortcomings listed in the *Lien Chiang* documents emerge as a result of a campaign; many reflect the contradictions that have given rise to the campaign. Moreover, many of these shortcomings are campaign specific, that is, they relate only to the Socialist Education campaign.

The analysis revealed 22 out of 27 indicators fitting a scale pattern. They fell into two relatively distinct categories of ideological and physical shortcomings.

Ideological Shortcomings

Failure to reform or eliminate all the targets of the campaign

Excessive labeling of targets

Demotions or firings among nontarget groups

Shortcomings in the general political policy

Violations in the implementation of policies

Leftist or rightist deviations of policy

Cadre failure in implementing the campaign

Conflict among cadres regarding the campaign

Reinvestigation following the campaign

Work or study slowdowns

Occurrence of bribery

The first three indicators concern campaign targets. Achieving total success in the elimination of campaign targets, whether groups or ideas, is problematic at best. Although all the targets, or problem focal points, are frequently not overcome, this is not seen as a critical shortcoming.

More serious, however, is the mislabeling of targets. For example, during Agrarian Reform it was not uncommon to find cases of improper classification—for instance, rich peasants classified as landlords or vice versa (Human Resources, 1955c: 48). The importance of mislabeling, particularly during struggle campaigns, is not to be underemphasized, for a person's whole future was at stake. Regardless of how explicit the classification guidelines were, there were always some borderline cases. Thus, in Long Bow, Hinton reports that the classification process was done three times, precisely to reduce error in this important matter. In a county conference of work team members, County Party Secretary Chen underlined the importance of proper classification:

> This is the most important work of the whole movement. He who leads the classification holds the knife in his hand. If you class a middle peasant as a rich peasant, it is as serious as killing him. You push the family into the enemy camp. You violate the policy of uniting with the middle peasants to isolate the enemy. If, on the other hand, you classify a landlord as a middle peasant, you protect a landlord. You clasp a viper to your bosom. You violate the policy of destroying feudalism [Hinton, 1968: 411].

Nonetheless, in spite of the care taken in this process, incorrect classification appears to have been a relatively common error in struggle and rectification campaigns. Less common were demotions among nontarget groups. For example, during the excesses of the GPCR and Agrarian Reform, people who had not been previously labeled as targets were suddenly removed from their jobs or had their property taken away. Alternatively, during Agrarian Reform cadres were improperly removed from positions because of minor errors committed in the campaign.

Another type of shortcoming relates to the problems of policy and overall implementation. Shortcomings could be the result, in part, of the overall failure of the general policy of the campaign. Here the current social conditions were not analyzed correctly and therefore the program developed could not be properly implemented in accordance with mass line politics. This became the most difficult indicator to interpret. The Maoist perspective does not acknowledge that the basic political policy of any campaign was incorrect, not even that of the GLF. In his self-criticism, Mao specifically attributed the problems of the GLF to the implementation of policy. Peng Te-huai and Liu Shao-chi have argued otherwise (Schram, 1967: 289). Thus, the response to this indicator became heavily dependent on one's perspective. Informants who had been targets of a campaign were more willing to argue that it was the campaign policy that was at fault, rather than how they or others went about implementing the campaign.[2]

The violation of or inability to implement campaign policy correctly appears to have been a more likely event. This involved specific cases of failure as well as more general types such as the inability to promote and achieve an understanding of the collective needs, which is part and parcel of virtually every policy promoted by the Communists. A survey conducted in 1951 at the time of the Resist America—Aid Korea campaign by a member of the Communist Party's County Committee in Chekiang reveals this more general type of implementation failure:

> In a survey of 405 peasants in one village, only 42 peasants knew that love of country is prior to love of family. The rest, 363 peasants, didn't even know the meaning of "country." About 95% of the peasants in the village made a general plan for increasing production in the Patriotic Pact, but 70% of them didn't even know the content of the Pact. The peasants when asked why they intended to increase production, answered "for better living." ... One middle peasant asked, "In the Patriotic Pact, we agreed that the public grain should be paid, the sooner the better. Why doesn't the government sign a pact with us to lend us the seed and other supplies on time?" [*JFRB*, October 23, 1951, in Human Resources, 1955c: 50].

Deviations in the implementation of policy were often classed as *leftist* or *rightist*. Leftist deviations result from exceeding existing social conditions,

---

[2] Not surprisingly, this was the most marginal indicator in the scale. It had the highest error ratio. If further statistical improvement in the scale had been required, this indicator would have been eliminated. It was not included in the calculation of scale steps used to determine correlations.

conditions that are determined by the Party leadership using mass line techniques. For example, instead of recognizing that mutual aid and cooperation
must proceed on a voluntary basis, leftist deviationists might argue that it is
necessary to coerce peasants to join. During the Mutual Aid campaign, although
the policy stated that membership was to be on a voluntary basis (Schurmann,
1968: 416–420), some cadres forced recalcitrant peasants to join. Leftist deviations are also associated with the insufficient use of persuasion and education
and improper use of coercion or force.

Rightist deviations (*tailism*), on the other hand, result from an inability to
keep pace with existing social conditions. For example, during the establishment
of cooperatives, Mao in his 1955 speech accused many cadres of

> tottering along like women with bound feet and constantly complaining, "You're
> going too fast." Excessive criticism, inappropriate complaints, endless anxiety, and
> the erection of countless taboos—they believe this is the proper way to guide the
> socialist mass movement in the rural areas [1971: 389].

Cadres might fail to implement policies properly in other ways as well. A
common problem, especially during the early campaigns, was corruption. For
example, during Agrarian Reform some cadres saw their new leadership roles in
the traditional light as more those of power and privilege than of responsibility.
Hence, with the expropriation of land, it was a natural error to dip a little deeper
into the till for one's own benefit or to see that one's family received the best
plot of land (Hinton, 1968: 233, passim; Human Resources, 1955c: 52–53).

Other kinds of cadre errors occurred. During periods of high mobilization and
"adventuristic" atmosphere could lead to overzealous reporting of production
figures—an occurrence not only during the GLF, but in other campaigns,
including the Cooperatives campaign (J. Chen, 1957: 64–65).

In a few campaigns there were conflicts between cadres. During Agrarian
Reform, for example, friction developed between cadres of peasant origin and
those of urban origin (Hinton, 1968: 335–336; Human Resources, 1955c: 51).
Some of this friction may well have been an early sign of the split that was to
develop between Liu and Mao and their respective followers. In any case, by the
time of the Socialist Education—Four Cleans campaign, and certainly by the
GPCR, conflict between groups of cadres was quite clear.[3]

Nearly half the campaigns studied included some effort at reinvestigation,
often involving groups or teams sent out to examine excesses of the campaign.
This was a major responsibility of the work team that William Hinton observed

[3] Informant responses and documentary evidence reflect cadre conflict only for the
GPCR and the Three-Anti campaign. If this indicator had been coded as present for Agrarian
Reform and Socialist Education, it would have moved the indicator two steps further down
the scale. The ordering of campaigns would be unchanged as would any statistical relationships, since this indicator was not used in subsequent statistical calculations because of its
borderline utility of differentiating only two cases.

in Long Bow. In this case, the errors were sufficiently numerous that a rectification campaign followed the work team's reinvestigation of Agrarian Reform.

Ideological problems could also be evidenced in work and/or study slow-downs. The most obvious example occurred in the communes, when people became lazy and worked less, knowing that wages were to be given primarily according to one's needs rather than one's work. It thus made little difference how much one worked. This reflection of dissatisfaction was due, at least in part, to insufficient ideological work, an unwillingness to make a sufficient commitment to achieve the changes called for by the campaign.

Finally, the presence of bribery also reflects insufficient commitment to the Communist work-style. A common practice in traditional China, it seems to have occurred more frequently during the early campaigns such as the Suppression of Counter-revolutionaries, Resist America–Aid Korea, and Agrarian Reform (Hinton, 1968: 164). The Five-Anti campaign focused on the elimination of bribery in evidence during earlier campaigns, especially the attempt of capitalists and other monied interests to buy "protection," to escape being labeled as a target, or to be dealt with leniently. After these early years bribery seems to have been less of a problem, at least during campaigns, although it apparently reemerged during the Socialist Education campaign.

The ideological shortcomings discussed here have occurred during, as well as apart from, campaigns. However, they are probably more frequent and more severe during campaigns. This is certainly the case with physical shortcomings.

Physical Shortcomings

Destruction of property

Substantial unsanctioned mass migration to the cities or out of the country

Individuals receiving insult or abuse

Suicides

Acts of violence to resist change

Physical conflict between classes and/or groups

Armed clashes resulting in injury

Armed clashes resulting in death

People indiscriminately killed

Physical harm inflicted on cadres

Activation of the army to maintain order and/or organization

The destruction of property occurred, for example, when landlords, capitalists, and peasants were forced to give up their properties. It also occurred during the GPCR, as well as a few other campaigns, when in the early stages, the Red

Guards went forth to "destroy the old and establish the new." Then the prime targets were artifacts of traditional culture in temples and homes.

A report by Liu Jui-lung, vice-chairman of the East China Agrarian Reform Committee, indicates the destructive character of some landlords:

> Not a few landlords destroyed their productive implements, dismantled houses, wrecked all furnishings, felled trees and bamboo groves, sabotaged farm implements, killed draft animals and fallowed lands [Human Resources, 1955c: 54].

During Agrarian Reform many landlords fled to the cities, as did other counterrevolutionary elements, such as bandits and spies. This type of unsanctioned migration also occurred in the early 1960s, partly because of the natural disasters in the countryside and, apparently, the campaign to mobilize urban people to go to the countryside to Aid Agriculture. This same type of problem still occurs, as many of the urban youth who were sent to the countryside in the closing phase of the GPCR in 1968 have surreptitiously migrated back to the cities or to Hong Kong to avoid the hardships encountered in agricultural life.

One potential cause of the unsanctioned migration is insult or abuse (*wu ru*) suffered by individuals. This occurs during most struggle campaigns when targets are often forced to "wear a hat," or to engage in other acts of public humiliation. Some of these acts are within the bounds of acceptable conduct during a campaign, but often they went beyond these bounds, humiliating those who should not have been targets, or humiliating targets to unsanctioned extremes (see, e.g., Bennett and Montaperto, 1971: 38–49).

Humiliation can lead to suicide. Suicides signal a failure to bring ideological change through persuasion, on the one hand, or on the other, to moderate and control excesses. The latter was evidenced, for example, during the Agrarian Reform campaign. Hinton alludes to the

> tremendous pressure which had been brought to bear on the Party members (in the villages) to make them acknowledge the failure of the *Fanshen* movement and concede their part in it. The pressure was so great and carried with it such overtones of revenge that many honest Communists felt they had no way out. Attempts at suicide had occurred in village after village [1968: 367].

In addition to destroying their own property, landlords might also attempt other violent acts, such as sabotaging the work of others by destroying seeds and even blowing up buildings. Bandits and spies, during these early years, might try to slow down or blow up trains carrying supplies to Korea as a part of the Resist America–Aid Korea campaign. This kind of activity often led to clashes between the counterrevolutionary groups and groups of peasants, workers, or soldiers who tried to stop them. Also, during the GPCR, clashes (*wu dou*) occurred between Red Guard groups.

Sometimes, as a result of these clashes, bystanders uninvolved in the conflict at hand were indiscriminately killed. That the conflict had escalated to this point indicated a more serious level of shortcomings than when the conflict was localized to the groups directly involved.

Cadres might also receive physical abuse. Hinton has described an attempt on a work team member's life (1968: 256–258). If cadres were suffering physical harm (as against mental or ideological pressure that might legitimately occur during rectification campaigns), shortcomings had proceeded to a level where the leadership had lost some measure of control.

The final indicator is the call-up of the army to restore or maintain order and organization. The data suggest this occurred during only two campaigns, the Suppression of Counterrevolutionaries and the GPCR. The need to use the army as a coercive force is a rather clear indication that the level of shortcomings is relatively high.

Most of these physical shortcomings probably occurred more during campaigns than at other times. In any case, physical acts opposing the campaign are more serious than ideological shortcomings. Thus, it is expected that ideological shortcomings should differentiate the low end of the scale, with physical shortcomings found more at the upper end as the levels of shortcomings rise. The distinction is in fact reflected in the observed pattern of shortcomings across the campaigns studied.

A MEASURE OF SHORTCOMINGS

We can proceed on the same basis used to develop a measure of mobilization (see Chapter 4). It is necessary to assume only that each indicator taps some additional level of shortcomings without specifying the actual amount contributed by each indicator. On this basis the 22 indicators formed a Guttman scale (Figure 5.1) across all campaigns measuring relative levels of shortcomings.[4]

This scale is somewhat weaker than the mobilization scale in that it fails to

[4] Seven indicators, not marked with an asterisk on the scale, were eliminated in determining the scale steps used for statistical calculations—five because of ties, one because of high unreliability, and one because of a high error ratio. The elimination of this last indicator meant that steps 8 and 9 were combined into a single step in the statistical calculations. Otherwise, the ordering of the campaigns is unchanged.

An attempt was also made to examine regional differences. Although data were collected specifically for three cities (Peking, Shanghai, and Canton) and three provinces (Kwangtung, Szechwan, and Shensi), they were insufficiently uniform to permit systematic analysis of regional differences. There is some basis, however, upon which to hypothesize that northern rural areas might have fewer shortcomings than southern ones: "In the areas of Agrarian Reform carried out in the north before liberation anyone who earned less than half their income by labor was a rich peasant and treated as an enemy. But after 1950, instead of attacking them (i.e., the rich peasants), the Revolution tried to neutralize them. Their surplus property was not confiscated and their profits were guaranteed [Hinton, 1968: 404]."

TABLE 5.1
Shortcomings Indicators and Levels of Shortcomings

Type of indicator	Level of shortcomings		
	Low	Medium	High
Physical	0	1	10
Ideological	0	7	4

differentiate the bottom 10 cases (the lower cutting point, differentiating the low and medium categories of shortcomings).[5]

The upper cutting point, differentiating medium and higher levels of short-comings, was made to maximize the distinctions between ideological and physical shortcomings. As suggested earlier, physical shortcomings imply more problems than ideological ones and hence should be reflected in higher levels of shortcomings. (See Table 5.1.)

The observed pattern of shortcomings suggests that struggle campaigns have higher levels of shortcomings than economic or ideological campaigns. (See Table 5.2.)

However, four of the five indicators that did not fit the scale pattern were economic in character.[6] Only two other indicators with some economic aspects

Thus, in these areas, liberated before 1949, the rich peasant question had been essentially resolved, but in other areas, including virtually all of southern China, rich peasants retained at least some of their influence. They possessed more resources with which to oppose the changes inherent in the agricultural transformation process.

In addition, in the south as well as in the cities after 1949, there was a dearth of local cadres sufficiently steeled in the ideological precepts of Chinese Communism, committed to and understanding of the process of criticism/self-criticism and the mass line. This meant that more cadres in these areas would either be from the outside and less capable of communicating in another dialect, or, if from the area, might be more likely (especially when compared to northern rural areas) to be less experienced.

Finally, the significantly shorter planting season in the north may be a cause of lower levels of shortcomings. This gave the villages more time free from the pressures of agricultural work seasons to prepare more carefully for and carry out campaigns.

These three factors suggest that, were data available for a systematic comparison, northern rural areas should have lower levels of shortcomings in comparison to other areas.

[5] Its selection is somewhat arbitrary since the development of additional indicators to differentiate the lower end of the scale might reveal that the most defensible cutting point would be a few cases on either side of the present one.

[6] The rejected indicators are as follows: production suffering as a result of the campaign; an economic loan necessary to offset the effects of the campaign; assignment of arbitrary production quotas; a rise in the actual tax rates (a percentage of collective earnings or production sent to the state without compensation). The fifth indicator, a return to old methods or patterns of organization following the campaign, was an attempt to tap the problem of campaign changes failing to be integrated into ongoing organizational patterns. Perhaps because it was vague and general, its error ratio was marginally high enough to exclude it from the overall pattern.

Campaign List No. (see Appendix 1)	Campaign Type	Campaigns	Scale step	I 19 targets remain*	I 12 violation of policy implementation*	I 10 re-investigation following campaign*	I 9 leftist or rightist deviations*	I 17 cadre failure in policy implementation*	P 22 people receive insult or abuse*	I 28 excessive labeling of targets*	I 21 policy shortcomings
		High									
33	S	GPCR	17	0	1	1	1	1	1	1	1
5	S	Suppress Counterrev.	16	1	1	1	1	1	1	1	1
2	S	Agrarian Reform	15	1	1	1	1	1	1	1	1
28	S	Socialist Education	14	1	1	1	1	1	0	1	0
13	E	Higher Level Coops	13	1	1	0	1	1	1	1	0
8	S	Five-Anti	12	0	1	1	1	1	1	1	0
7	I	Three-Anti	11	1	1	1	1	1	1	1	0
19	E	Great Leap Forward	11	1	1	1	1	1	1	1	1
18	S	Anti-Rightist	10	1	0	1	1	0	1	0	1
		Medium									
22	I	Cultural Revolution 58	9	1	1	1	1	1	1	1	1
17	I	Rectification 57	8	1	8	1	1	0	1	1	0
15	I	100 Flowers	7	1	1	0	1	1	1	0	0
4	I	Resist U.S.–Aid Korea	6	0	1	1	0	1	0	8	0
9	E	Cooperatives	6	0	1	1	1	1	0	0	0
20	E	Communes	6	0	1	1	1	1	0	0	0
21	F	Backyard Furnaces	6	0	1	1	1	1	0	0	0
6	E	Mutual Aid	5	0	1	1	1	0	0	0	0
29	I	Successor Generation	5	1	1	1	1	0	0	0	0
11	E	Business Reform	4	1	1	1	0	0	0	0	0
34	I	Rectification 68	4	1	0	1	0	0	0	+	0
12	S	Eliminate Counterev.	3	1	1	0	0	0	+	0	0
14	E	Combat Four Evils	2	1	0	0	0	0	0	0	0
24	I	Rightist Sympathies	2	1	0	0	+	0	0	0	0
25	I	Anti Japan-U.S. Treaty	2	8	0	0	0	0	0	8	0
30	E	Learn from Tachai	2	1	0	0	0	0	0	0	0
31	E	Learn from Taching	2	1	0	0	0	0	0	0	0
		Low									
1	E	Buy Victory Bonds	1	0	0	0	0	+	0	0	0
3	I	Peace Signatures	1	0	0	0	0	0	0	0	0
10	I	Study Constitution	1	0	0	0	0	0	0	0	0
16	I	Study Mao "On Contra. . . ."	1	0	0	0	0	0	0	0	0
23	E	Urban Communes	1	0	0	0	0	0	0	0	0
26	E	Aid Agriculture	1	0	0	0	+	0	0	0	+
27	I	Learn from the PLA	1	0	0	0	0	0	0	0	0
32	I	Study Mao Thought	1	0	0	0	0	0	0	0	0
35	I	Support the Army	1	0	0	0	0	0	0	0	0
36	E	Barefoot Doctors	1	0	0	+	0	0	0	0	0
		Errors		7	2	3	2	4	2	2	5
		Nonmodals Down		17	17	17	18	16	12	11	7

Indicator Type
Indicator No.
(see Appendix 5, Section F)

Figure 5.1 Guttman scalogram of shortcomings (scalability = .652).

Indicators

P 15	I 2	P 6	P 20	P 25	P 1	I 18	P 23	I 13	P 7	P 3	P 4	P 5	I 26
suicides*	work or study slowdowns	destruction of property*	violent acts of resistance*	physical conflict between classes or groups	unsanctioned mass migration*	occurrence of bribery*	people indiscriminately killed	demotions among non-target groups*	army activated to maintain order*	physical harm inflicted on cadres	armed clashes resulting in death*	armed clashes resulting in injury	conflict among cadres
1	1	1	1	1	1	~~0~~	1	1	1	1	1	1	1
1	1	1	1	1	1	1	1	1	1	1	0	0	0
1	~~0~~	1	1	1	1	1	1	1	0	~~0~~	0	0	0
1	1	~~0~~	1	1	~~0~~	1	0	0	0	0	0	0	0
~~0~~	1	1	1	1	1	1	0	0	0	0	0	0	0
1	1	1	1	1	0	0	0	0	0	0	0	0	0
1	1	1	0	0	0	0	0	~~+~~	0	0	0	0	~~+~~
~~0~~	1	1	0	0	0	0	0	~~+~~	0	0	0	0	0
1	1	0	0	0	0	0	0	0	0	0	0	0	0
0	0	0	0	0	0	0	0	0	0	0	0	0	0
0	0	0	0	0	0	0	0	0	0	0	0	0	0
0	0	0	0	0	0	0	0	0	0	0	0	0	0
0	0	0	0	~~0~~	0	~~+~~	0	0	0	0	0	0	0
0	0	0	0	0	0	0	0	0	0	0	0	0	0
0	~~+~~	0	0	0	0	0	0	0	0	0	0	0	0
0	0	~~+~~	0	0	0	0	~~+~~	0	0	0	0	0	0
0	0	0	0	0	0	0	0	0	0	0	0	0	0
0	0	0	0	1	0	0	0	0	0	0	0	0	0
0	0	0	0	0	0	0	0	0	0	0	0	0	0
~~+~~	~~+~~	0	0	0	~~+~~	0	0	0	0	0	0	0	0
~~+~~	0	0	~~+~~	0	0	0	0	0	0	0	0	0	0
0	0	0	0	~~+~~	0	0	0	0	0	0	0	0	0
0	0	0	0	0	0	0	0	0	0	0	0	0	0
0	~~+~~	0	0	0	0	0	0	0	0	0	0	0	0
0	0	0	0	0	0	0	0	0	0	0	0	0	0
0	0	0	0	0	0	0	0	0	0	0	0	0	0
0	0	0	0	0	0	0	0	0	0	0	0	0	0
0	0	0	0	0	0	0	0	0	0	0	0	0	0
0	0	0	0	0	0	0	0	0	0	0	0	0	0
0	~~+~~	0	0	0	~~+~~	0	0	0	0	0	0	0	0
0	0	0	0	0	0	0	0	0	0	0	0	0	0
0	0	0	0	0	0	0	0	0	0	0	0	0	0
0	0	0	0	0	0	0	0	0	0	0	0	0	0
	5	2	1	2	3	2	2	1	0	0	0	0	1
	12	8	7	8	6	4	5	4	2	2	1	1	2

Code: 0 = absent   1 = present   8 = missing data   ~~0~~ or ~~+~~ = error
Campaign Type: I = ideological   E = economic   S = struggle
Indicator Type: I = ideological   P = physical
* = indicator used for calculating correlations

127

TABLE 5.2
Campaign Types and Levels of Shortcomings[ab]

Type of campaign	N	Level of shortcomings		
		Low	Medium	High
Struggle	7	0%	14%	86%
Economic	14	29	57	14
Ideological	15	40	53	7

[a]Chi-square = 17.75.
[b]$p < .001$.

did fit the scale pattern: work or study slowdowns and bribery. Might there be another dimension of economic shortcomings that does not fit the present scale pattern? Moreover, in the present scale of shortcomings, might the higher level of shortcomings for struggle campaigns relative to economic campaigns be due merely to the dominance of physical shortcomings and the absence of economic ones? Perhaps the observed pattern is a mere accident of the indicators used?

With the four economic indicators that did not scale plus the two economic indicators that did, an attempt was made to build a scale just of economic campaigns. The indicators differentiated only the upper end of the scale, so the observations are necessarily limited. One indicator, a rise in actual tax rates, did not occur in any of the economic campaigns. The other five produced a pattern at the upper level of the scale to include not only the HAPCs and the GLF but the associated campaigns of the GLF as well, the Communes and the Backyard Furnaces.

The attempt was then made to build a scale with these six indicators across all the campaigns. Two indicators had to be eliminated. A rise in actual tax rates, although it occurred in two cases, failed to differentiate any cases as a part of the scale pattern. The assignment of arbitrary production quotas likewise occurred in four cases but failed to differentiate any cases as a part of the scale pattern. The remaining four indicators, two of which were in the main scale, differentiated only the upper end of the scale. But this was enough to observe whether there would be a major shift of the pattern such that economic campaigns would have high economic shortcomings and struggle campaigns would have relatively lower (than economic) levels of economic shortcomings. There was no major shift. With three exceptions, the original pattern held. All the struggle campaigns in the upper level of shortcomings in the original scale remained in the upper level in the scale of just economic shortcomings, except for Agrarian Reform. Besides the GLF and the HAPC, already at this level, only two other economic campaigns, the Communes and Backyard Furnaces, moved into the upper level of economic shortcomings.

This suggests that even if other economic indicators that did fit the scale pattern were developed, there would be no major shift in the high level of shortcomings of struggle campaigns relative to economic ones. Struggle campaigns, in short, possess all levels of shortcomings—ideological, physical, and economic—in relatively greater levels than economic or ideological campaigns.[7]

THE INFORMANT'S PERSPECTIVE

During each interview the informant was asked to list the most important shortcomings of the campaign under discussion. Although the responses were necessarily subjective and not totally independent of the scale, they provide a somewhat different approach to assessing relative levels of shortcomings. Notable differences in the trend of response were found between the three types of campaigns.

Overall, informants indicated that shortcomings increased from ideological to economic to struggle campaigns. This corresponds to the observed scale.

Ideological Campaigns

With the exception of one ideological campaign ranking at the upper end of the shortcomings scale, and three campaigns for which the single informant could not recall any shortcomings, the shortcomings of virtually all the other ideological campaigns were characterized by expressions such as "having no lasting impression," "being too short," "a single blast of wind" (yi jen feng), "never fully implemented," "failed to carry to conclusion," "no real changes resulted," "happened very quick, with little awareness of the problem," "it was not internalized." Although there were other shortcomings, particularized for

[7] Separate scales were also constructed for the three major types of campaigns, using all indicators in the original scale. Since each type of campaign should be more homogeneous than the whole, some improvement in scalability might be expected. There is, however, remarkably little change, suggesting a strong underlying dimension binding the three types of campaigns together.

For economic campaigns, the shift of only one indicator produced a scalability of .679, a marginal improvement of only .027. The elimination of three indicators, one physical and two ideological, increased the scalability to .786. In neither case did any shift in the relative ranking of campaigns occur. For struggle campaigns, a shift of 6 of the 22 indicators produced a scalability of .75, an improvement of .098. The relative ordering of campaigns remained the same. Three indicators were shifted for ideological campaigns to produce a scalability of .717, an improvement of .065. Again, the relative ordering of campaigns remained the same. For all three types of campaigns, near-perfect scales could be built using just a few of the indicators.

each campaign, no other trend was apparent. Shortcomings of ideological campaigns represent one central trend; as a group these campaigns tended to be insufficiently thorough in implementation and to lack enduring impacts on the population. Their shortcomings tended to be ones of omission rather than commission. This may, in part, explain why the lower end of the scale, mostly ideological campaigns, is not differentiated by the selected indicators, since the indicators identified primarily errors of commission.

Economic Campaigns

Some economic campaigns at the lower end of the scale were also characterized as being insufficiently implemented, as suffering from shortcomings of omission (three of four at the lowest level and two of eight at the middle level). Informants characterized five of the economic campaigns as detrimental to production. They included the two economic campaigns at the upper level of the scale plus the three economic subcampaigns of the GLF in the middle level of the scale. This would tend to support the discussion in the previous section to the effect that had there been more indicators of economic shortcomings, the Communes and Backyard Furnaces campaigns might have ranked higher on the scale of shortcomings.

However, the dominant trend was the informants' repeated mention of ideological shortcomings. With the exception of the GLF and its associated campaigns, the feeling tended to be that although the economic goals were often reached (i.e., production increases), and changes were successfully made in organization structure (e.g., Mutual Aid Teams, Cooperatives), people were often not ideologically convinced of the positive value of these changes.

This type of shortcoming is characterized by "inadequate propaganda work," "still putting self above collective," or "an unwillingness to speak out." This suggests, as does the scale, that ideological shortcomings tend to predominate among most economic campaigns.

Struggle Campaigns

The trend presented by struggle campaigns is clear. Every one of these campaigns is characterized predominantly by its excesses. Excesses took three basic forms: overclassification, physical abuse, and the use of coercion instead of persuasion. (Similar characterizations were made of the GLF, the HAPC, and the Communes campaigns.) Indicators of these excesses predominate at the upper end of the scale. Informants' impressions clearly confirm that struggle campaigns should cluster at the upper end of the shortcomings scale.

Informants felt that individuals had been unfairly classified in many of these campaigns. The cost of erroneously classifying rich peasants as landlords or vice versa has already been noted.

The problem of physical abuse is characterized in Hinton, for example, when one peasant, so enraged by the process of recounting the abuses of an errant cadre during a struggle meeting, attempts to strangle the cadre to death (1968: 470). Similar abuses were frequent in the treatment of landlords during Agrarian Reform as well as in other struggle campaigns such as the GPCR.

In the previous chapter, I have stressed the Chinese commitment to persuasion. Coercion is to be used only in cases where the class enemies fail to respond to persuasion (Mao, 1967: Vol. 4, 419). Yet, for many of the campaigns, especially those with high levels of shortcomings, there seems to be a substantial amount of coercion. Walker notes the reluctant use of coercion as described by one cadre during the HAPC campaign:

> We know coercion is bad but the tasks are urgent and time is short; there are few alternative methods; you are anxious and therefore cannot avoid using a little coercion [in Walker, 1968: 425].

Why do physical and coercive excesses seem to occur among these campaigns and not others? Many of these campaigns also have high levels of mobilization. It would appear that the intensity of activity found at the highest levels of mobilization produces pressures that breed coercion and physical abuse. Skinner and Winckler (1969: 424–425) have noted this phenomenon, which seems to begin at the peak of "high tide" and carries over into the period of "deterioration." These data suggest, however, that for most economic and ideological campaigns their peak or level of mobilization is relatively lower than the level for struggle campaigns and that such pressures are not forthcoming, eliminating the physical and coercive excess found in struggle campaigns.

At these periods of high mobilization, or "high tide," pressures emerge for an incisive and quick resolution of the contradiction or problem at hand. The leadership may even encourage it, believing that the possible excesses will be offset by quicker and hopefully more thorough solutions (Mao, 1971: 29–30). Extreme solutions seem more attractive, and persuasion gives way to coercion. Hinton describes this problem in his portrayal of how the work team members improperly dealt with the four cadres who had committed serious errors:

> They had attempted to crush the people's new oppressors, not remake them. In working thus they had distorted the essence of the "purification movement," and had followed in the wake of those impetuous poor peasants who demanded only revenge for past injuries and had no vision of the potential of leaders who had temporarily gone astray [1968: 471].

SUMMARY

Evidence presented in this chapter has identified a rather clear pattern of shortcomings, reflecting increasing levels of shortcomings in ideological, economic, and struggle campaigns. That there should be a pattern or, even more, that campaigns have many shortcomings, should surprise no one, least of all the Chinese. Mao acknowledged that excesses will occur (1971: 29). The problem is not to eliminate the inevitability of the excesses, and certainly not to hide them. The problem is to analyze them in order to correct them. Hinton describes how Little Li, the vice–work team leader, drove this point home in chastizing the work team leader for offering to resign his post because of the errors he had committed:

> Such a thing is quite wrong. You just want to escape in the face of trouble. A Communist should never think like that. Mistakes are unavoidable. The thing to do is to examine and correct them, not run away [Hinton, 1968: 391].

And here, in the face of errors or shortcomings, lies the kernel of achievement. A shortcoming properly analyzed and corrected can be turned into an achievement.

6

Achievements

Achievements and shortcomings, difficulties and the bright future—these are aspects of a single process and are the unity of opposites. . . . We would . . . be blindly clinging to the shortcomings and difficulties if we overlook our achievements and lose sight of the bright future, and this would lead us to passiveness and pessimism and eventual abandonment of struggle because of loss of hope in victory.

—*PR*, January 14, 1972: 9–10

The preceding chapter stressed the emphasis the Communists place on shortcomings and their correction. It is out of the resolution of shortcomings that achievements may come. Achievements should not be seen in isolation. They are interrelated, their effect is multiple. Achievements in one area can lead to achievements in other areas. The correction of ideological problems may produce the atmosphere for better economic accomplishments. Like mobilization and shortcomings, therefore, indicators of achievements should be applicable to all three types of campaigns.

THE INDICATORS OF ACHIEVEMENTS

What are some of these achievements and how might they be compared across campaigns? Following the pattern and logic used in Chapter 5 to present shortcomings, I have identified indicators of achievements potentially common to all campaigns so that a measure of the relative levels of achievements can be constructed.

In identifying potential indicators of achievements, I relied primarily on the writings and statements of the national leadership. It is they who set the tone, who outline national goals. Where the leadership is divided, the statements most closely associated with Mao Tse-tung have been selected as standard, for his

133

thought, more than any alternative view, has inspired and emphasized the mobilization approach central to the campaign.[1]

Two types of indicators are present. One emphasizes ideological achievements and the other emphasizes economic achievements.[2] However, indicators of both types include elements of the other. In fact, for some indicators it is not easy to discern exactly where the emphasis should be placed. This may be due to the close interaction between ideological and economic factors.

Ideological Achievements

Raising of political consciousness

Written individual citations

Written group citations

Increase in collective orientation in unit

Increased interunit cooperation

Increase in Party membership

Improvement in anti-bureaucratic styles

Improvement in communication networks between upper and lower levels of organization

Increased decentralization of decision making

Reduction in rural–urban differences

Penetration of campaign to backward areas

Increased equality between groups

Political consciousness is a frequently used term in the Chinese political vocabulary. It refers at once to the whole educational process of understanding socialist practice and Communist theory. Yet, at any given time, an increase in political consciousness can result from a better understanding of a relatively specific set of interrelationships. For example, as a result of the Anti-Traitor campaign of 1945,

> half the landlords and rich peasants in the district were attacked and punished with the confiscation of some or all of their property, thus cutting back considerably the

[1] I decided against using alternative standards such as those associated with development models, or values of a "developed" capitalist society, or even a mixed set of standards imposed by the evaluator; that approach seemed grossly unfair. If one is to judge the achievements of the mobilization system in China, or any other system, realistically, one should judge them only on what that system aims to accomplish, not what it has never tried to do or never wanted to do.

[2] Another type of indicator, control achievements, emerged in the course of discussion with informants. The impact of failing to include this type of indicator is discussed later in this chapter.

holdings on which the old system was based. Many people were mobilized, organized, and educated by these events and learned to see some connection between collaboration and the dominant feudal class [Hinton, 1968: 125].

Political consciousness emerged from active participation in a struggle campaign. Active participation can be quite important in the process:

> All the members of the [work] team felt that the intangible results were far more important. They saw the *gate* as a turning point in the political *fanshen* ("turning over") of the people. . . .
> The most important result of the whole campaign was certainly this drawing into meaningful action of hundreds of peasants who, because of various inhibitions and fears, had remained passive throughout the revolutionary years, or had lapsed back into passivity once the big struggle against the landlords had been victoriously concluded [Hinton, 1968: 363].

Some people will merely participate, others will take a leading or "activist" role. The activists, especially if they have not taken on such roles before or if their contributions are particularly notable, often become candidates for written citations for outstanding performance in ideological and/or manual work. Work groups may be similarly cited for their collective activism. Collective activism can also lead to an increase in the level of collective orientation in a unit. When people increase their willingness to work together it is reasonable to expect that they will also increase their sense of belonging, or orientation to the collective whole. This sense of activism and collective orientation may go beyond the unit as well, leading to greater cooperation between units.

Individual activists can become candidates for formal leadership positions as cadres and/or Party members. This recruitment of fresh talent is seen as a means to constantly revitalize the bureaucracy. Mao himself was aware of the bureaucracy's unresponsiveness to the Maoist emphasis on mobilization (see, e.g., Barnett, 1968: passim, especially 432–445; Whyte, 1973):

> Hostility to bureaucracy crops up again and again in Chinese Communist history and reached its high point during the Great Leap Forward when the leadership appeared convinced that the economic revolution could more or less dispense with the instruments of formal administration [Schurmann, 1968: 112].

Others have pointed to Mao's belief that bureaucracy retards economic achievements rather than promoting them (RMRB, August 7, 1957). Also,

> [Mao regarded] . . . the state bureaucracy as the biggest obstacle to the growth of an appreciation among the population generally of the basic identity of individual and communal interests which the Party's economic planning was supposed to enshrine [Gray, 1969: 131].

The enduring and pervasive drive to counteract bureaucracy has not been easy given the mandarin cultural tradition of China and the observed entrenchment of bureaucracies in other socialist countries, especially the Soviet Union (Schram,

1967: 264). Although concrete achievements in combatting bureaucracy have been realized in several campaigns, it is the rectification campaigns that focus most directly on this effort (Teiwes, 1971: 62–65).

During rectification campaigns, it is stressed that cadres and bureaucrats must get out among the poeple they are supposed to be serving, talk with them, investigate at the local level, and spend a good part of their time laboring with peasants and workers in order to understand better their thinking, their needs, and their livelihood. Bureaucrats must learn that the responsibility granted to them in leadership roles cannot be converted into irresponsible use of influence to further their own interests.

To the extent this kind of interaction is fostered between leaders and led (bureaucrats and masses) it may also lead to the improvement of communication between upper and lower levels.

Moreover, the de-emphasis on bureaucratic styles is tied to the emphasis on decentralization, not only in the location of industry, for example, but in the process of decision making as well. Although the responsibility to make broad policy decisions and establish overall production goals remains that of the central government, the implementation of these decisions and goals is to be decentralized to the extent possible (Gray, 1969: 124–129).

Major attention is paid to the effort to reduce urban–rural differences:

> It is perhaps in the idea of the "destruction of the three great differences"—
> among industry and agriculture, town and country, and mental and manual labor—
> that Mao's point of view on social and economic change is best summed up. . . . In
> Mao's thought, their elimination becomes . . . the most critical step toward successful
> economic development [Gray, 1969: 142].

For example, industry is introduced into the countryside not only to educate the peasantry on the potential of industrialization, but also to give peasants the chance to participate in that industrialization process, to create their own mechanization technology.

Obviously the greatest differences between city and countryside are seen in the "backward" rural areas. Some campaigns, although undertaken in most rural areas, nevertheless fail to penetrate to the more backward areas. The penetration of a campaign to backward areas suggests the potential of further reducing existing differences. For example, one informant said that if the sociopolitical changes that took place during the Commune campaign were equal to 20 years in most communes, then the changes wrought in the backward areas, at least those she visited and worked in, were equal to 100 years.

Great importance is attached to decreasing urban–rural differences; equal stress is attached to decreasing differences betwen classes and groups in the society. No two goals more clearly characterize dominant elements of the socialist transformation process.

The Maoist standard of equality is, of course, the peasant and the worker. In this respect the process of *xia fang*, going down to the lower levels, furthers achievements in the equalization process:

> One of the important tasks of the [Youth] League organizations is to mobilize and organize League members and other young people to firmly take the road of integration with the workers and peasants. Chairman Mao pointed out long ago: "How should we judge whether a youth is a revolutionary? How can we tell? There can only be one criterion, namely, whether or not he is willing to integrate himself with the broad masses of workers and peasants and does so in practice." Several million educated young people have settled in the countryside. . . . This phenomenon has pounded hard at traditional contempt for physical labor and for workers and peasants [*RMRB*, February 22, 1973, in *PR*, March 2, 1973: 14–15].

The *xia fang* process is thus designed to ensure that distinctions in role responsibility between leader and led, between intellectual and worker, will not be turned into hierarchical benefits of privilege and power of one group over another. (See also *HQ*, 1965: 8, in *PR*, August 20, 1965: 20–21.) The effort to eliminate distinctions between classes or groups has been substantial in the process of women's liberation. Before liberation, women were virtual chattels of men in spite of their contributions to productive and social life, they were even referred to as the "wife of ____" or "the mother of ____." Whatever influence a woman might have obtained in the centuries of recorded history in China came virtually without exception from her relationship to a man (e.g., as a mother-in-law or dowager empress). In the rural areas Agrarian Reform struck the first major blow at this oppressive system. For the first time some women could and did own land and were referred to by their own names. Other campaigns, including the GLF, have chipped away at this system of inequality, still embedded in the thinking of many who lived before liberation as well as some who were born after.

> There were many women who saw in the [urban] communes an opportunity for themselves. Women played an active role in the street Party committees and in the leadership of mass organizations. They became the cadres of the new organizations, just as women earlier dominated the urban residents committees. . . .
>   The Great Leap Forward was a time of psychological liberation for many peasants: probably many women, one of China's suppressed populations, must have felt that the millenium was at hand, when they could freely enter the great public world on a par with men [Schurmann, 1968: 396–397].

One press report from the time stated that some women

> got so excited in working that they forgot to eat, forgot to sleep, forgot to return home. . . . Housewives who simply took care of their own homes now cared about each other and helped each other [Schurmann, 1968: 397].

Of course, the millenium did not come. Although great changes have been made, for a number of critical reasons embedded in the history, leadership, structure, and ideology of the society the complete liberation of women in

China is still a long way off (Johnson, 1976). It is simply not, for example, an easy task to change centuries of tradition and old attitudes passed down from generation to generation. For example, with the liberation of Long Bow and Agrarian Reform accomplished, most women still thought it wrong for a woman to ask for a divorce—not to mention the men. Hinton reports in a most dramatic fashion the first divorce ever recorded in Long Bow to be requested by a woman. The women of the village agreed to support the divorce claim in exchange for this woman's willingness to testify against the bad actions of her husband, an erring cadre whom so many had come to fear that none were willing to testify against him (1968: 455–459).

The reduction of differences between urban and rural areas and the reduction of inequalities between classes and groups have been dealt with at length because they are central standards set by the leadership for the transformation of society. Thus, for a campaign to realize achievements in these areas is of substantial significance, more so perhaps than most of the other indicators. Because of the incremental gain in achievements implied by the presence of these two indicators, they have been taken as the cutting points on the scale of achievements.[3]

Economic Achievements

Improvement of collective economic conditions

Improvement of work methods

Production records broken

New material achievements

Decrease in living costs

Acquisition of new skills

Increase in occupational opportunities

Increase in occupational grade

Improvement of family conditions

Increase in individual income

The improvement of collective economic conditions as a result of the campaign is a direct indication of economic achievement. This improvement could result from better harvests brought about by changes in collective forms of

---

[3] The argument that these two indicators should be the cutting points is less obvious than the rationale for the cutting points for mobilization and shortcomings. With achievements, no similar distinction emphasizing types of indicators emerged from the data. Thus indicators were selected that seemed to represent higher increments of achievements and would differentiate the scale into three parts, roughly equivalent in number to the mobilization scale.

organization, or from increased industrial production brought about by improvements in the system of industrial organization. For example, during the Five-Anti campaign, which sought to control the abuses of large industrial and business enterprises, the success in combatting such abuses as graft, cheating, and bribery resulted not only in additional resources for investment but in greater control over the production process. These results in turn often led to a heightened sense of collective orientation within the unit and hence to greater efforts to increase production.

As indicated in the previous section, campaigns often produce greater activism on the part of individuals and groups. In the productive process this activism often leads to greater efforts invested into increasing production through improvement in working skills, and, in turn, the breaking of old production records.

This emphasis on the productive process can also lead to new material achievements, such as the construction of large buildings, factories, and sports arenas, or, in agriculture, the building of large-scale water conservation projects—usually in "record" time and with great inputs of labor power from the general population. This type of achievement was quite pronounced during the GLF.[4]

In a couple of campaigns there was a reported decrease in living costs. A great deal of time is spent monitoring living costs. Most prices are controlled according to economic plan rather than supply and demand. This means that there need not be, nor has there been, much fluctuation in living costs; they have remained very stable over the past 20 years even as income has increased. However, living costs have been reduced on occasion—as when the changes wrought by a campaign appeared to warrant such a reduction.

In the effort to minimize differences between groups, it is considered an achievement to learn new skills. For example, an intellectual who has learned to operate a factory machine has learned something of another role. Alternatively, a peasant who has learned to read may be able to begin to sense the role of a student or intellectual.

Four of the economic indicators emphasize the improvement of family or individual conditions. Such improvements are not seen as concurrently detrimental to the collective interest, for they tend to result from incremental achievements in the collective sector. Of course, at any given moment some individuals will benefit more than others. The aim, however, is to benefit those who have less. For example, some factory managers have relatively high wages because they have held their positions for many years; some even antedate liberation. When wages are increased the aim is to increase them more at the lower levels and less (or not at all) at the highest levels.

[4] Thus, although the GLF did suffer setbacks in other areas of the economic infrastructure (e.g., the accounting and reporting system), in the area of capital construction there were some long-term gains to offset shortcomings.

In rural areas, however, one earns according to one's capabilities and time invested. Improvements in individual income can in turn lead to improvements in the family's material well-being (e.g., the addition of a sewing machine, bicycle, radio). However, these achievements nevertheless occur in a basically *collectivized* economy based primarily on *collective* earnings. In short, one is encouraged to increase one's own income by working to increase that of the collective whole.

Collective considerations are also primary in changes in occupational grades and opportunity. One is likely to advance to a higher level in a factory pay scale or be evaluated at a higher work point level for agricultural work precisely because one has been actively involved in a campaign or other effort to increase production. Increased activity in individual sideline production (e.g., private garden plots) is quite obviously not grounds for being promoted or evaluated at a higher work point level. Likewise the increase in occupational opportunities is more likely to result from collective effort, such as the construction of commune dining halls, the establishment of street factories during the GLF, the popularization of higher educational opportunities, or the expansion of medical services.

As I mentioned earlier, it is not always clear whether an achievement should be considered ideological or economic; there is some overlapping. For the most part, it has been possible to distinguish them on the basis of primary emphasis. The fact that many indicators contain elements of both types may in fact be reflected in the mixed ordering of economic and ideological indicators in the scale.

A MEASURE OF ACHIEVEMENTS

Proceeding on the same basis used to develop measures of mobilization and shortcomings, we need assume only that each indicator taps some additional level of achievement. On this basis the 22 indicators formed a Guttman scale (Figure 6.1) across all campaigns measuring levels of achievements.[5]

---

[5] Six potential indicators failed to fit the scale pattern. Three (early fulfillment of quotas or production targets, increase in self-reliance, and the presence of self-confession) had a marginally higher error ratio than the acceptable minimum. The use of additional informants might have improved the error ratio and led to the inclusion of these indicators. The improvement of environmental conditions, such as sanitation, health care, and security, occurred in many campaigns but was apparently limited to only certain types of campaigns—see the next section, "The Informant's Perspective." So too, is the indicator of whether politics is more important than economics. This was judged the case for all but one of the struggle and ideological campaigns (Five-Anti), but it was not so judged for five economic campaigns. Finally, the indicator of *work point value increase* was potentially limited to only a few agricultural campaigns after the Cooperatives campaign, and was

TABLE 6.1
Campaign Types and Levels of Achievements[a][b]

Type of campaign	N	Level of achievement		
		Low	Medium	High
Economic	14	14.3%	28.6%	57.1%
Struggle	7	28.6	28.6	42.9
Ideological	15	26.7	53.3	20.0

[a]Chi-square = 4.64. [b]
[b]$p < .33$.

As indicated earlier, two indicators, reduction in urban–rural differences and increased equality between groups, which imply high incremental levels of achievements, were selected for cutting points. On this basis, the observed data show a somewhat greater level of achievements for economic campaigns, and lower levels for struggle and ideological campaigns, although the results are not statistically significant, suggesting that all types of campaigns are likely to be found at the different levels of achievements. (See Table 6.1.)

When separate scales are constructed for each type of campaign the rank order of campaigns for the scale of each type of campaign is unchanged.[6] This would indicate an underlying achievement dimension common to all campaigns, regardless of type.

The observed pattern of achievements reflected a slightly greater level for economic campaigns than for struggle or ideological ones. Might this simply be an artifact of the indicator order? Perhaps ideological indicators simply differentiated the lower end of scale, whereas economic ones differentiated the upper end. (See Table 6.2.)

judged to have actually occurred in only one campaign. The last three indicators violate the standard that all indicators should have a potentially equal chance of occurring in any campaign.

Of the 22 indicators that did fit the scale pattern (within the minimum scalability of .65), six were eliminated in determining the step levels used to calculate correlations. Five were eliminated because of ties. Three of these plus one other were eliminated because their disagreement ratios were unacceptably high (above an arbitrary .15—see Chapter 3).

[6] For the economic campaigns only three indicators had to be re-ordered to produce a minimum scalability of .658, insignificantly higher than the overall scale's scalability of .651. For the struggle campaigns the re-ordering of four indicators produced an improved scalability of .722. Ideological campaigns showed an improved scalability of .696 even without re-ordering any indicators. The re-ordering of four further raised the scalability to .775. The fact that at least two subtypes had higher levels of scalability should be expected. Even though there is a common underlying dimension that permits all three types of campaigns to fit on a single scale, it is also the case that there should be greater homogeneity among campaign types.

				I 21	I 16	I 19	I 13	E 2	I 22	E 11	E 9
Campaign List No. (see Appendix 1)	Campaign Type	Campaigns	Scale step	raise political consciousness*	improve communication networks*	improve collective orientation*	more people enter party*	improve collective economic conditions	increase equality between groups*	work methods improve*	break production records*
		High									
7	I	Three-Anti	17	1	1	1	1	1	1	1	1
8	S	Five-Anti	17	1	1	1	1	1	1	1	1
19	E	Great Leap Forward	16	1	1	1	1	1	1	1	1
33	S	GPCR	16	1	1	θ	1	1	1	θ	θ
2	S	Agrarian Reform	15	1	1	1	1	1	1	1	θ
11	E	Business Reform	15	1	1	1	1	1	1	1	1
36	E	Barefoot Doctors %	15	1	1	1	1	1	1	1	θ
6	E	Mutual Aid	14	1	1	1	1	1	1	1	1
13	E	Higher Level Coops	14	1	1	1	1	1	1	1	1
20	E	Communes	14	1	1	1	1	1	1	1	1
23	E	Urban Communes	13	1	1	1	1	1	1	1	1
15	I	100 Flowers	13	1	1	1	θ	1	1	1	1
21	E	Backyard Furnaces	13	1	1	1	1	1	1	1	1
27	I	Learn from the PLA	12	1	1	1	1	1	θ	1	1
		Medium									
4	I	Resist U.S.–Aid Korea	11	1	1	1	1	1	1	1	1
22	I	Cultural Revolution 58	11	1	1	1	1	1	1	1	1
30	E	Learn from Tachai	11	1	θ	1	1	1	1	1	1
31	E	Learn from Taching	11	1	θ	1	1	1	θ	θ	1
5	S	Suppress Counterrev.	10	1	1	1	1	1	1	θ	1
32	I	Study Mao Thought	10	1	θ	1	1	1	1	1	1
26	E	Aid Agriculture	9	1	θ	1	1	1	1	θ	1
9	E	Cooperatives	8	1	θ	1	1	1	1	1	θ
24	I	Rightist Sympathies	7	1	1	θ	1	1	θ	1	1
29	I	Successor Generation	7	1	1	1	1	1	1	1	θ
34	I	Rectification 68	7	1	1	θ	1	θ	1	1	
10	I	Study Constitution	6	1	1	θ	θ	θ	1	1	1
17	I	Rectification 57	6	1	1	θ	1	1	1	1	1
28	S	Socialist Education	5	1	θ	1	1	1	1	0	0
		Low									
18	S	Anti-Rightist	4	1	1	1	1	0	0	0	0
1	E	Buy Victory Bonds	3a#	1	1	1	0	0	0	0	0
12	S	Eliminate Counterrev.	3	1	1	0	0	0	0	0	0
3	I	Peace Signatures	2	1	0	0	0	0	0	0	0
16	I	Study Mao "On Contra...."	2	1	0	0	0	0	0	0	0
25	I	Anti Japan–U.S. Treaty	2	1	0	0	0	0	0	+	0
14	E	Combat Four Evils	1	0	0	0	0	+	0	0	0
35	I	Support the Army	1	0	0	0	0	0	+	0	0
		Errors		0	6	5	2	3	4	5	5
		Nonmodals Down		2	11	11	9	9	10	12	14

Indicators

Steps 3 and 3a are combined in the scale used for correlational analysis.
% The Barefoot Doctor campaign ranks at step 17 in the scale used for correlational analysis.

Figure 6.1 Guttman scalogram of achievements (scalability = .651).

E 12	I 20	E 4	I 3	I 24	E 10	I 25	I 26	E 1	E 6	E 5	I 14	I 15	E 28
new skills learned*	greater cooperation between units*	new material achievements	individuals receive citations*	groups receive citations*	occupational opportunities increase*	decrease rural–urban differences*	campaign carried to backward areas*	family material conditions improve*	individual/family income increase	occupational grade increase*	improve anti-bureaucratic work styles	decision-making decentralized*	living costs decrease
1	1	1	1	1	1	1	1	1	θ	1	1	1	8
1	1	1	1	θ	1	1	1	1	1	1	1	1	1
1	1	1	1	1	1	1	1	1	1	1	1	1	0
1	1	1	θ	θ	θ	1	1	θ	θ	1	1	1	0
1	1	1	1	1	1	1	1	1	1	1	0	0	0
1	1	1	1	θ	θ	1	1	1	1	1	0	0	0
1	1	1	1	1	1	1	1	1	θ	1	0	0	+
1	θ	1	1	1	1	0	1	1	1	0	0	0	0
1	1	1	θ	θ	1	1	1	1	1	0	0	0	0
1	1	1	1	1	1	1	1	1	1	0	0	0	0
θ	1	1	1	1	1	1	1	0	0	0	+	0	0
1	1	1	1	1	1	1	1	0	0	0	+	0	0
θ	1	θ	1	1	θ	1	0	0	0	0	0	0	0
1	1	1	1	1	1	0	0	0	0	0	0	0	8
1	1	1	1	1	1	0	0	0	0	0	0	0	0
1	1	1	1	1	1	0	0	0	0	0	0	0	0
1	θ	1	1	1	1	0	0	0	0	+	0	0	0
θ	1	1	1	1	0	0	0	0	0	0	+	0	8
1	1	1	1	1	0	0	0	0	0	0	0	0	0
1	1	1	1	0	0	+	0	0	0	+	0	0	0
1	1	8	0	0	0	0	+	+	+	0	0	0	0
1	0	0	0	0	0	0	0	0	0	0	0	0	0
1	0	0	0	0	0	0	0	0	0	+	0	0	0
1	0	0	0	0	0	0	0	0	0	+	+	0	0
0	0	0	0	0	0	0	0	0	0	0	0	0	0
0	0	0	0	0	0	0	+	0	0	0	+	+	0
0	0	0	0	0	0	0	0	0	0	0	+	0	0
0	0	0	0	0	0	0	0	0	0	0	+	0	0
0	0	0	0	0	0	0	+	0	0	0	0	0	8
0	0	0	0	0	0	0	0	0	0	0	0	0	0
0	0	0	0	0	0	0	+	0	0	0	0	0	8
0	0	0	0	0	0	0	0	0	0	0	0	0	0
0	0	0	0	0	0	0	0	0	0	0	0	0	0
0	0	0	+	+	0	0	0	+	0	0	0	0	8
0	0	0	0	0	0	0	0	0	0	0	0	0	0
3	2	1	3	5	3	2	4	3	4	4	7	1	1
14	16	15	16	17	15	14	17	12	9	11	11	5	2

Code: U = absent 1 = present 8 = missing data θ or + = error
Campaign Type: I = ideological E = economic S = struggle
Indicator Type: I = ideological E = economic
* indicator used for calculating correlations

TABLE 6.2
Achievement Indicators and Levels of Achievement

Type of indicator	Level of achievement		
	Low	Medium	High
Economic	0	6	4
Ideological	4	4	4

This does not, however, appear to be the case. Although there are no economic indicators differentiating the lower end of the scale, two economic campaigns rank at the level. Moreover, though slightly more economic than ideological indicators are found at mid-levels, there is in fact a higher proportion of ideological than economic campaigns at mid-level. Nor does the high level of achievement show any pattern suggesting a spurious relationship.

In a further check to elicit any spurious relationships, two separate scales were constructed. One used just ideological indicators, and the other just economic indicators. This was done first across all campaigns, and then across subtypes of campaigns to see if separate sets of indicators cause groups of campaigns to shift into different levels of achievements in a systematic fashion.

With one exception, no shift in categories was observed when each type of campaign was scaled separately using either kind of indicator.[7] However, when all campaigns were scaled together, one campaign shifted categories when just ideological indicators were used.[8] Five campaigns shifted categories when just economic indicators were used to scale all campaigns. Even in the latter case there was no sharp observable change in the overall pattern.[9]

In short, the data do not support the proposition that the observed higher levels of achievement in economic campaigns are due to a spurious relationship of economic indicators differentiating the upper end of the scale, nor does the use of one kind of indicator without the other produce an alternative pattern.

---

[7] When using economic indicators for ideological campaigns, one campaign ranks in a higher category and another ranks in a lower one.

[8] One economic campaign ranks in a higher category, suggesting, *if anything*, that economic campaigns *might* have higher ideological achievements than ideological campaigns.

[9] One economic campaign and one ideological campaign moved up from the middle to high category. One struggle and one ideological campaign moved down from the high category to the middle. One economic campaign moved up from the lower to the middle category. On balance, then, two economic campaigns moved up a category and one struggle campaign moved down one category, by using just economic indicators—not a very sharp trend and one that makes little difference in the overall pattern. If anything, it lends further credence to the observed pattern of greater achievements for economic campaigns.

Thus, economic and ideological indicators are seen as potentially common to all types of campaigns.

THE INFORMANT'S PERSPECTIVE

To what extent do informants corroborate this view that economic and ideological achievements are common to all types of campaigns? During each interview the informant was asked to list the most important achievements of the campaign under discussion. Their responses were categorized by the type of response. Although these responses are subjective and not totally independent, they do provide an alternative approach to assessing the pattern of achievements, particularly with respect to what extent types of indicators are common to types of campaigns.

Ideological Campaigns

Most informants listed predominantly ideological achievements for ideological campaigns. The most common was an increase in political consciousness. Others included greater unity, activating or mobilizing the masses, the advancing of ideological work, and the increased integration of theory and practice. Some did list economic achievements as well. Moreover, there was a tendency for informants to list economic achievements in direct relationship to the campaigns' overall measured level of achievements. (See Table 6.3.)

This pattern supports the scale. Ideological campaigns in the lowest scale category are differentiated by ideological indicators. On the other hand, ideological campaigns listed by informants as having economic achievements tended to be differentiated on the scale by economic as well as ideological achievements.

TABLE 6.3
Informant's Achievement Items and Levels of Achievements

	Level of achievement		
Item	Low	Medium	High
Ideological and two or more economic items listed	0	1	2
Ideological and only one economic item listed	1	2	1
Only ideological items listed	4	4	0

Struggle Campaigns

Informants' lists for struggle campaigns contained both economic and ideological items. However, the list for one campaign, the Anti-Rightist campaign, which ranks in the low category of achievements, contains only ideological achievements. Again, this pattern tends to support the observed scale suggesting that struggle campaigns having fewer achievements tend to be more ideological, whereas those with more achievements tend to have both ideological and economic achievements.

There is, however, another phenomenon. Informants have listed many achievements emphasizing increased control—for example, increased security, wider government authority, elimination of the power of bad groups or classes (e.g., the capitalists or landlords), and the defeat of those opposed to Mao. With the exception of the Suppression of Counterrevolutionaries campaign in 1950, the emphasis on control-type achievements does not predominate over other kinds of achievements. Moreover, in spite of their frequent mention for struggle campaigns, control achievements were mentioned by informants only 3 other times in 140 listings of achievements for economic and ideological campaigns. Here, then, is one phenomenon that might not be common to all types of campaigns. Indeed, the one potential indicator that did try to tap this, the improvement in environmental conditions, failed to scale because of a very high disagreement ratio.

Might there be another dimension common only to struggle campaigns that would suggest they have a greater level of achievement than the scale reflects? In the absence of a suitable measure, a refutation of this possibility is difficult. Clearly, it is an oversight that this research did not include these control indicators. How serious is this oversight? With the sole exception of the Suppression of Counterrevolutionaries campaign, the more frequent listing by informants of economic and ideological achievements over those of control suggests that struggle campaigns may already be adequately represented on the scale. If control indicators could be developed that are common to all types of campaigns, they would probably be mixed along economic and ideological indicators. Hence, there would be no significant change in the overall pattern of relative achievement. The presence of control achievements may even be overstated, since the informal list comes from informants whose negative attitudes toward the government may reflect a skewed emphasis. Even though precise contradictory evidence is lacking, one must nonetheless be cautious about the extent these *ex post facto* explanations justify the thrust of the conclusions that economic campaigns overall have higher levels of achievements than struggle campaigns.

Economic Campaigns

Although ideological achievements are listed by all informants for every economic campaign, there is a clear predominance of economic achievements listed for every economic campaign save three. This would suggest, as does the scale, that both types of achievements are common to these campaigns. If informants are correct it also seems reasonable to argue that economic achievements may be more important. The three exceptions, where ideological achievements are more frequently listed, are the GLF and its associated campaigns, the Communes and Backyard Furnaces. For these, in the absence of substantial economic achievements, the emphasis given by informants, as well as by other analysts, is on ideological achievements (Schurmann, 1968: 498).[10]

SUMMARY

The data presented in this chapter suggest a pattern of somewhat higher achievements for economic campaigns relative to struggle or ideological campaigns. Ideological campaigns tend to emphasize ideological achievements: economic campaigns, economic achievements; struggle campaigns are mixed and include, according to informants, some control-type achievements as well. At the same time these tendencies, especially for ideological campaigns, are moderated by the position of the campaign on the scale. Campaigns at lower levels of the achievements scale emphasize primarily ideological achievements, whereas campaigns at higher levels are more mixed in their achievements.

Achievements do not, however, occur in the absence of shortcomings. Both may occur at the same time. One may even cancel the other out. It is important, therefore, to look at the net effects, and to understand the overall outcomes of campaigns in the context of mobilization activity. This is the remaining task.

[10] This would support the evidence in Chapter 5 that suggests that Communes and Backyard Furnaces might in fact rank at a higher level of shortcomings when only economic indicators are used. Although there is no assumption in the measurement of shortcomings and achievements that high economic shortcomings necessarily mean low economic achievements, this appears to have been the case for Communes and especially for Backyard Furnaces.

7

Net Effects:
The Utility of
the Campaigns

It was obvious that without victory gained in these campaigns it would have
been impossible for us to gain a basic victory in the socialist revolution in so
short a time after the birth of New China.
                                    —Chou En-lai, in *PC*, July 16, 1957: 5–6, supplement

Chou En-lai's praise of the campaigns represents the leadership's strong
endorsement of the campaigns' ability to foster change, specifically socialist
transformation.

The preceding chapters have presented the data and the techniques used to
evaluate the campaigns. It is now possible to "test," to throw some light on the
utility of the campaign. Do different types of campaigns produce substantially
different outcomes? How much do campaigns assist in the process of socialist
transformation? Might the goals of socialist transformation be better and more
quickly achieved without them?

These are the central questions confronted in this chapter. To evaluate the
first question, on the variability between the three types of campaigns, the test
results are compared with the 14 hypotheses presented in Chapter 1.

DO CAMPAIGNS HAVE MARGINAL UTILITY?

Hypothesis 1:   Campaigns having predominantly ideological goals produce higher levels of achievements relative to short-comings.[1]

Skinner and Winckler, along with other Western analysts, seem to believe that if campaign mobilization is going to be utilitarian anywhere it should be with ideological campaigns. Thus achievements ought to be higher than shortcomings for ideological campaigns. Actually the data show no significant differences. (See Table 7.1.)

A shift of two cases could completely eliminate any differences. The data do not support hypothesis 1.

Hypothesis 2:   Campaigns having predominantly economic goals produce lower levels of achievements relative to shortcomings.

Although the results are statistically significant, they are significant because they support trends opposite from those predicted. (See Table 7.2.) Skinner and Winckler have implied that remunerative power, which does *not* predominate in campaigns, is more conducive to the achievement of economic goals; therefore, economic goals are best achieved in noncampaign periods. Thus it would appear that the use of normative power at least in revolutionary China is quite efficacious in realizing economic goals.

Hypothesis 3:   Struggle campaigns having predominantly order goals produce higher levels of shortcomings relative to achieve-ments.

This hypothesis generated by the Skinner and Winckler model is not statistically supported. (See Table 7.3.) However, to the extent that there is some tendancy for struggle campaigns to have higher levels of shortcomings, that tendancy is more likely due to the inherent distinctions between the struggle

---

[1] In a conversation, University of Wisconsin sociologist Russell Middleton has correctly pointed out that when comparing levels of achievements and shortcomings it is not possible to be absolutely sure there is a one-to-one correspondence between levels. For example, low levels of achievements may not correspond to low levels of shortcomings. This problem results from having different indicators within each scale and consequently from the inability to be certain that the cutting points are exactly the same. However, this is believed to be a potentially serious problem only for the shortcomings scale, where there are no indicators to differentiate the lower end of the scale (see later). If there were such indicators, the logical cutoff point might be somewhat lower, throwing some campaigns from low to middle levels of shortcomings. This problem exists for hypotheses 2 and 3 as well, but does not apply to hypotheses 4 and 5, since only a single scale is used to test these hypotheses.

TABLE 7.1

Levels of Achievement and Shortcomings for Ideological Campaigns[a][b][c]

	Level on scale		
	Low	Medium	High
Achievements	27%	53%	20%
Shortcomings	40	53	7

[a]Chi-square = 1.4.
[b]$p < .50$ (N.S.).
[c]$N = 15$.

TABLE 7.2

Levels of Achievements and Shortcomings for Economic Campaigns[a][b][c]

	Level on scale		
	Low	Medium	High
Achievements	14%	29%	57%
Shortcomings	29	57	14

[a]Chi-square = 5.60.
[b]$p < .10$.
[c]$N = 14$.

TABLE 7.3

Levels of Achievements and Shortcomings for Struggle Campaigns[a][b][c]

	Level on scale		
	Low	Medium	High
Achievements	29%	29%	40%
Shortcomings	0	14	86

[a]Chi-square = 3.34.
[b]$p < .20$ (N.S.).
[c]$N = 7$.

campaigns and the other types of campaigns rather than the logic of the compliance model.

An alternative way to look at these relationships is to compare the three types of campaigns across their relative levels of achievements and shortcomings. Some of Mao's opposition along with some Western analysts discussed in

TABLE 7.4
Levels of Achievements for Economic, Struggle, and Ideological Campaigns[a][b]

Type of campaign	N	Level on scale		
		Low	Medium	High
Economic	14	14%	29%	57%
Struggle	7	29	29	42
Ideological	15	26	53	20

[a]Chi-square = 4.64.
[b]$p < .33$. (N.S.)

Chapter 1 (including Skinner and Winckler) believe there should be higher achievements for ideological campaigns than for struggle and certainly economic campaigns.

Hypothesis 4: Levels of achievements are higher for campaigns having predominantly ideological goals than for campaigns having predominantly struggle or especially economic goals.

These results are also not statistically significant. (See Table 7.4.) Thus, support is again lacking for the hypothesis generated by this perspective which encompasses the Skinner–Winckler model. Whatever discernible trend exists is exactly the opposite of the predicted trend, with ideological campaigns clearly having fewer achievements than struggle and especially economic campaigns.

Hypothesis 5: Levels of shortcomings are lower for campaigns having predominantly ideological goals than for campaigns having predominantly struggle or especially economic goals.

The statistically significant results shown in Table 7.5 suggest that although ideological campaigns do indeed have lower levels of shortcomings than do

TABLE 7.5
Levels of Shortcomings for Ideological, Economic, and Struggle Campaigns[a][b]

Type of campaign	N	Level on scale		
		Low	Medium	High
Ideological	15	40%	53%	7%
Economic	14	29	57	14
Struggle	7	0	14	86

[a]Chi-square = 17.75.
[b]$p < .001$.

struggle campaigns, the same cannot be said in any significant way for the difference between ideological and economic campaigns, where the shift of a single ideological or economic campaign would produce no difference. Again, with the exception of struggle campaigns, the hypothesis, generated by this perspective which includes the Skinner and Winckler model, lacks support.

In summary, the data do suggest that shortcomings may be no less likely or only slightly less likely to occur in ideological campaigns than in economic ones. The data quite clearly suggest, however, that achievements are higher for economic than for ideological campaigns.

Why should the data fail to support these hypotheses? Many who argue against the utility of economic campaigns think only of economic goals. It has been shown in Chapter 6 that achievements for economic campaigns include both economic and ideological goals. However, this mixture cannot account for the lack of support for these hypotheses. It has already been shown in Chapter 6 that if just economic indicators or goals are used the results are substantially the same. Even if ideological indicators are used to rank ideological campaigns, and economic indicators used to rank economic campaigns, the rankings remain unchanged.[2]

At least five possible explanations for the discrepancy between data and hypotheses are apparent. First, Skinner and Winckler, as well as others, seem to overemphasize negative outcomes. For them, participant involvement in the campaigns necessarily moves from commitment to alienation.

> As the campaign comes to seem more and more shrill in its threats and promises and less and less substantial in its accomplishments, an increasing number of lower participants move over into alienation [Skinner and Winckler, 1969: 418].

They hypothesize that the only way to end this alienation is to end the campaign and return to remunerative power and remunerative rewards.

Second, by using only rural campaigns they have perhaps unwittingly excluded any consideration of one major type of campaign—ideological. Ideological campaigns, which tend to involve all sectors of the society, are by Etzioni's logic the ones that have the highest potential for achievement. Their exclusion from Skinner and Winckler's data partly explains these authors' emphasis on negative outcomes.

Third, is the heavy emphasis most writers holding this view place on the campaign for HAPCs and especially the GLF as the main sources for examples (see Bennett, 1976: 76). (Skinner held this view in an earlier version of the study—1965.) My data in fact show that these campaigns represent the excep-

---

[2] This would not call into question comparability (see note 1) since an overall pattern combining both ideological and economic indicators has already been established for achievements.

tion among economic campaigns (see below). Thus, at least for economic campaigns, Skinner and Winckler and others are generalizing not from the norm, but from the exceptions, the outliers.

Fourth, as with so much of contemporary research on China, there is an inability to use or to generate testable data, forcing a reliance on persuasion and argument.[3] Even Skinner and Winckler's efforts to be systematic suffers from the lack of testable data.

Finally, it appears that Skinner and Winckler erred in using the Etzioni model. If congruence is held to be the most effective form of compliance, one cannot hold problematic the possibility that noncongruent sets, at least in terms of goals and power, may be more utilitarian than congruent ones, and certainly are not less so. Etzioni's model may be correct in terms of Western large-scale complex organizations. However, the evidence available to date suggests that the model cannot pass the test of universality when applied to a collectivist society such as China, where normative appeals may be at least as or even more utilitarian in achieving order and especially economic goals. In the case of others who question the utility of economic campaigns, the same problem can be more broadly stated: There is often, implicitly or explicitly, an erroneous expectation that the institutions and processes that work in the Western/capitalist world may be equally well suited for the non-Western and/or socialist world.

THE ALTERNATIVE VIEW:
MOBILIZATION—THE KEY TO CAMPAIGN RESULTS

The Chinese leadership views the campaign as confronting and attempting to resolve contradictions within the society. To resolve these contradictions, solidarity is important. This is gained through mobilization of the masses. It is logical that the levels of mobilization be commensurate with the size of the contradiction and that the greater the contradiction, the greater will be the results both positive and negative.

Hypothesis 6:   Levels of campaign mobilization are directly correlated with levels of shortcomings.

Hypothesis 7:   Levels of campaign mobilization are directly correlated with levels of achievements.

By implication,

Hypothesis 8:   Levels of shortcomings and achievements are directly correlated.

[3] I am indebted to John Lo for this observation.

The tau$_b$ correlations for these three relationships are .46, .45, and .31 respectively. Other influencing factors seem to be present. These hypotheses have not predicted the whole story. As indicated in Chapter 1, significant differences may well prevail between the three types of campaigns. The results of the following six hypotheses will be grouped by shortcomings and achievements, rather than by the order of hypotheses presented in Chapter 1.

Achievements

Mobilization and achievements correlated .60 for ideological campaigns, .52 for struggle campaigns, and .37 for economic campaigns compared to .45 for all campaigns. Ideological campaigns are more supportive of hypothesis 7 than are other types of campaigns.

Hypothesis 13: For ideological campaigns, levels of achievements are directly related to levels of mobilization.

Figure 7.1, a scatter diagram of mobilization and achievements, shows that ideological campaigns deviate less from a diagonal line intersecting the diagram.[4] Only two ideological campaigns deviate substantially from the line. Moreover, the number of ideological campaigns above and below the diagonal line is relatively equal (six versus nine).

For struggle campaigns, however, only four cases fall close or relatively close to the line. The remainder, which deviate substantially from it, are all above the line. This suggests that in the case of struggle campaigns it takes higher levels of mobilization to reach equivalent levels of achievements when compared to other types of campaigns.

Hypothesis 10: For struggle campaigns, the level of achievements is lower than the level of mobilization and is lower for struggle campaigns than for other types at equivalent levels of mobilization.

---

[4] If all points fell directly on the line, hypothesis 13 would be fully supported. (For other hypotheses, the line represents the continuous points above or below which campaigns should fall to support any given hypothesis fully. Whether they fall above or below the line depends on the types of campaigns and whether shortcomings or achievements are being considered.) However, since ordinal scale steps are not necessarily equal and since there are more steps here for mobilization (29) than for achievements (17), it is impossible to be sure that this line ought to exactly bisect the plot. However, in the absence of other data suggesting, for example, that one step of mobilization is equal exactly to one step of achievements, it is assumed here that the full range of achievements is approximated in 17 steps and the full range of mobilization is approximated in 29 steps. Other diagrams presented in this chapter show the same reasoning.

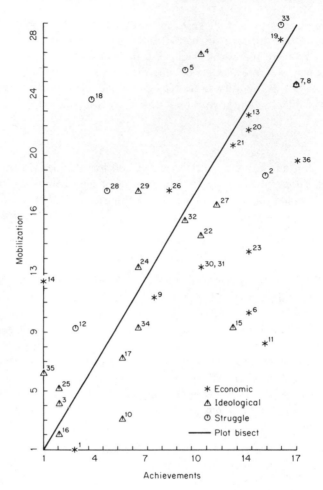

Figure 7.1   Scatter diagram of mobilization and achievements. The numbers next to the symbols correspond to the campaign numbers in Appendix 1. The numbers on the axes are the scale steps.

The data in Figure 7.1 suggest that there is in fact an asymptotic relationship between mobilization and achievements for struggle campaigns. It seems to take a great deal of mobilization to reach any level of achievement, after which mobilization begins to level off while achievements may continue to increase. Although I cannot conclusively state the exact nature of this relationship given the use of ordinal data and the limited number of observations (struggle campaigns), it does appear that for struggle campaigns, the mobilization effort must be greater to reach equivalent levels of achievements when compared to other types of campaigns.

Quite the opposite appears to be the case for economic campaigns. At equivalent levels of mobilization there are disproportionately higher levels of achievements.

> *Hypothesis 11:* For economic campaigns, the level of achievements exceeds the level of mobilization and is higher for economic campaigns than for other types at equivalent levels of mobilization.

Only 3 of the 14 economic campaigns are above the line in Figure 7.1. This suggests that at similar levels of mobilization most economic campaigns produce more achievements than do other types of campaigns. Schram has suggested one important reason for the relatively higher level of achievements:

> If we look closely at the "philosophical articles" written by workers and peasants who claim to have benefitted from this study, we discover that "assimilating Chairman Mao's dialectics" means looking at all sides of a problem, and that "revolutionary zeal" means working hard. In other words, "Mao's thought" is also a slogan and a sanction to justify the inculcation of certain attitudes long current in the West and useful for promoting experiment and economic growth [Schram, 1966: 26].

Whyte (1970: 298) has found the use of study groups more pronounced during periods of campaigns. The data gathered here on mobilization confirm the presence of these groups in virtually every campaign. Moreover, there are many other indicators of mobilization that involve the dissemination of Mao's thought and its intended internalization by the masses (e.g., increased political consciousness and group commitment).

The Skinner–Winckler and Etzioni compliance model, along with the views of many other Western analysts on the utility of using campaigns to fulfill economic goals, may be valid for capitalistic societies where the emphasis is on individual effort and benefit. There remunerative rewards may be dominant in the realization of economic goals. However, for collectivist societies like China, commitment obtained through normative inputs, like those suggested by Schram, may be equally important if not more so in fulfilling economic as well as ideological or order goals.

Shortcomings

Over all categories of campaigns, mobilization and shortcomings are correlated .45. However, the tau_b correlation is .62 for struggle campaigns, .27 for economic campaigns, and .39 for ideological campaigns. Contrary to the hypothesized relationships, the struggle campaign, rather than the ideological, appears most supportive of hypothesis 6, suggesting a direct relationship between mobilization and shortcomings.

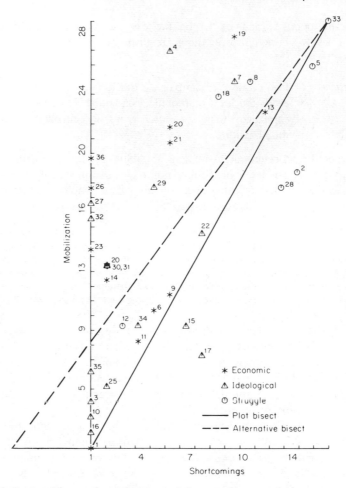

Figure 7.2 Scatter diagram of mobilization and shortcomings.

Hypothesis 9: For struggle campaigns, the level of shortcomings exceeds the level of mobilization and is higher for struggle campaigns than for other types at equivalent levels of mobilization.

Looking at the line bisecting the scatter diagram (Figure 7.2) of mobilization and shortcomings, it is apparent that an equal number of struggle campaigns fall above as below the line (with one on the line), although the hypothesis predicts that more will fall below. It is noteworthy, however, that for struggle campaigns a much greater percentage of the total number falls below the line than for the other types of campaigns, and, more important, that most campaigns with a high level of shortcomings are struggle campaigns.

The observations for ideological campaigns also do not support the predicted hypothesis:

Hypothesis 14: For ideological campaigns, levels of shortcomings are directly related to levels of mobilization.

Although there appears to be no clear pattern, most of the ideological campaigns (13 of 15) fall above the bisecting line, suggesting that ideological campaigns produce lower levels of shortcomings relative to their levels of mobilization.

Only for economic campaigns does the hypothesis accurately predict the observed relationships between mobilization and shortcomings.

Hypothesis 12: For economic campaigns, the level of shortcomings is lower than the level of mobilization and is lower for economic campaigns than for other types at equivalent levels of mobilization.

Again, although there is not a clear correlational pattern, all the economic campaigns fall on or above the bisecting line, suggesting that shortcomings for economic campaigns are indeed lower given comparable levels of mobilization and tend to be lower than other campaigns at similar levels of mobilization.

Why have two of the three hypotheses failed to predict the observed relationships? The answer may be due to the confounding inability of the shortcomings scale to differentiate nearly a third of the campaigns (see Chapter 5). Ten campaigns lie along the lowest observed step. Assume for the moment that other indicators could be found to differentiate most of the 10 campaigns. Step 1 would then become a higher step and the shortcomings scale would be extended further down. The addition, say, of five or six more steps at the lower level would produce a new line (see dotted line, Figure 7.2) also bisecting the plot but with very different consequences. Ideological campaigns would fall above and below the line in nearly equal numbers producing a higher linear correlation (although still with great variance). The correlation for struggle campaigns between mobilization and shortcomings would be reduced, with 66% of the campaigns now falling below the line. At the same time, most economic campaigns would still fall above the line. In short, all three hypotheses would be more predictive of these alternative relationships.

Either way, however, there is the interesting phenomenon of struggle campaigns dominating the upper levels of shortcomings with shortcomings for ideological and economic campaigns falling at medium and low levels.

Given the relatively few cases under study, this becomes a rather significant relationship ($p < .001$—see Table 7.5). To understand why, it is necessary to

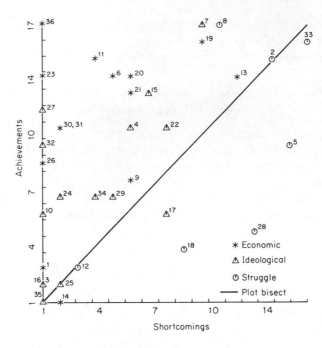

Figure 7.3 Scatter diagram of achievements and shortcomings.

allude briefly to the earlier discussion in Chapter 1. Struggle campaigns are the working out of antagonistic contradictions. By their very nature greater problems are involved. Emotions are more easily aroused. Excesses are more easily spawned. Ideological campaigns, which deal with nonantagonistic contradictions, do not create these pressures and thus do not have as much potential for producing shortcomings. Economic campaigns have even less potential for producing shortcomings, especially given their level of mobilization, because of their orientation toward achievements.

Net Effects

How does the pattern of shortcomings compare with that of achievements? A positive linear relationship was originally predicted:

Hypothesis 8:   Levels of shortcomings and achievements are directly correlated.

The observed tau_b correlation over all campaigns is only .31.[5] However, when

[5] The absence of a strong correlation also has its rewards. The relatively low correlation suggests that the same underlying dimension is not being represented by both variables.

correlating each campaign subtype separately an increase in the value of each subtype is observed: .44 for ideological, .38 for economic, and .55 for struggle.

Different patterns prevail for each type of campaign. The scatter diagram of achievements and shortcomings (Figure 7.3) suggests that for ideological campaigns the increase in achievements tends to be slightly faster relative to the increase in shortcomings. Struggle campaigns, however, reveal that an exponential relationship may exist. Shortcomings increase much more rapidly relative to achievements, up to a point where achievements begin to increase more rapidly than shortcomings. Economic campaigns reflect exactly the opposite pattern from struggle campaigns. Here an asymptotic relationship prevails with achievements increasing rapidly relative to shortcomings up to a point, only to taper off as shortcomings begin to rise more rapidly relative to achievements.

In short, the data suggest that shortcomings and achievements more nearly balance each other out for ideological campaigns than for struggle or economic campaigns. The optimum levels for maximizing achievements for economic campaigns are at the mid-levels of mobilization. For struggle campaigns, achievements and shortcomings seem to be equalized at the upper and lower levels, but at mid-levels of mobilization, shortcomings are greater. In terms of net effects, economic campaigns, particularly at mid-levels of mobilization, appear to be the most utilitarian in the campaign process.[6]

Carrying this analysis one step further, it is possible to construct a pattern of net effects. If levels of shortcomings are subtracted from levels of achievements, how would they compare with levels of mobilization?[7]

Previous observations suggest that though there may be variations between campaign types, the pattern within each type should be fairly constant even as mobilization increases. This is because, with two exceptions, shortcomings and achievements balance each other. The two exceptions are economic campaigns, which should show some increase at mid-levels, and struggle campaigns, which should show some decrease at mid-levels relative to lower and upper levels. Therefore, relative to mobilization, net effects should be lower for struggle campaigns than for other types, higher for economic campaigns, and somewhere in between for ideological campaigns.

---

[6] Beyond this larger generalization, too much weight ought not be attached to the exact dimensions of the observed patterns. Parallel to the previous discussion (notes 1 and 4), not only are ordinal scales being used, with the possibility of misplaced assumptions regarding the equal size of each step, but there is also the confounding character of the shortcomings scale, which does not differentiate the bottom 10 campaigns.

[7] Since some campaigns have greater negative levels than positive ones, to avoid a negative net effect score for purposes of statistical calculations (−8 was the "lowest," for Socialist Education), 9 was added to each result so that all net effects would be positive, ranging from 1 to 25. Although this statistical adjustment has no effect on the relative rankings or the plot description, the problem of assuming equal distances between steps for ordinal scales remains. Therefore, though the precise pattern must not be overemphasized, it is nonetheless possible to make some observations regarding the overall trends.

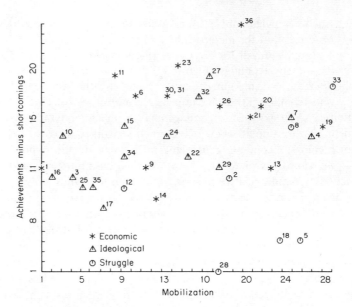

Figure 7.4 Scatter diagram of mobilization and achievements minus shortcomings.

These expectations are borne out in the scatter diagram of mobilization and achievement minus shortcomings (Figure 7.4), although for struggle campaigns the drop at mid-levels is not as readily apparent. This diagram suggests that economic campaigns have greater utility, relative to ideological and, certainly, struggle campaigns.

Beyond the role of antagonistic and nonantagonistic contradictions and the inherent character of different campaign types (emphasizing positive or negative factors more), what other alternative explanations might there be for these observed relationships?

CAMPAIGN PATTERNS: ALTERNATIVE EXPLANATIONS

In the effort to elicit possible alternative explanations, attention was paid to the length of the campaign (number of months duration), the order of occurrence or chronology (from 1949 to 1973), urban versus rural emphasis, primary emphasis in an institutional area (agricultural, industry/commerce, intellectuals, party, or more than one primary area), and Alan Liu's categories of functional specificity versus diffuseness with or without a target.[8] (See Chapter 3 to

[8] Alan Liu (1971: 185–196) developed these categories to account for difference between campaigns. There are four: functionally diffuse campaigns with targets, func-

identify categories for each campaign.) Might these factors or a combination of them actually account for the observed differences between types of campaigns and the three variables, mobilization, achievements, and shortcomings?

Taking all campaigns together, with five exceptions, there are no tau_b correlations above .20 (or no chi-square significance levels less than .10 for cross tabulations with nominal categories) for any of the variables listed in the previous paragraph when correlated with each other or with mobilization, achievements, or shortcomings.

The most significant of these low correlations is the relation between the types of campaigns and the order in which they occurred. The arguments set forth in Chapter 1 suggest that Apter, Barnett, MacFarquhar, and Tsou believe that campaign mobilization, while possibly useful in the early years, loses its utility in later years. If this is the case, the data should show a positive correlation between order of occurrence and shortcomings, and a negative correlation between the order of occurrence and achievements. The tau_b correlation between achievements and chronology is $-.023$, but between shortcomings and chronology it is also a $-.183$. Both correlations are rather weak. The first is far too weak to suggest any relationship between order and achievements. The second, if anything, suggests that the earlier campaigns have in fact greater levels of shortcomings.

The first exception to a low correlation is length. Mobilization is correlated with length of campaigns at .35, and achievements with length at .30 (shortcomings and length are correlated only at .11). Not surprisingly, longer campaigns provide time for more mobilization and greater achievements. However, it would seem that factors such as the nature of the contradictions, rather than length, contribute to produce shortcomings. At least in the case of achievements, other factors, such as levels of mobilization, bear a stronger relationship to achievement than does length.

Second, campaigns that touch on either urban *or* rural sectors, rather than both sectors combined, are more likely to have higher achievements. (See Table 7.6.) Perhaps when all parts of society are involved, it is more difficult to adapt the guidelines of the campaign to meet the needs of each institutional area. This emphasis on single sectors is more common with economic campaigns.

The third exception concerns Liu's conceptualization. On the basis of Liu's categories, it appears that campaigns without targets have fewer shortcomings whereas those with targets have more shortcomings. (See Table 7.7.) In fact, this appears to be merely a more complicated way to say that struggle campaigns

---

tionally diffuse campaigns without targets, functionally specific campaigns with targets and functionally specific campaigns without targets. However, unlike Yu's three campaign types which reflect major differences in this study, there is insufficient evidence to give Liu's categories the same attention.

TABLE 7.6
Level of Achievements and Urban/Rural Emphasis[a][b]

Level of achievements	Number of campaigns	Emphasis		
		Urban	Rural	Both
High	14	28.6%	42.9%	28.6%
Medium	15	14.3	21.4	64.3
Low	7	0	0	100

[a]Chi-square = 10.53.
[b]$p < .033$.

have more shortcomings, since over half of these campaigns are struggle campaigns.

The fourth exception involves the comparison of the urban–rural dimension with the three types of campaigns. (See Table 7.8.) Economic campaigns tend to be rural and rural campaigns tend to be economic; ideological and struggle campaigns tend to involve both sectors simultaneously.

For the fifth exception it appears that Liu's categories are strongly descriptive of Yu's categories, although Liu's variables appear unrelated to most other variables in this study. (See Table 7.9.) Of the 14 economic campaigns, 13 account for all but 4 of specific campaigns without targets; 4 of 7 struggle campaigns account for all but 2 diffuse campaigns with targets. And 7 of 15 ideological campaigns account for all but 1 of the diffuse campaigns without targets. However, in the absence of significant correlations with other variables, Liu's categories seem to be little more than descriptions of economic, struggle, and ideological campaigns plus a residual category (of specific campaigns with targets).

TABLE 7.7
Liu's Categories and Shortcomings[a][b]

Level of shortcomings	Number of campaigns	Category			
		Diffuse with target	Diffuse without target	Specific with target	Specific without target
High	9	33.3%	0%	33.3%	33.3%
Medium	17	17.5	17.5	12	53
Low	10	0	50	0	50

[a]Chi-square = 13.20.
[b]$p < .04$.

TABLE 7.8
Urban/Rural Emphasis and Campaign Type[a][b]

		Emphasis		
Type of campaign	N	Urban	Rural	Both
Ideological	15	20%	0%	80%
Struggle	7	14	14	72
Economic	14	14	57	29

[a]Chi-square = 13.57.
[b]$p < .009$.

Rather than produce alternative explanations, these relationships can for the most part be subsumed under the distinctions between the three major variables. What little additional specification they provide does not seem to alter the basic findings significantly. They suggest that achievements are more likely in campaigns of high mobilization that include either urban or rural sectors but not both. Campaigns of this type are most likely to be economic campaigns, which also tend to have specific goals and be without targets.

Ideological and struggle campaigns tend to include both urban and rural sectors at the same time, which results in lower achievements. Shortcomings are higher for struggle campaigns, which have targets and diffuse goals.

In short, these relationships are basically reflected in the relationships observed between types of campaigns and achievements and shortcomings.

Economic campaigns tend to have high achievements, ideological campaigns tend to be medium, and struggle campaigns are mixed. For shortcomings, on the other hand, struggle campaigns are high, economic campaigns tend to be medium, and ideological campaigns tend to be medium to low.

TABLE 7.9
Liu's Categories and Campaign Type[a][b]

		Category			
Type of campaign	N	Diffuse with target	Diffuse without target	Specific with target	Specific without target
Struggle	7	57%	0%	29%	14%
Ideological	15	13	47	20	20
Economic	14	0	7	0	93

[a]Chi-square = 29.9.
[b]$p < .000$.

WHY HAVE STRUGGLE CAMPAIGNS?

These data have clearly indicated that, given the leadership's definition of shortcomings and achievements, there is a distinct order of descending utility: economic, ideological, and struggle campaigns. Economic campaigns produce the highest overall achievements compared to other types and relative to levels of shortcomings. Ideological campaigns occupy the middle ground, in some cases with slightly higher achievements relative to shortcomings, but in general having these effects offset each other. Struggle campaigns have mixed levels of achievements, but these tend to be offset by high levels of shortcomings.

Some have noted the high costs of the great struggle campaigns: the Suppression of Counterrevolutionaries (Mu, 1962: 142), the Anti-Rightist campaign (e.g., Hsia, 1961; Johnson, 1961); and above all, the GPCR (Lewis, 1968). (See Pfeffer, 1971, for others.) Their data have provided legitimate reasons to question the utility of these campaigns, diffuse in character, perhaps hard to control, and confronting "enemy" targets that represent antagonistic contradictions. If the utility of these campaigns is relatively low, why do these campaigns continue? Is there not a more utilitarian method to resolve the problems confronted by these campaigns, one that might produce less rancor, fewer shortcomings, while accomplishing the same ends?

The end in mind is, of course, the establishment of a fully socialist society. At the conclusion of each interview the informant was asked, "Was this campaign more or less or about as important as other campaigns in fulfilling socialist transformation goals?"[9] They were asked to give other campaigns as referents. From their replies three levels emerged. Significant differences are observable between the campaign types. (See Table 7.10.)

The informants clearly believed that struggle campaigns were the most significant type in the overall goal of working toward a socialist society. This is in spite of the fact that they also attributed high levels of shortcomings to these campaigns *and* were sometimes the targets of these very same campaigns! What

---

[9] This question suffers from subjective vagueness. Each informant's interpretation of socialist transformation might be slightly different. If anything, however, this should only confuse and reduce rather than accentuate the observed differences.

One might wish to argue that the 1955 campaigns actually achieved "socialism." Thus, with the goal of a fully socialist society already reached in 1955, this question would not apply for the campaigns after 1955. Such would essentially be the case for the system of ownership—except for private plots (Mao, 1971: 463). However, in other areas Mao himself noted in 1957 the continuing "ideological struggle between socialism and capitalism in our country [1971: 463]." Of course Mao saw the GPCR, in part, as confronting those who wished to take China back to capitalism. In ideological terms the attitudes of the masses, particularly the peasantry, are not fully socialist (*PC*, June 16, 1957: 7; Whyte, 1970: 335). "The class struggle in the ideological field . . . will continue to be long and tortuous and at times will even become very acute [Mao, 1971: 464]."

TABLE 7.10
Informant Ranking of Campaign Types in the Utility of the Socialist
Transformation Process[a] [b]

Type of campaign	N	Utility		
		Low	Medium	High
Ideological	15	47%	33%	20%
Economic	14	14	50	36
Struggle	7	0	14	86

[a]Chi-square - 12.27.
[b]$p < .015$.

may be high costs in terms of shortcomings exceeding achievements may in fact
be the necessary cost in confronting antagonistic contradictions in the quest for
a socialist society. In short, although the immediate effects of struggle campaigns
may not seem to have a high overall utility, the long-run effects do seem to be
rather important in the achievement of larger goals.

If this is the case, the question then is not whether struggle campaigns are
worth the long-run costs relative to other types of campaigns. Rather, the
question should be whether any type of campaign is that utilitarian, whether a
system without campaigns would not have moved China further toward its own
goal of a fully socialist society at an even faster pace than it is now moving. This
is not an easy question to answer. There is no alternative "experimental"
society. The response must necessarily be to hypothetical conditions.

THE UTILITY OF THE CAMPAIGN MOBILIZATION STRATEGY

The Chinese leadership is quite clear about the importance it attaches to
campaigns.[10] What did informants think about this? If anything, their own
dissatisfaction, which led most of them to leave China, should make them the
most critical of the campaign mobilization system. At the conclusion of each
interview each informant was also asked, "Without the campaign would the
shortcomings and achievements have been the same?" Again, one is faced with
hypothetical answers to hypothetical situations. Still, for 27 of the 36 campaigns, informants generally felt the achievements would not have been realized
without the campaign, or at least would have been a longer time in coming. For
all but one of the struggle campaigns, they saw the overall achievements as very

[10] Bennett (1976) also argues for the utility of the mass mobilization campaign strategy.
He notes that China's nationalist ideology, desire to change, and its resources (high labor
inputs and low technology) all lend themselves to the campaign strategy.

important. Had there been no campaigns the consequent problems would have been much greater. For example, for the early years they stressed the role of the Five-Anti campaign in fostering economic authority and the Suppression of Counterrevolutionaries in fostering political authority. Some went so far as to suggest that had these campaigns not occurred when they did, the Communists might not have been able to maintain control.

On balance for struggle campaigns, informants thought that if the Anti-Rightist Campaign and the GPCR had not occurred, achievements might have been less. However, for both of these campaigns, they also pointed to shortcomings that would not have occurred had there been no campaign. For example, in both cases they pointed to short-term consequences for production because of the campaign.

Economic and ideological campaigns both tend to be characterized as producing changes only somewhat faster given the campaign and as producing changes that tended to be less significant compared to struggle campaigns.

For three campaigns, all part of the Great Leap (Communes, Backyard Furnaces, and the 1958 Cultural Revolution), informants felt that had there been no campaign the shortcomings that would have been eliminated would be greater than achievements resulting from the campaign. Here, then, for these three campaigns, is the only indication, at least on the part of the informants interviewed, that the absence of campaigns would have been more utilitarian in moving China toward a socialist society.

For six ideological and economic campaigns, informants felt that had they never occurred, the impact on society, in terms of changes in shortcomings or achievements, would have been no different. They felt that the organization of street industry could have occurred without the attempts to organize Urban Communes. They saw little impact of the Four Evils campaign in improving health conditions (in contrast to the Barefoot Doctors campaign, where they saw the impact to be very great). The Study of the Constitution and the campaign to oppose the Japan—United States military treaty were both so fleeting as apparently to leave no impact.

Finally, two campaigns, Learn from the PLA and Train Revolutionary Successor Generation, had little impact beyond a slight rise in people's consciousness. They certainly did not deal successfully with the problem of "revolutionizing" a new generation of Chinese youth, especially those from urban areas, who know little of the trials of the liberation struggle and the bitterness of the years before 1949. Today this problem remains still basically unresolved in spite of the massive efforts to revolutionize the youth by sending them down to the factory and the countryside (Townsend, 1967: 210). Surely the effort to resolve this problem will be one significant challenge to the campaign system in the years to come.

In short, informants felt that most campaigns helped to move China along the road of socialism. This is particularly pronounced with struggle campaigns in spite of their high levels of shortcomings. Conclusions here must, however, be made cautiously because they are based on material that is both subjective and speculative.

Some acknowledgment must also be made of the argument that this test of the campaign strategy misses the point. In the effort to quantify, the argument goes, this research has erroneously equated one campaign with another, as if all were equal. For example, the shortcomings of the GLF and the GPCR may be far greater than the achievements of many smaller campaigns combined. To be sure, there is much truth in this criticism of the research, especially when interpreted in terms of short-term effects. But when seen over the longer run, there is mounting evidence (e.g., for industry see Riskin, 1971; Lo, 1976; also Bennett, 1976: 77) that these two campaigns, in spite of their immediate shortcomings, may have set the stage for greater achievement, including productivity gains, in the years to come. Although this does not fully respond to the criticism, it does suggest that when taking a long-term perspective, it may be that whatever error there is, due to the quantification used here, it is in one direction. Thus, achievements may consistently be more important than shortcomings, especially for most of the larger campaigns.

It is now time to summarize the conclusions suggested by the data and to speculate briefly on their implications both for China's progress and for wider areas of development theory and reality in third world societies.

8

The Meaning
and Message of
the Campaign Strategy

A single spark can start a prairie fire.
—Mao, 1967: Vol. 1, 177

CAMPAIGNS IN CHINA: THE RESEARCH FINDINGS

A balance sheet is not easy to construct. A random sample covering the entire population of all campaigns, national, regional, and local, irregular and periodic, is lacking. Thus inferences to the entire population of campaigns in China must be qualified. Measurement problems make it impossible to prove beyond doubt that reasonably reliable measures of mobilization, shortcomings, and achievements have been constructed. Nor have the long term effects of campaign outcomes been systematically analyzed. There are related problems of measurement, disagreement, and unreliability discussed in Chapter 3. Nor has this research systematically compared campaign and noncampaign periods. This limitation is especially a problem in examining the overall utility of campaigns. Lacking comparable evaluations of the degree of changes, shortcomings, and achievements of programs and policies not implemented through campaigns, conclusions drawn about the overall utility of campaigns must be more tentative.

These represent some of the more important limitations qualifying the conclusions summarized. Yet, even in the face of these qualifications, the data analyzed here reveal some clear trends and findings, albeit some emerge more forcefully than others:

171

1. The campaign system as a whole is a utilitarian method for China's goal of socialist transformation. Although there may be some exceptions, most notably the GLF, in terms of short-term outcomes, the evidence collected here emphasizes, on balance, the positive rather than the negative effects of the overall campaign process. More apparent is the rapid pace the campaigns have been able to establish in the transformation process. The limited evidence available here also suggests that without the campaigns China would today be considerably further away from socialist transformation.

2. There are different types of campaigns. Three, economic, struggle, and ideological, seem most apparent. They are distinguished by the goals primarily emphasized. Some emphasize economic construction; others stress ideological change. Most important, there is a distinction based on antagonistic and nonantagonistic contradictions.

3. Struggle campaigns confront antagonistic contradictions. The friction, pressures, and consequent shortcomings generated are much greater than those produced by other types of campaigns, and achievements tend to be lower. Shortcomings are higher. This is understandable given the greater problems inherent in dealing with antagonistic contradictions. However, in spite of the greater problems, informants agree that these campaigns are the most important in the overall process of China's transformation into a fully socialist society.

4. Economic campaigns at given levels of mobilization show greater levels of achievements and lower levels of shortcomings compared with other types of campaigns. This finding is contrary to the arguments in much of the Western literature on contemporary China. The high levels of achievements appear to stem from the emphasis economic campaigns place on building up, on constructing, on the positive, and on the importance attached to collective involvement and loyalty, to solidarity, to the willingness to sacrifice for others. The GLF and its associated campaigns are exceptions, at least in the short run, in the overall pattern of economic campaigns.

5. Ideological campaigns produce the lowest level of achievements as well as shortcomings, although their concurrent levels of mobilization are equally low. The issues and problems dealt with in these campaigns are seen to involve less thorough and immediate change, at least in the short run. They lack the antagonistic contradictions characteristic of struggle campaigns, and the need to build new productive structures characteristic of most economic campaigns.

These five points represent the specific findings of this research. Beyond the five points are considerably more speculative issues—issues that were not in any sense tested in the course of the research. These issues do arise, however, in considering the implications of the research findings. Among these issues are the extent to which the campaign mobilization system has contributed to the vast changes in Chinese society in the quarter-century from 1949 to 1976 and the impact the Chinese example may have on the rest of the world.

CAMPAIGNS IN CHINA: ASSET OR LIABILITY?

No one should doubt that the transformation of Chinese society has been far-reaching and dramatic. In the Chinese countryside of the 1940s and earlier, the single overriding issue on the agenda of a peasant was to keep alive. There was no talk of adequate medical care or learning to read and write. It was simply to stay alive from one day to the next.

Today the peasant worries not about the next meal, the food for the next year, or even the social and economic security of the future and old age. On the agenda is a new sewing machine, a new bicycle, increasing the *amount* of education for all, the achievement of even higher levels of health care, and so on.

These are simple items and thoughts, but how massive the transformation of Chinese society must have been to bring so totally different an agenda to the mind of the average peasant.

Even the most cursory of travelers to China today cannot but be impressed with its great achievements in health care, education, industrial production, and, above all, the greater spread of economic and political resources to the people. Given the incredible morass of Chinese society inherited by the Communists, no society has done so much in so short a time.

> In China a fourth of the human race has found the solution to the twin scourges of Asia: poverty and ignorance. Not completely, to be sure, but these have ceased to be the big problems of survival that they are in the rest of Asia. In evaluating the achievement of man, his ideology, the elimination of poverty and ignorance and disease—in a nation peopled by 700 million—is a feat [not to be ignored] [Abaya, 1967].

At the heart of many of these changes is the campaign mobilization strategy. This is not to say that this strategy, based on mass line politics, should be credited with all the achievements. It is impossible to determine what portion of China's achievements should be attributed to the campaigns. Other factors also account for achievements, such as early Russian assistance, the absence of war, and economic stability.

Moreover, the campaign strategy must also carry its share of the shortcomings and problems, some of which remain as serious obstacles. For example, China has yet to resolve contradictions posed by the roles and responsibilities of intellectuals and youth. China readily admits to its backwardness in mechanization, particularly in agriculture. China has yet to rid itself of inequalities between old and young, between minority and majority populations, and especially between men and women, and between rural and urban areas. Overriding all these and other unsolved problems is China's own question of which road to take. Will it continue to move along the road of rapid change characterized by the campaign mobilization system or will change be moderated through more stable and perhaps more bureaucratic structures?

To suggest that these are not easy problems to resolve may be the understatement of the era. Yet, for all its problems the visitor to China is left with another impression. Of some 40 societies I have visited over the past decade, it is the Chinese and the Chinese alone who convey an overwhelming sense of optimism about the future. They are not always sure how they can solve any given problem, large or small, but they, especially the workers and peasants, seem to exude great confidence in their ability to solve the problem—and solve it in a way that it will benefit all people, equally. Perhaps they are convinced that mobilization campaigns will continue to work to their advantage. Certainly, under Mao, the Communists have been wedded to the continued use of the campaign mobilization strategy.

CAMPAIGNS IN CHINA: THE MESSAGE TO OTHERS

The success of the Chinese example has certainly led many in the third world and elsewhere to question the relevance of Western capitalist models of development.

How can remaining problems of third world societies be best resolved? For example, how do the collective orientations of a socialist society compare in their ability to foster change with the opportunities of individual entrepreneurship? Is conflict harmful in bringing needed changes, or if it is harnessed can it assist in making these changes? When the choice of emphasis must be made, is mass discussion and involvement preferable to bureaucratic institutions and the delegation of authority through the ballot box? Can technological problems be best resolved by emphasizing diffusion processes or local self-reliance strategies? To achieve industrialization, are urbanization and its attendant problems inevitable? When the choice must be made, should more emphasis be placed on stability and institution building or on the process of constant change?

There are no simple answers to these questions. Which strategy can best resolve problems of third world societies: capitalist development or socialist transformation? To this continuing debate, this research has made a contribution. Where some question the campaign mobilization strategy's ability to foster economic growth, this research has produced counterevidence. So, too, does this research add evidence of the campaigns' abilities to foster other types of change—political and social as well as economic. This research, in short, has contributed systematic evidence of the utility of a very different alternative strategy in the "development" process.

The debate over which strategy is best is increasingly more complex. The Chinese have brought forcefully and dramatically to the world's attention a vibrant, dynamic, alternative strategy for economic, political, and social change. The social scientists wishing to lay claim to the universality of development theory can no longer ignore the Chinese example. They must reckon directly with this very different strategy and the implications it poses for other strategies of social, political, and economic change.

As the theorist must reckon, so too will the masses and leaders of Asia, Africa, and Latin America reflect on the choices before them. For if they are to get on with the agenda of resolving the festering questions of political, social, and economic injustices that surround so many of these societies, these people in their own ways must come to grips with the choices.

Tanzania's Julius Nyerere, upon his visits to America and China, commented on the differences. In America he was impressed by the great technology of the huge automobile factories turning out thousands of cars a day, which Tanzania could not afford. In China he was impressed by a worker sitting outside of his small house assembling by hand a bicycle, which Tanzania needs. Above all, though, he was impressed by the pride and confidence of the latter and the boredom and indifference of the worker in the auto plant.[1] These lessons are not lost on the people of the villages and slums around the world, nor are they lost on the leaders, although many, out of immediate self-interest, refuse to act on them.

Yet, in spite of the apparent utility of the campaign mobilization strategy, China cannot and will not provide the blueprint for action for other societies. China cannot because of differences between societies in culture, history, and natural environment. All societies have different organization structures, political institutions, leadership capabilities, and so on. Each of these factors breeds different problems, which in turn need different solutions. Lin Piao, among others, made clear in his famous 1965 speech that China will not provide a blueprint. Each society must pull itself up and stand up on its own. Another society can only assist, can only inspire. Here is the message. Has the spark of inspiration, no longer in the hands of the massive industries and Western electoral systems of the North Atlantic, now been passed to the collective efforts of the villages dotting the vast reaches of China's Yangtze and Yellow River watersheds? If so, the long, long spring of struggle and revolution has just begun.

[1] Relayed to me by Lady Chesham, member of the Tanzanian parliament and close friend of Julius Nyerere, in a conversation, March 1967.

Epilogue

Whither China's Revolutionary Spring?

> Today we are separating into two worlds. I am old and will soon die.... Human life is limited, but revolution knows no bounds. In the struggle of the past ten years I have tried to reach the peak of revolution, but I was not successful....
> —From Mao's last message to his wife, Chiang Ching, 1976

The year 1976 witnessed the greatest change in leadership the People's Republic of China has seen since its founding. Within the space of 10 short months, eight of its top leaders died or were removed from office, including all those who at the outset of 1976 were thought to be the likely successors to Chou and Mao.

What does this mean for China's future? How much is China's future linked to its leaders? To the people of China? To the interaction between the two? What are the dreams, aspirations, thoughts, and plans of its leaders and people? How much are the people and their new leaders committed to Maoist orientations and revolutionary change? Do they desire a more comfortable, stable society, less fraught with the anguish and struggle that often accompany mass mobilization campaigns? What would be the consequences of this kind of Chinese society? These are only some of the important issues at stake in China's future, and they are complex and intertwined.

Clearly, we will look back on 1976 as a watershed year. In the starkest and simplest of terms, the issue is this: Will the revolution continue? Will the new leaders and the Chinese people continue down the Maoist revolutionary road, or will they chart a new course? The stakes are immense. The evidence is far from gathered, and may not be for several years. Few answers to these important questions can be found in the closing days of 1976. At this early stage it is only

177

possible to examine the issues at stake. This will hopefully provide some basis on which to evaluate the future, to determine which road China is taking.

THE MAOIST VISION

What has been the Maoist revolutionary road? From its grand schemes to noble dreams to specific institutions of change, there is probably no event that more definitively symbolizes the Maoist road than the GPCR and the institutions and programs that either sprang from it or were promoted by it. In every field of life changes were made during and after the GPCR, changes that have had a profound impact on the shape of Chinese society and changes that might well be reversed on a road different from Mao's. To illustrate the depth and significance of the Maoist changes, five areas of society will be briefly considered: industry, agriculture, health care, education, and leadership.

Factory life and leadership have changed significantly as a result of the GPCR. Such institutions as the revolutionary committee, technical innovation groups, and worker–management teams have had a profound impact on the spread of power and the nature of interaction between workers and management. Although in areas of larger political policy the managers and Party leadership retain substantial control, on technical, social, and even local political questions a substantial amount of power has passed into the hands of workers (Lo, 1976). A Maoist China would probably continue and enhance this pattern of decentralized power and control. A non-Maoist China might see reversals, with workers once again having less say and managers and Party leaders once again—as before the GPCR—becoming more powerful and more entrenched.

Agriculture probably saw fewer changes as a result of the GPCR than did other areas of society. Nonetheless, in the years following the GPCR, Tachai, noted for its lack of private plots, for its greater equality in income distribution, and above all for its effort to endure tremendous physical hardship and political struggle to achieve higher economic goals, has along with other politically advanced agricultural units been a model for others to follow. Although others such as Chou heavily supported the Tachai model, Mao also clearly endorsed it as part of the continuing revolutionary process. A Maoist China would see agriculture continuing to make these types of changes throughout China's rural population. A non-Maoist China might well revert to other methods of sustaining and increasing agricultural productivity, such as material incentives and larger private plots.

Health care has seen tremendous achievements since the GPCR, not the least of which is the use of acupuncture anesthesia. Even more significant, however, has been the spread of medical facilities to urban neighborhoods and to the rural countryside via the Barefoot Doctors campaign. Although the effort to spread medical services to the countryside was under way by 1965, if not before, the actual Barefoot Doctors program did not begin until the closing years of the GPCR. Moreover, the tremendous emphasis of the GPCR on reducing status differences, such as that between doctors and patients, has contributed immeasurably to the success of the Barefoot Doctors program. A Maoist China is likely to see the continued spread of medical services, including the frequent movement of highly trained medical teams in and out of the countryside. A non-Maoist China, though perhaps retaining the form, and in many respects even the content, of the Barefoot Doctors program, might place less emphasis on servicing the countryside. More resources might be once again devoted to improving specialized medical care in major urban hospitals.

There is perhaps no area of China in which the GPCR was more profound and far-reaching than in education. Textbooks were rewritten. Teachers and professors have for the most part begun to interact more as friends, partners, and co-learners than in an elite leader–follower relationship. A tremendous emphasis has been placed on practical experience and the direct application of knowledge to everyday work situations. Of great importance has been the requirement that all urban youth, upon graduation from high school (after 9 years of schooling) accept a permanent work assignment. This is usually in the countryside, often in a remote and very backward—for the urban youth—part of China. Although the peasant thinks about how much better his life has become, the urban youth often thinks about how much harder life in the countryside is compared to the city. Some of the urban youth adjust, make tremendous physical and mental sacrifices, and through struggle and hardship come to understand in the deepest way the realities of peasant life. In this way the Maoist goal of preparing youth for collective commitment and achievement through sacrifice and struggle is realized. Others fail and become disaffected, performing a negative role on the communes, or drift back to a marginal role in the cities; some may leave China altogether. When successful, this program has clearly had tremendous benefits for producing the anti-elitist youth crucial for the continuance of a Maoist China. However, a non-Maoist China, dependent more on elites, hierarchy, and technical expertise, could do without such a program and indeed might find it advantageous to end it.

Equally important in their impact on the questions of elitism and collective work orientation have been the May Seventh Cadre Schools, established throughout China in all divisions of government as a result of a 1968 directive by Mao. All cadres, or leaders, are expected to spend time periodically at a rural school established by their institution or organ of government. Although agricultural work and physical labor are clearly a function of the experience, more important is the undergoing of study, reflection, criticism, and self-criticism. A cadre leader is also expected to spend shorter periods (e.g., a day each week and/or a week every few months) doing manual labor in a factory or commune near his or her work. The overall goal is to cut back on the growth of elitist orientations and thinking and the desire for greater privilege, in order to enhance the process of continuing equality between leaders and led. A Maoist China would find the continuation of this process crucial. A non-Maoist China might well find it an anathema, preventing such important goals as the rapid increase in technical expertise and continuity of leadership.

The foregoing has been only a brief review of some of the central institutions and programs resulting from or enhanced by the GPCR, in some of the more important sectors of society. There are many other sectors (e.g., minorities, man–woman relationships, the army) as well as programs that I have not considered. The ones considered should, however, indicate the type of specific programs and institutions characterizing a Maoist China. These are the programs and institutions at stake in China's future.

More generally, at stake is a cluster of very important goals that characterize the broader aims of a Maoist revolutionary China. There is no question that at the heart of the Maoist vision is the equalization of resources, services, and power among the people *and* the leaders of China. Virtually every program ever endorsed by Mao and his ideological supporters has had as part of its goals the furtherance of this equalization.

This is the case whatever the issue or contradiction, whether between the rich and the poor as in the Agrarian Reform campaign, or in improving the spread of medical services, both areas where there have been great strides. Even with other contradictions, such as those between city and countryside and especially between men and women, where there have been fewer achievements, the goals remain and the achievements that have been made are in the direction of greater equality.

But nowhere has the issue of equality been more pronounced than in the effort to reduce elitism and privilege, especially among the leadership. The attacks on bureaucracy and the efforts to move leaders to rectify their work-styles have been all too frequent to be seen as anything but a direct, consistent, and persistent effort to equalize status if not work roles. Although Mao never dismissed technical expertise as unimportant, he was quite willing to see its progress slowed, especially if failing to do so would mean further entrenchment of elitism, bureaucracy and privilege. No China committed to a Maoist vision could fail to continue its attack on factors so antithetical to the process of increased equalization.

Central to this process of achieving greater equality, as well as to the other programs and institutions described previously, has been the mass mobilization campaign. In terms of the process of change, there simply has been no institution more central and important than this one. To conceive of a Maoist China without the campaign is impossible. To suggest that a non-Maoist China may well wish to do without them or to dilute them is quite reasonable. (This occurred in effect with some of the ideological campaigns discussed above.) As suggested in this study, the campaigns, especially the larger, more significant ones, involved a great deal of struggle, often searing personal confrontations, and substantial shortcomings. Many, including the rectification campaigns, become direct attacks on the leaders themselves. Although my research has provided direct evidence that the campaigns may well move China along the road of greater equality faster, the leadership of a non-Maoist China might wonder whether the costs of the campaign strategy are worth the advantages; whether a slowed pace in the achievement of greater equality might be worth the sacrifice to avoid the upheavals wrought by the Maoist mass mobilization strategy.

THE NEW LEADERSHIP

Having briefly suggested, in broad terms, the nature of the Maoist strategy, and having characterized some of the issues at stake, I can now take a brief look at the leadership and the people of China. Where does its leadership stand and what are in the thoughts of China's people today? Impossible questions to answer with any degree of certainty, but ones that are critical. It is possible, nonetheless, to provide some information about these questions and to suggest some of the issues that must be confronted in the months and years ahead.

Given China's continuity of leadership from 1935 and the Yenan period up to the eve of the GPCR—some 30 years—and even through part of the 1970s, the changes in the leaderhsip during 1976 have been tremendous.

Virtually all in the Standing Committee of the Politburo, China's most central and powerful body, have been eliminated. All those thought likely to replace Mao and Chou are no longer in power (although Teng Hsiao-ping could possibly return). Hua Kuo-feng, by the end of 1976 undisputedly the most powerful person in China, was in early 1976 the minister of Public Security, a relatively recent arrival on the national scene.

Who is Hua Kuo-feng, and what are his politics and those of the men around him? Hua is thought to be a "moderate," more left than Teng, but less so than Chang and the others from Shanghai. He had been thought to be a compromise choice to replace Chou En-lai as premier. Politically he has been and remains very closely identified with the Tachai model of agriculture as well as with efforts to maintain the decentralization process. These are Maoist tenets of action. (However, since Hua's association with the Tachai model, there appears to be more stress on mechanization and less on physical sacrifice.) But if Hua is Maoist in his politics, how then is it possible to explain not only the removal from power of the three leaders from Shanghai (Chang, Yao, and Wang) along with Mao's wife, Chiang Ching, but the often virulent campaign denouncing them that has followed their removal?

Many explanations have been offered, all the way from suggesting that the four were rightists in disguise and attempted a military coup against Hua and threatened civil war on the one hand, to arguing that Hua is an out-and-out revisionist and capitalist roader on the other. The actual reason may well lie somewhere between these two poles.

Given the intensity of the campaign against the four (by the end of 1976 it had clearly entered the stage of an antagonistic contradiction), it is obvious that not only was Hua in sharp disagreement with them, but that he felt his newly acquired power base threatened. He may well have also been under pressure from the military.

One possible explanation is that Hua was reacting to the four's reaction to Teng Hsiao-ping. During the campaign against Teng, Teng was accused of ignoring politics for the benefit of production in his development of the Fifth Five-Year Plan, set to begin in January 1976. In the recent criticism of the Gang of Four, accusations were made that they simply reversed this process, ignoring production for the benefit of politics. Hua Kuo-feng and the current leadership, it has been suggested, are trying to steer a middle course combining politics and production, thus following the legacy of Chairman Mao.

There is some evidence both supporting and questioning this explanation. On the one hand the new leadership has indeed paid great attention to the need for increasing production, arguing, for example in agriculture, that the Maoist principle of learning from Tachai be followed. (The Second National Conference to Learn from Tachai opened during December 1976 and a national conference on the industrial model, Taching, is scheduled for spring 1977.) A great deal of emphasis has been placed on continuing to promote Chairman Mao's thoughts, notably by the formation of a commission to edit and publish his complete works. Detractors of the new leadership argue that this is just window dressing. They argue that if the errors of the four had been essentially those of too heavily emphasizing politics, the virulent character of the attacks on the four, especially the slanderous and very personal attacks on Chiang Ching, would not have been necessary. Whether this explanation is the correct one only time and history can confirm.

What is clear at this time is the uncertainty of the current transition period, which in terms of top leadership is greater for the Party than at any time since 1935. In a period of such transition, especially when the reconstruction needs following the incredibly destructive earthquakes of 1976 are considered, it is only natural for the new leadership to emphasize stability, moderation, consolidation, and the need for economic construction; to de-emphasize the reliance on political struggle, upheaval, and the mass mobilization campaign as vehicles for continuing change and revolution. The go-slow attitude is reasonable for certain periods. Mao said as much in his last interview with Edgar Snow. But it can also lead to permanent reversals. Too much stability for too long allows the bureaucracy to become entrenched, permits those with greater responsibility to, little by little, almost unnoticed, turn that responsibility into privilege, improperly associating their political and technical expertise with their rights to greater privileges. These are the makings of elitism, makings Mao saw emerging in the mid-1950s and again in the early 1960s. When inertia does set in, only a great deal of sacrifice and struggle on the part of the people and a strong, committed leader can reverse the tide. China had this combination in the past quarter-century, as evidenced in the rectification campaigns and the GPCR. It is not so clear this combination will be available again.

This is the dilemma. One does not have to believe that the new leaders are in any way capitalist roaders, or some kind of other "evil anti-Communists." They can be very committed Communists, committed to the same egalitarian goals as Mao. But if they move too slowly, too cautiously, even with good reason, it may in the long run be too late to sustain the revolution.

Some argue that a gradual ebbing of a revolution can always be reversed; just as things move to the right, so can they move back to the left. But it is always much easier to move to the right than to the left. Inertia, stability, consolidation, and the like naturally portent slides to the right; a left movement takes conscious action, struggle, sacrifice, and commitment that is not always possible to bring about.

THE CHINESE PEOPLE

What of the people of China? Are they satisfied? Dissatisfied? Prepared to act? Complacent? Again, from this distance and at this time it is impossible to know with certainty their thoughts, let alone to summarize the thoughts into a unified whole. At the same time, some speculation seems possible on the basis of China's past and knowledge of human action. There should be little doubt that the Chinese people wholeheartedly support the visible achievements of the Chinese revolution, in areas such as health care, a secure livelihood especially for the young and old, and universal education. Beyond this there is even substantial evidence to warrant the belief that most workers and peasants have more access to power and authority than ever before. When compared to the horrors of the pre-liberation period, which is the perspective of many if not most of the elder generation of Chinese people—those over 40—the present does seem good indeed.

Less clear is the acceptance of the costs of struggle endured for the benefits secured. For everyone who has benefited there may be some who had to sacrifice. Resources are not infinite. There may be some slack available, but it is not without limits. For example, the peasants surely welcome the Barefoot Doctors programs and the great influx of well-trained mobile medical teams. But these medical workers had to make sacrifices for the peasants to benefit. Many made the sacrifices willingly, but It cannot be assumed that all did so. The point is that even for the older generation there may be limits to sacrifice, to how much struggle is acceptable at any given time. Like the leadership, they may in fact welcome a temporary respite, especially since in the short run the benefits may well continue.

In some ways the younger generation—those under 40—may be even more willing to accept the present situation. They had little, if any, firsthand experience of the horrors of pre-liberation China. As they grow up, they come to accept conditions as they know them as the primary basis for judging the present and the future. (In this context, one can understand the disaffection of many of the youth sent to the countryside, who complain that they are only making sacrifices without the benefits realized by others.) The years since the GPCR have been especially beneficial in the equalization of both material and political resources (power) among the population. Not that true equality is anywhere near. This is not the point. The point is that just to maintain the present benefits the leadership will have to continue to struggle against inertia and backsliding. To *increase* the benefits, and presumably the continued wholehearted endorsement of the population, the leadership will eventually have to make even greater sacrifices and work even harder. In short, against the present baseline the entire Chinese population may have overly optimistic expectations that the new leadership may simply be unable to meet.

Does this mean that if the new leadership does not progress along a Maoist revolutionary road a popular uprising or a genuine popular GPCR can be expected? This cannot be assumed, for attitude is not the same as behavior. Assuming popular attitudes generally run in favor of the new leadership, should they change at a later date the population may be unable or unwilling to organize on their own and to act. The same may hold true right now, if indeed there is widespread disaffection with the new leadership. (There is little confirmed evidence of widespread *behavior* opposing the new leadership since the death of Mao.)

Although Chinese history is rife with examples of popular uprisings, there are few examples of popular efforts that succeeded in making long-term gains against a strong, effective leadership. Yet the social origins of the Chinese Communist revolution, its political base, and the mass mobilization process of struggle and popular involvement all lead one to caution against too pessimistic an outlook on this point. The Chinese people are more politically conscious and potentially prepared to act than perhaps any other people have ever been. This is Mao's legacy to his people. This does not mean they will act, even if they want to; but it does mean that their potential ability to act cannot be easily dismissed.

In short, one cannot be sure today of China's future, even the immediate future of the next few years. Will China continue to follow Mao's revolutionary vision? Or will the institutions such as the May Seventh Cadre Schools and the sending of youth to the countryside be slowly reduced and replaced by another road of action, with all the consequences an alternative road may have? These pages have been able to suggest little more than what is at stake in China's future and what might be the key issues that will determine and indicate which road China will take.

Mao was 82 when he died. He once told André Malraux that "old men live too long." It is too early to know how enduring his impact will be on China's future. What is clear is his impact on China's past. It is simply impossible to speak of China during the middle half of the twentieth century without speaking of Mao Tse-tung. One does not have to accept the "great man" theory of history to say this. Mao was one of the greatest social revolutionaries ever to live, perhaps the greatest. Great social revolutionaries owe their greatness not to some hidden genius, but to their ability to capture the moments of history, to seize the dreams of their people and to translate them into concrete action in the service of the people they govern. This is Mao's greatest legacy to China and the kernel of his greatness.

But what of China's support for Mao? Did Mao live too long? Many Western as well as Chinese observers cited in the early pages of this book have implied that he did. They argue that Mao and Maoist politics, dominated by the mass mobilization campaign, outlived their usefulness.

In a radiobroadcast the day Mao died, the moderator asked me if things would "settle down now," if China would become "more stable?" "Perhaps so," I responded, "but at the same time one could perceive of no greater gift of the Chinese people to Mao's legacy than to have another GPCR." Perhaps not this year or next, when stability and consolidation may be the necessary guiding themes, much as they were in the early 1960s after the Great Leap Forward and the natural disasters at that time; but soon, before bureaucracy becomes entrenched and responsibility is turned into elitism and privilege. It is too early to tell whether there will be more mass mobilization campaigns of a genuinely enduring and penetrating character. But it is not too early to predict that if there are not more of these kinds of campaigns in the years to come, Mao's revolution as the world and the Chinese people have known it will be at an end.

Appendix 1

National Campaigns in Research Sample

st no.	Campaign	Start date	End date	Duration (months)	Yu type[a]	Liu type[b]	Urban rural[c]	Institutional sector[d]
1	Buy People's Victory Bonds	6/50	?[e]	18	E	FS	B	M
2	Agrarian Reform	6/50	11/52	30	S	FST	R	A
3	Peace Signatures	4/50	4/50?	4	I	FS	B	M
4	Resist America–Aid Korea	10/50	7/53?	31	I	FD	B	M
5	Suppression of Counterrevolutionaries	11/50	8/51?	9	S	FDT	B	M
6	Mutual Aid Teams	12/51	12/54?	24	E	FS	R	A
7	Three-Anti (corruption, waste, bureaucracy)	12/51	7/52	8	I	FST	U	P
8	Five-Anti (bribery, tax evasion, theft of state property, cheating on government contracts, stealing economic information for speculation)	12/51	11/52	11	S	FST	U	C

(*continued*)

[a] Yu campaign types: E = economic; I = ideological; S = struggle.
[b] Liu campaign types: FS = functionally specific without targets; FST = functionally specific with ets; FD = functionally diffuse without targets; FDT = functionally diffuse with targets.
[c] Urban/rural dimension: U = urban emphasis; R = rural emphasis; B = both areas.
[d] Sector of primary emphasis: A = agriculture; C = commerce/industry; P = party; I = intellectual; M = e than one sector.
[e] A question mark signifies either uncertainty or disagreement over dates. For these cases the ulation of the duration must be an approximation. However, since only ordinal statistics are used, the ential for unreliable correlations is reduced.
[f] Campaign was still continuing at the end of 1976. The duration in months is calculated through ember 1976.

List no.	Campaign	Start date	End date	Duration (months)	Yu type[a]	Liu type[b]	Urban rural[c]	Institutio sector[c]
9	Agricultural Producers Cooperatives	7/53?	?	27	E	FS	R	A
10	Study of the PRC Draft Constitution	6/54	9/54	2	I	FS	B	M
11	Socialist Reform of Private Business	1/56	5/56?	5	E	FS	U	C
12	Elimination of Counterrevolutionaries	12/54	12/55	12	S	FDT	B	M
13	Higher-Level Agricultural Producers' Cooperatives	8/55	8/57	24	E	FS	R	A
14	Combat the Four Evils (rats, flies, mosquitos, sparrows)	4/56?	6/56?	2	E	FS	B	M
15	Hundred Flowers	5/56	2/57?	9	I	FD	U	I
16	Study Mao's "On Handling Contradictions Among the People"	2/57	3/57	1	I	FD	B	M
17	Rectification	5/57	6/57	1	I	FST	B	P
18	Anti-Rightist	6/57	4/58?	10	S	FDT	B	I
19	Great Leap Forward	10/57	1/61	39	E	FS	B	M
20	Communes	7/58	11/60	28	E	FS	R	A
21	Backyard Furnaces	6/58?	8/58?	3	E	FS	B	M
22	Cultural Revolution	9/58?	3/59?	6	I	FD	B	M
23	Urban Communes	9/58	?	11	E	FS	U	M
24	Counter Rightist Sympathies	8/59	3/60	7	I	FST	B	M
25	Oppose U.S.–Japan Military Treaty	5/60	5/60	1	I	FD	B	M
26	Aid Agriculture	11/60	11/65	60	E	FD	R	A
27	Learn from the PLA	2/63	3/65	25	I	FD	B	M
28	Socialist Education	9/62	11/65	38	S	FDT	B	P
29	Train Revolutionary Successor Generation	5/64?	5/66	24	I	FD	B	M
30	Learn from Tachai[f]	4/64		153	E	FD	R	A
31	Learn from Taching[f]	4/64		153	E	FD	U	C
32	Study and Apply Chairman Mao's Thought	3/64	5/66	26	I	FD	B	M
33	Great Proletarian Cultural Revolution	5/66	4/69	35	S	FDT	B	M
34	Rectification	7/69?	12/69	5	I	FST	B	P
35	Support the Army, Cherish the People	1/68?	12/68?	11	I	FD	B	M
36	Barefoot Doctors	9/68	12/71?	40	E	FS	R	M

Appendix 2

Other National Campaigns (1950-1975)

Year of inception	Campaign
1950	Ideological Remolding
	Reduction of Rents and Interest
	Tax Collection
	Marriage Law
	Support the Troops and Well Treat Their Families
	Winter Clothing Donation
	Tax Collection
	Enrollment in Military Schools
1951	Democratic Reform
	Oppose Rearmament of Japan
	Study of Wu Hsun
	Public Security Rectification
	Donations for the Purchase of Airplanes and Heavy Artillery
1952	Oppose Germ Warfare
	Sino–Soviet Friendship
1953	Marxist–Leninist Study
	Party Rectification
1954	Criticize the Thought of Hu Shih
1955	Oppose the Use of Nuclear Weapons
1956	Study Marxism–Leninism
	Voluntary Military Service
	Investigation of Cadres
1957	Mass Irrigation
	Socialist Education
1958	Turn Over the Heart to the Party
	Physical Fitness
	Oppose U.S. Provocations

(*continued*)

Year of inception	Campaign
1960	Strengthen the PLA New Three-Anti Technical Transformation
1963	New Five-Anti
1970	Leap Forward in Production
1971	Mass Scientific Research
1973	Criticize Lin Piao and Confucius
1975	Study the "Dictatorship of the Proletariat"

Appendix 3

Some Regional and Local Campaigns

Year of Inception	Campaign
1950	Denounce American Imperialism and Crimes of Aggression (Nanking)
	Ban Secret Societies (Taiyuan)
	Ban Secret Societies (Northwest)
	Payment of Taxes Due (Chungking)
	Winter Study (Shanghai)
	Ban Listening to "Voice of America" (Yen Ching University, Peking)
	Self-Salvation Through Production (Hainan)
1952	One Irrigation Project for Every Village (Kwangtung and Hunan)
	Literacy in PLA Units (South)
1958	Textbook Reform (Tsinghua University, Peking)
	Pedagogical Reform (Peking University)
	Academic Criticism and Academic Research
1961	Love and Protect the Peking University Library
1970	Construction of the Lotung Hydroelectric Station (Kwangsi)

Appendix 4

Informants

Status in China	Sex	Year of birth	Class origin	Home city or province	Education	Year left China	Campaigns interviewed for
Student	m	1949	Worker	Kwangtung	Secondary	1967	33
Student	m	1947	Medical	Kwangchow	Secondary	1969	14, 21, 33, 36
Teacher	f		Petty bourgeoisie	Peking	College	1964	4, 16, 17, 18, 19, 20
Teacher, rightist	m	1933	Landlord	Kwangtung	Secondary	1967	1, 3, 4, 5, 7, 8, 10,
Student, cadre, rightist	m	1931	Capitalist	Kwangtung	College	1967	2, 18, 33
Student, cadre	m	1933	Landlord	Kwangtung	College	1968	1, 3, 5, 7, 8, 9, 10, 11, 12, 16, 22, 23, 24, 25, 26, 27, 28, 29, 30, 31, 32
Peasant, merchant	m	1928	Rich peasant	Kwangtung	Primary	1967	2, 6, 11, 12, 13, 14, 20, 28
Student, teacher	f		Bourgeoisie	Kwangchow	College	1970	21
Student, teacher, rightist	m	1932	Landlord	Kwangtung	Secondary	1972	13, 36
Student, peasant, teacher	m	1942	Overseas Chinese	Kwangchow	College	1967	12, 15, 20, 23
Student	m	1938	Capitalist	Shanghai	College	1962	10, 15, 22
Student, worker, peasant	m	1947	Petty bourgeoisie	Kwangchow	Primary	1970	28, 29, 30
Student, worker	m	1946	Worker	Kwangchow	Secondary	1970	27, 32, 34, 35

Appendix 5

Interview Data Collection Schedule

Campaign _____

Informant Number _____

Interview/Data Collection Date _____

SECTION A: GENERAL BACKGROUND OF INFORMANT

1. When and where born
2. Where grew up
3. Educational history (number of years and types of schools)
4. Occupational history (especially prior to and during the campaign in question)
5. Informant's personal status classification (*ge ren zheng fen*)
6. Family's social class categorization (*jie ji chu shen*) (If informant grew up in another family, their categorization)
7. While in China could informant:
   a.   Read or listen to newspaper reading, etc.; how often?
   b.   Write (letters, articles, essays, etc.)?
   c.   Participate in current affairs study groups? how often?
8. Did informant:
   a.   Attend movies (how often, where, and with whom)?
   b.   Listen to public broadcasts (how often, collectively, with family, or individually)?

    c.   Listen to the radio (how often, collectively, with family, or individually)?

9. Marital status (family still in China)?

10. Did informant participate in small group activities? Before the campaign? During? Describe the nature of participation (e.g., formal? informal? much criticism/self-criticism?)

11. When did informant leave China?

12. Current occupation in Hong Kong

For sections B, C, D, E, F, and G one campaign will be selected for focus. The questions relate only to the specific campaign in question. Any given informant may be interviewed several times for different campaigns.

SECTION B: QUESTIONS PERTAINING TO THE MONTHS PRIOR TO THE CAMPAIGN

1. Describe the specific nature and purpose of informant's overall unit (e.g., factory or commune, products produced, where it was located, approximate size—e.g., number of people; if agricultural, size in kilometers).

2. How would the informant describe the economic well-being of his or her unit relative to neighboring ones at the outset of the campaign? In general, in comparison with the overall national level? Had it been improving or declining relative to others (e.g., was the level of remuneration Increasing or decreasing)?

3. Communication within the unit preceding the campaign:
   - a.   Was there a newspaper reading group? Which parts of the paper was read? How often (e.g., daily, weekly)?
   - b.   Frequency and content of reporter's meetings (more related to immediate occupation or larger political issues)?
   - c.   Amount and character of small group activity?
   - d.   Frequency of movies?
   - e.   How were incidents of worker complaints handled by those in responsible positions?
   - f.   What percentage of the people in the unit does informant estimate could read a newspaper? How many did?
   - g.   What percentage had a newspaper read to them?
   - h.   What percentage attended some primary school? Of this, what percentage before liberation? After?

    i.   What percentage completed primary school? Of this, what percentage before liberation? After?

    j.   What percentage viewed the movies?

    k.   What percentage listened to radio sets?

    l.   What percentage listened to radio broadcasts?

4. In the months before the campaign began was there ever any discussion regarding problems that later became the focus of the campaign? Which problems? What kind of discussions?

5. Did the unit participate in any trial or experimental efforts to "test" the campaign? If so, describe the nature of the activities. Did the informant know of any other units which did?

SECTION C: GENERAL QUESTIONS ON THE CAMPAIGN

1. How it began:
   a.   When (season if not date)?
   b.   Was it related to a seasonal or annual event (e.g., planting, harvesting, anniversary celebration)?
   c.   Through what means was the first announcement made (e.g., broadcast, radio, newspaper, local leadership)?

2. At the outset of the campaign, did the informant know of or see a plan, rules, or guidelines governing the conduct of the campaign? (These would be more specific than general "directives" or "instructions"—e.g., during land reform, such regulations were issued to deal with the disposition of expropriated property.)

3. What were the goals of the campaign?

4. Were goals ever officially announced? If so, at what point in the campaign? How?

5. Process of the campaign: the number and character of stages. (This is an open-ended question calling for a brief characterization of the campaign including a differentiation of stages and the labeling of the period of "high tide" if possible.)

SECTION D: INDICATORS OF MOBILIZATION

NOTE: The following symbols have been used throughout Sections D, E, and F:

*The indicator almost fit into the final scale used for statistical calculations.

†The indicator was used to determine scale rankings to calculate relationships with other variables.

‡The indicator has a high disagreement ratio. Because of the high ratio, the indicator was eliminated from the final scale used to determine correlations with other variables.

	Disagreement ratio[1]	Indicator type[2]
1. Was there a class or "anti-productive" group labeled as an enemy or campaign target (e.g., landlords, capitalists, capitalist roaders)?*	.08	I
2. Were errors of thinking or acting characterized as targets of the campaign?*	.13	I
3. Were there movements of large numbers of people to implement the campaign (e.g., *xia fang*, volunteers)?†	.13	M
4. Were there individual work models?*, ‡	.24	M
5. Were there individual labor heroes?	.08	I
6. Were there group work models?*, ‡	.26	M
7. Were written pledges made to promote the campaign (e.g., higher production goals, production pacts, ideological or propaganda work)?‡	.18	M
8. Were regular occupational activities ceased to attend meetings or otherwise participate in the campaign?	.09	M
9. Was off-hours work time given to work in the campaign (beyond meetings)?†	.09	M
10. Were personal material donations made to others (e.g., money)?	.07	M
11. Did outsiders visit the family to discuss the campaign?	.11	M
12. Were there formally organized discussions about the campaign?‡	.25	M
13. Were there individual competitions or emulation drives to support the campaign?	.15	M
14. Were there collective competitions or emulation drives to support the campaign?‡	.21	M
15. Did national leaders participate in local campaign work/visits?‡	.18	O

[1] For a definition of the disagreement ratio see Chapter 3.
[2] I = informational; O = organizational; M = mass participation.

16. Were there stories of sacrificing life?[†] .09 I

17. Were films used to promote the campaign?[*,‡] .28 I

18. Were postage-stamps used to promote the campaign? .15 I

19. Were there national rallies, demonstrations, parades in Peking?[†] .11 M

20. Were there rallies, demonstrations, parades in provincial centers or major cities?[†] .10 M

21. Were there rallies, demonstrations, parades in local villages or district centers?[†] .10 M

22. Were slogans used to promote the campaign (e.g., "Grasp revolution, promote production")?[†] .08 I

23. Were wall papers, blackboard bulletins, or *dazibao* (big character posters) used to promote the campaign? .11 I

24. Were pamphlets, booklets, etc., written especially for the campaign?[†] .06 I

25. Were propaganda teams used to promote the campaign?[‡] .16 I

26. Were drama troupes organized to perform for the campaign?[‡] .16 I

27. Were books written especially for the campaign?[†] .14 I

28. Were there statements (e.g., articles, directives, speeches) given by national leaders in support of the campaign?[‡] .20 I

29. Were there major editorials whose primary purpose was to support the campaign?[*] .01 I

30. Were there statements by organizations (e.g., writers, students, labor) supporting the campaign?[‡] .18 I

31. During holidays (e.g., Spring Festival) did the content of banners relate specifically to the campaign?[†] .10 I

32. Were there songs promoting the campaign? .14 I

33. Were articles written to promote the campaign?[*] .00 I

34. Were there radio broadcasts to support the campaign (other than news or the reading of newspaper articles or editorials)? .02 I

35. Were there slide shows to support the campaign (e.g., "lantern slides")?[†] .09 I

36. Were illustrated drawings (e.g., cartoons) used in papers, wall posters, or movies to support the campaign?‡   .20   I

37. Were photograph displays used to support the campaign?†   .08   I

38. Were ad hoc newspapers published as a part of the campaign?†   .12   M

39. Did students or the general population (other than major figures or newspaper commentators) write essays on the campaign?‡   .18   M

40. Were poems written to promote the campaign?   .12   I

41. Were slogan posters used to promote the campaign?   .08   I

42. Were dances developed primarily for the campaign?   .11   I

43. Were there exhibitions to support the campaign?*,‡   .25   I

44. Were short stories written primarily to support the campaign?†   .07   I

45. Were woodcuts, clay figures, or other handicrafts made specifically for the campaign?*   .08   I

46. Were there propaganda posters primarily relating to the campaign?   .10   I

47. Were letters written to newspapers primarily dealing with the campaign?   .12   M

48. Were badges or buttons used for the campaign?| .02   M

49. Were there small group or study meetings used to discuss the campaign?†   .04   M

50. Were there public trials or accusation meetings?*   .05   M

51. Were there "recall bitterness—think sweetness" meetings?*,‡   .25   M

52. Were there meetings of criticism/self-criticism?†   .10   M

53. Were there conferences/policy meetings to discuss the campaign?‡   .34   O

54. Were there large general meetings (within the local unit) to promote the campaign?   .10   I

55. Was there a special study of current events in relation to the campaign?   .06   M

56. Was a special organization or office established for the campaign?‡   .22   O

57. Did cadres enter from the outside to assist in the organization and implementation of the campaign (e.g., work teams)?[†] .12 O

58. Were special training centers established to train people to assist in the implementation of the campaign (e.g., work teams)?[‡] .38 O

59. Were special schools established to reeducate targets of the campaign? .02 O

60. Did cadres participate in special meetings to prepare for the campaign? .11 O

61. Was there special mention of minority group participation?[*,‡] .17 M

62. Was there special mention of participation of women's groups?[‡] .19 M

63. Was there special mention of youth participation?[†] .14 M

64. Were mobile units/work teams used in the campaign?[*,‡] .18 O

65. Did a reorganization of the basic unit occur?[†] .13 O

66. Did the campaign require a substantial change in the established plans or operations of the unit (e.g., revising production targets, school schedules, or closing a school or factory for several days)?[†] .06 O

67. Was there a financial reallocation of resources to support the campaign?[†] .03 O

68. Were plans or programs established before the campaign curtailed for financial reasons in order to promote the campaign?[†] .02 O

69. Were there struggle meetings?[†] .06 M

70. Were there meetings to pass judgment? .08 M

71. Were there meetings of criticism?[*] .07 M

72. Were there condemnation meetings?[†] .04 M

73. Were quotation signboards or quote cards used? .03 I

74. Were there mobilization meetings?[†] .02 I

75. Were there banners or flags with slogans on them?[†] .10 I

76. Were homes visited to carry out investigations? .05 M

77. Did people visit other (model) areas to learn about the campaign? .02 M

SECTION E: INDICATORS OF ACHIEVEMENTS

	Disagreement ratio	Indicator type[3]
1. Did personal or family conditions improve (e.g., addition of a new radio or bicycle)?†	.10	E
2. Did collective economic conditions improve (e.g., bigger grain harvest, increased production)?*,‡	.17	E
3. Did individuals receive written citations (e.g., cited as a labor hero)?†	.13	I
4. Were there new material achievements (e.g., construction of new buildings, irrigation system or machinery)?*,‡	.24	E
5. Did people increase their occupational grade as a result of the campaign?†	.13	E
6. Did individual income increase as a result of the campaign?*	.09	E
7. Did the value of work points increase?	.02	E
8. Were quotas/targets fulfilled early?‡	.20	E
9. Were production records broken?*,‡	.19	E
10. Were occupational opportunities increased (e.g., jobs, schools)?†	.11	E
11. Did working methods improve (i.e., better at old skills)?†	.11	E
12. Were new skills acquired (e.g., learning to read, operate a new machine)?†	.14	E
13. Were more people accepted into the Party as a result of the campaign?†	.03	I
14. Did anti-bureaucratic styles improve?*	.08	I
15. Did the decentralization of decision making increase?†	.03	I
16. Did communication networks improve?†	.08	I
17. Did environmental conditions improve (e.g., sanitation, health care, security)?	.08	E

[3] I = ideological; E = economic.

18. Was there increased self-reliance?	.07	I
19. Was there a strengthening of collective orientation in the basic unit as a result of the campaign (rather than a heightening of individualistic desire, competition)?*,‡	.22	I
20. Was there greater cooperation between units?†	.13	I
21. Did political consciousness increase?†	.06	I
22. Did equality between groups increase (e.g., women–men, youth–elders, cadres–masses)?†	.11	I
23. Were there self-confessions?	.02	I
24. Did groups receive citations (e.g., Four Good Classes)?†	.09	I
25. Was there a reduction in rural–urban differences ?†	.12	I
26. Were backward areas penetrated?†	.10	I
27. Was politics more important than economics?	.05	I
28. Did living costs decrease?†	.01	E

SECTION F: INDICATORS OF SHORTCOMINGS

	Disagreement ratio	Indicator type[4]
1. Was there substantial unsanctioned mass migration to the cities or out of the country?†	.08	P
2. Did work or study slowdowns occur?*	.11	I
3. Was physical harm inflicted on cadres?*	.04	P
4. Were there armed clashes resulting in death?†	.02	P
5. Were there armed clashes resulting in injury?*	.01	P
6. Did the destruction of property occur (e.g., the slaughter of draft animals)?†	.03	P
7. Was the army activated for the purpose of maintaining order or organization?†	.03	P
8. Was there a rise in actual tax rates (percentage turned over to the state)?	.09	E

[4] I = ideological; P = physical; E = economic.

9. Were there leftist or rightist deviations as a result of the campaign?[†]   .09   I

10. Were there reinvestigation groups or measures following the campaign to correct problems and/or excesses of the campaign?[†]   .08   I

11. Were arbitrary production quotas assigned?   .02   E

12. Were there violations in the implementation of policies pertaining to the campaign?[†]   .09   I

13. Were there demotions or firings among nontarget groups?[†]   .05   I

14. Was an economic loan or outside assistance necessary to get through the campaign or its effects?   .05   E

15. Were there suicides resulting from the campaign?[†]   .03   P

16. Was there a return to the old methods or patterns of organization following the campaign?   .04   I

17. Did cadres fail in aspects of implementing the campaign?[†]   .05   I

18. Did bribery occur as a consequence of the campaibn?[†]   .03   I

19. Was there a failure to reform or eliminate all the targets of the campaign?[†]   .05   I

20. Were acts of violence used to resist?[†]   .07   P

21. Were there shortcomings in the general (political) policy?[*]   .05   I

22. Did people receive abuse or insult?[†]   .04   P

23. Were people indiscriminately killed?[*]   .01   P

24. Did production suffer as a result of the campaign?   .04   E

25. Was there physical conflict between classes/groups?[*]   .03   I

26. Were there conflicts between cadres over the campaign?[*]   .03   I

27. Was the labeling of targets excessive?[†]   .05   I

SECTION G: GENERAL QUESTIONS OF CAMPAIGN EVALUATION

1. Was this campaign more or less or about as important as other campaigns in fulfilling the socialist transformation process? (What other campaigns are being used by the informant as a referent?)

2. Did this campaign directly relate to others? If so, how, and which ones?

3. How did the campaign terminate (date or season, did it just fade away; if termination was via an announcement, what means were used—see Section C, question 1)?

4. How would activities during the campaign (e.g., number and frequency of meetings) compare with activities before and after?

5. If there were changes during the campaign, for example, in personnel, in interpersonal relations, in the status of specific individuals (e.g., acceptance into the party), to what extent did these things return to their precampaign state after the termination of the campaign?

6. If there were changes during the campaign in the organization of the unit, to what extent did these changes return to their precampaign state after the termination of the campaign?

7. What were the main shortcomings and achievements of the campaign? Which were more important?

8. Without this campaign would the shortcomings and achievements have been the same?

9. How did the informant react to the campaign? Were there excesses or was it too moderate (e.g., if there were guidelines, how much deviation was there from the guidelines)? How did others react?

10. In the informant's unit what percentage participated in the campaign?

11. What percentage of the total population participated In the campaign?

SECTION H: QUESTIONS ON INFORMANT'S VIEWS ON CHINA

1. Were any family members ever in trouble with the authorities? If so, describe the character of the problem.

2. Feelings of the informant about his/her occupation. Was the pay adequate? Working conditions? What was the feeling toward political activities?

3. How long was coming to Hong Kong under consideration before leaving?

4. How and why did the informant leave?

References

ABBREVIATIONS

CZRB   *Chang Zih Ri Bao* [Chang Zih Daily]. Chang Zih, Shansi.

FBIS,   Foreign Broadcast Information Services *Daily Report: People's Republic of China,* Springfield, Va. National Technical Information Service, U.S. Department of Commerce.

HQ   *Hong Qi* [Red Flag]. Peking.

JFRB   *Jie Fang Ri Bao* [Liberation Daily]. Shanghai.

KMRB   *Kuang Ming Ri Bao* [Bright Daily]. Peking.

NFRB   *Nan Fang Ri Bao [Southern Daily]. Canton.*

NCNA   New China News Agency. *News Dispatches.* Peking.

PC   *People's China,* 1950–1957. Peking.

PR   *Peking Review,* 1958–. Peking.

RMRB   *Ren Min Ri Bao* [People's Daily]. Peking.

SCMM   *Survey of China Mainland Magazines,* 1955–. Hong Kong: American Consulate General.

SCMP   *Survey of the China Mainland Press,* 1950–. Hong Kong: American Consulate General.

URI,   Union Research Institute, Classified Files 1950–1970

WHB   *Wen Hui Bao* [Literary News]. Shanghai.

XQRB   *Xin Qiang Ri Bao* [Sinkiang Daily]. Sinkiang.

Abaya, Hernando
  1967 *The Untold Philippine Story.* Quezon City.
Apter, David E.
  1965 *The Politics of Modernization.* Chicago: University of Chicago Press.
Armstrong, Marrianne
  1967 "The campaign against parasites." In Peter H. Juviler and Henry W. Morton (eds.), *Soviet Policy Making: Studies of Communism in Transition.* New York: Praeger.

Barnett, A. Doak
  1964 *Communist China: The Early Years, 1949–1955.* New York: Praeger.
  1968 *Cadres, Bureaucracy and Political Power in Communist China.* New York: Columbia University Press.
Baum, Richard
  1967 "Ideology redivivus." *Problems of Communism* 16 (May–June).
Baum, Richard, and Frederick Teiwes
  1968 *Ssu-Ching: The Socialist Education Movement of 1962–1966.* Berkeley, California. Center for Chinese Studies.
Bennett, Gordon A.
  1976 *Yundong: Mass Campaigns in Chinese communist leadership.* China Research Monographs, Berkeley, Center for Chinese Studies.
Bennett, Gordon A., and Ronald Montaperto
  1971 *Red Guard: The Political Biography of Dai Hsiao-ai.* Garden City, New York: Doubleday.
Bernstein, Thomas P.
  1967 "Leadership and mass mobilization in the Soviet and Chinese collectivization campaigns of 1929–30 and 1955–56: A comparison." *China Quarterly* 31 (July–September).
Bridgham, Philip
  1967 "Mao's 'Cultural Revolution': Origin and development." *China Quarterly* 29 (January–March): 1–35.
  1968 "Mao's Cultural Revolution in 1967: The struggle to seize power." *China Quarterly* 34 (April–June): 6–37.
Burchett, Wilfred G.
  1966 *Vietnam North.* New York: International Publishers.
Canton People's Publishing House
  1958 *Wen Hua Ge Ming Kai Shi Le* [The Cultural Revolution Has Started].
Cell, Charles P.
  1974 "Charismatic heads of state: The social context." *Behavior Science Research,* IX:4: 255–305.
  1973–1974 "Transforming China's leadership." *China notes* 12 (Winter): 4–7.
Chaliand, Gerhard
  1969 *The Peasants of North Vietnam.* Baltimore, Maryland: Penguin.
Chang, Parris H.
  1969 "Mao's great purge: A political balance sheet." *Problems of Communism* 18 (March–April).
Chen, C. S., and Charles P. Ridley (eds.)
  1969 *Rural People's Communes in Lien-Chiang: Documents Concerning Communes in Lien-Chiang County, Fukien Province, 1962–63.* Stanford, California: Hoover Institution Publication 83.
Chen, Jack
  1957 *The New Earth: How the Peasants in One Chinese County Solved the Problem of Poverty.* Peking: New World.
Chi, Wen-shun (ed.)
  1963 *Readings in Chinese Communist Documents.* Berkeley: University of California Press.
Cleary, J. W.
  1965 "The Virgin Lands." *Survey* (July).
Cohen, Jerome A.
  1967 "Interviewing Chinese refugees: Indispensable aid to legal research on China." *Journal of Legal Education* (October).

Committee of Concerned Asian Scholars
  1972 *China! Inside the People's Republic.* New York: Bantam.
Crook, Isabel, and David Crook
  1966 *The First Years of Yangyi Commune.* London: Routledge and Kegan Paul.
Eckstein, Alexander
  1968 "Economic fluctuations in communist China's domestic development." In Ho
         Ping-ti and Tang Tsou (eds.), *China in Crisis.* Chicago: University of Chicago Press.
         Pp 691–729.
Etzioni, Amitai
  1961 *A Comparative Analysis of Complex Organizations.* New York: Free Press.
Fainsod, Merle
  1958 *Smolensk under Soviet Rule.* Cambridge: Harvard University Press.
Gardner, John
  1969 "The Wu Fan campaign in Shanghai: A study in the consolidation of urban
         control." In A. Doak Barnett (ed.), *Chinese Communist Politics in Action.* Seattle:
         University of Washington Press. Pp. 477–539.
Gillin, Donald
  1964 "Peasant nationalism in the history of Chinese communism." *Journal of Asian
         Studies* 23 (February).
Gittings, John
  1964 "The Learn from the PLA Army campaign." *China Quarterly* 18 (April–June):
         153–159.
Goldenberg, Boris
  1965 *The Cuban Revolution and Latin America.* New York: Praeger.
Goldman, Merle
  1962 "Hu Feng's conflict with the literary authorities." *China Quarterly* 12 (October–
         December): 102–137.
  1967 *Literary Dissent in Communist China.* Cambridge: Harvard University Press.
Gray, Jack
  1969 "Economics of Maoism." In *China after the Cultural Revolution.* New York:
         Random House.
  1973 "The two roads: Alternative strategies of social change and economic growth in
         China." In Stuart R. Schram (ed.), *Authority, Participation and Cultural Change in
         China.* Cambridge: Cambridge University Press. Pp. 109–158.
Green, Gil
  1970 *Revolution: Cuban Style.* New York: International Universities Press.
Gurley, John G.
  1970 "Capitalist and Maoist economic development." *Bulletin of Concerned Asian
         Scholars* 2 (April). 34–50.
Guttman, Louis
  1947 "The Cornell technique for scale and intensity analysis." *Educational and Psycho-
         logical Measurement* 7 (Summer): 247–280.
Harrison, James P.
  1969 *The Communists and Chinese Peasant Rebellions.* New York: Atheneum.
Hinton, William
  1968 *Fanshen: A Documentary of Revolution in a Chinese Village.* New York: Vintage.
  1972 "The Cultural Revolution at Tsinghua University." *Monthly Review* 24.
Ho Ping-ti, and Tang Tsou
  1968 *China in Crisis,* Vol. 1, Books 1 and 2. Chicago: University of Chicago Press.
Hsia, Ronald
  1961 "The intellectual and the public life of Ma Yin-ch'u." *China Quarterly* 6 (April–
         June): 53–63.

Huberman, Leo, and Paul Sweezy
   1967   "The Cultural Revolution in China." *Monthly Review* 18 (January).
Human Resources Research Institute
   1955a *Chinese Communist Anti-Americanism and the Resist-America Aid-Korea Cam-*
         paign. Lackland Air Force Base, Texas, Air Force Personnel and Training Research
         Center, Air Research and Development Command. Research Memorandum No. 36
         (May).
   1955b *The Strategy and Tactics of Chinese Communist Propaganda as of 1952.* Lackland
         Air Force Base, Texas, Air Force Personnel and Training Research Center, Air
         Research and Development Command. Research Memorandum No. 39 (June).
   1955c *Agrarian Reform in Communist China to 1952.* Lackland Air Force Base, Texas,
         Air Force Personnel and Training Research Center, Air Research and Development
         Command. Research Memorandum No. 41 (July).
   1955d *Chinese Farm Economy after Agrarian Reform.* Lackland Air Force Base, Texas,
         Air Force Personnel and Training Research Center, Air Research and Development
         Command. Research Memorandum No. 34 (August).
   1955e *Wartime "Mass" Campaigns in Communist China: Official Countrywide "Mass*
         Movements" in Professed Support of the Korean War. Lackland Air Force Base,
         Texas, Air Force Personnel and Training Research Center, Air Research and
         Development Command. Research Memorandum No. 43 (October).
Hunter, Neale
   1969   *Shanghai Journal: An Eye-Witness Account of the Cultural Revolution.* New York:
         Praeger.
Hunter, Neale, and Deidre Hunter
   1972   "Our man in Tachai: Chen Yung-kuei on the two-line struggle in agriculture."
         Monthly Review 24 (May).
Johnson, Chalmers A.
   1961   "An intellectual weed in the socialist garden: The case of Ch'ien Tuan-sheng."
         China Quarterly 6 (April–June): 25–52.
   1962   *Peasant Nationalism and Communist Power: The Emergence of Revolutionary*
         China 1937–1945. Stanford University Press.
Johnson, Kay Ann
   1976   "The Politics of Women's Rights and Family Reform in China," unpublished
         doctoral dissertation, Madison: University of Wisconsin.
Joint Publications Research Service
         Reports on China, Springfield, Va.: National Technical Information Service, U.S.
         Department of Commerce.
Kagan, Richard C.
   1973   "Father, Son and Holy Ghost: Pye, Solomon and the 'spirit of Chinese politics': A
         review article on Richard Solomon's *Mao's Revolution and the Chinese Political*
         Culture." Bulletin of Concerned Asian Scholars 5 (July).
Kim, Ilpyong, J.
   1969   "Mass mobilization policies and techniques developed in period of the Chinese
         Soviet Republic." In A. Doak Barnett (ed.), *Chinese Communist Politics in Action.*
         Seattle: University of Washington Press. Pp. 78–98.
Klein, Wells C., and Margorie Weiner
   1959   "North Vietnam." In George McT. Kahin (ed.), *Government and Politics of*
         Southeast Asia. Ithaca, New York: Cornell University Press.
Ko Ching-shih
   1960   "Mass movements on the industrial front." In *Ten Glorious Years.* Peking: Foreign
         Languages Press.

Kornhauser, William
1959 *The Politics of Mass Society*. New York: Free Press.
Lee, Rensselaer, W.
1966 "The Hsia Fang system: Marxism and modernization." *China Quarterly* 28 (October–December): 40–62.
Lewin, Moshe
1968 *Russian Peasants and Soviet Power: A Study of Collectivization*. Evanston, Illinois: Northwestern University Press.
Lewis, John W.
1963 *Leadership in Communist China*. Ithaca, New York: Cornell University Press.
1968 "Leader, commissar and bureaucrat: The Chinese political system in the last days of the revolution." In Ho Ping-ti and Tang Tsou (eds.), *China in Crisis*. Chicago: University of Chicago Press. Pp. 449–481.
Lifton, Robert J.
1968 *Revolutionary Immortality: Mao Tse-tung and the Chinese Cultural Revolution*. New York: Vintage.
Lingoes, James C.
1963 "Multiple scalogram analysis: A set-theoretic model for analyzing dichotomous items." *Educational and Psychological Measurement* 23(3): 501–524.
Lippit, Victor
1975 "The Great Leap Forward reconsidered," *Modern China* 1 (January): 92–115.
Liu, Alan P. L.
1971 *Communications and National Integration in Communist China*. Berkeley: University of California Press.
Liu Shao-chi
1945 "On the party's mass line." In *On the Party*, a report to the Seventh People's Congress of the CCP. (Reprinted in *PC*, July 1, 1950.)
1950 "Report on problems concerning agrarian reform." Second Session of the National Committee of the People's Consultative Conference, Peking. (Reprinted in *PC*, July 16, 1950.)
Lo, John Yen-chak
1976 "Workers' Participation and Industrial Democracy in China 1971–1974," unpublished M.A. Thesis, Madison: University of Wisconsin.
Lobkowicz, Nicholas
1967 *Theory and Practice: History of a Concept from Aristotle to Marx*. South Bend: University of Notre Dame.
MacFarquhar, Roderick
1969 "Communist China's twenty years: A periodization." *China Quarterly* 39 (July–September): 55–63.
Mao Tse-tung
1967 *Selected Works of Mao Tse-tung*, Vols. 1–4. Peking: Foreign Languages Press.
1971 *Selected Readings from the Works of Mao Tse-tung*. Peking: Foreign Languages Press.
Massell, Gregory
1968 "Law as an instrument of revolutionary change in a traditional milieu: The case of Soviet Central Asia." *Law and Society Review* 2 (February).
Matthews, Herbert
1969 *Fidel Castro*. New York: Simon and Schuster.
Meisner, Maurice
1971 "Leninism and Maoism: Some populist perspectives on Marxism–Leninism in China." *China Quarterly* 45 (January–March): 2–36.

Menzel, Herbert
  1953   "A new coefficient for scalogram analysis." *Public Opinion Quarterly* 17: 529–
         537.
Merriam, Charles E.
  1945   *Systematic Politics*. Chicago: University of Chicago Press.
Metzger, Thomas A.
  1972   "On Chinese political culture." *Journal of Asian Studies* 32 (November): 101–105.
Michael, Franz
  1967   "The struggle for power." *Problems of Communism* 16 (May–June).
Mills, Harriet
  1959   "Thought reform: Ideological remoulding in China." *Atlantic Monthly* 204 (De-
         cember): 71–77.
Milton, David, and Nancy Milton
  1976   *The Wind Will Not Subside*. New York: Pantheon.
Moravia, Alberto
  1968   *The Red Book and the Great Wall*. New York.
  1969   "A Mao for all seasons." *The New York Review of Books* 12 (January): 5–10.
Mote, F. W.
  1972   "China's past in the study of China today—Some comments on the recent work of
         Richard A. Solomon." *Journal of Asian Studies* 32 (November): 107–120.
Mu Fu-sheng
  1962   *The Wilting of the Hundred Flowers: The Chinese Intelligentsia Under Mao*. New
         York: Praeger.
Myrdal, Jan
  1966   *Report from a Chinese Village*. New York: Signet.
Myrdal, Jan, and Gun Kessle
  1970   *China: The Revolution Continued*. New York: Pantheon.
National Council of Churches of Christ
  1963   *Documents of the Three Self Movement*. New York: National Council of Churches.
Nee, Victor
  1969   *The Cultural Revolution at Peking University*. New York: Monthly Review Press.
Nee, Victor, and James Peck (eds.)
  1975   *China's Uninterrupted Revolution*. New York: Pantheon.
Nettl, J. P.
  1967   *Political Mobilization: A Sociological Analysis of Methods and Concepts*. London:
         Faber and Faber. (New York: Basic Book, Inc.)
Neuhauser, Charles
  1967   "The Chinese Communist party in the 1960's: Prelude to the Cultural Revolution."
         China Quarterly 32 (October–December): 3–36.
Nove, Alec
  1964   *Economic Rationality and Soviet Politics, or Was Stalin Really Necessary?* New
         York: Praeger.
Oksenberg, Michael
  1968   "Comments." Pp. 487–500 in Ho Ping-ti and Tang Tsou (eds.), *China in Crisis*, Vol.
         1, Book 2. Chicago: University of Chicago Press.
  1969   "Policy formulation in Communist China: The case of the mass irrigation campaign
         of 1957–1958." Unpublished doctoral dissertation. New York: Columbia Univer-
         sity.
Pfeffer, Richard
  1971   "Mao Tse-tung and the Cultural Revolution." In Norman Miller and Roderick Aya
         (eds.), *National Liberation*. New York: Free Press. Pp. 249–296.

1972 "Serving the people and continuing the revolution." *China Quarterly* 52 (October–December): 620–653.
Pike, Douglas
1966 *Viet Cong: The Organization and Techniques of the National Liberation Front of South Vietnam.* Cambridge: M.I.T. Press.
Richman, Barry M.
1969 *Industrial Society in Communist China.* New York: Random House.
Riskin, Carl
1971 "Small industry and the Chinese model of development." *China Quarterly* 46 (April–June): 245–273.
Robinson, Joan
1969 *The Cultural Revolution in China.* London: Penguin.
Rue, John
1966 *Mao Tse-tung in Opposition 1927–1935.* Stanford, California: Stanford University Press.
Schapiro, Leonard
1959 *The Communist Party of the Soviet Union.* New York: Random House.
Schram, Stuart R.
1966 "What is Maoism, a symposium." *Problems of Communism* 15 (September–October).
1967 *Mao Tse-tung.* Baltimore, Maryland: Penguin.
1971 "Mao Tse-tung and the theory of permanent revolution." *China Quarterly* 46 (April–June): 221–244.
1972 "Mao Tse-tung and Liu Shao-chi: 1939–1969." *Asian Survey* 12 (4): 275–293.
Schurmann, Franz
1961 "The roots of social policy." *Survey* 38 (October).
1966 "What's happening in China?" *The New York Review of Books* 7 (October).
1968 *Ideology and Organization in Communist China,* rev. ed. Berkeley: University of California Press.
Schwartz, Benjamin
1968a *Communism and China: Ideology in Flux.* Cambridge: Harvard University Press.
Selden, Mark
1969 "The Yenan legacy: The mass line." In A. Doak Barnett (ed.), *Chinese Communist Politics in Action.* Seattle: University of Washington Press. Pp. 99–151.
1971 *The Yenan Way in Revolutionary China.* Cambridge: Harvard University Press.
Selznick, Philip
1952 *The Organizational Weapon: A Study of Bolshevik Strategy and Tactics.* Glencoe, Illinois: Free Press.
Serruys, Paul L. M.
1962 *Survey of the Chinese Language Reform and the Anti-Illiteracy Movement in Communist China.* Berkeley, California: Center for Chinese Studies.
Skinner, G. William
1964–1965 "Marketing and social structure in rural China." *Journal of Asian Studies* 24 (1–3); 3–44; 195–228; 363–400.
1965 "Compliance and leadership in rural communist China." Mimeographed.
Skinner, G. William and Edwin Winckler
1969 "Compliance succession in rural communist China." In Amitai Etzioni, (ed.), *A Sociological Reader on Complex Organizations,* 2nd ed. New York: Holt, Rinehart and Winston. Pp. 410–438.
Snow, Edgar
1972 *The Long Revolution.* New York: Random House.

Solomon, Richard
   1971   *Mao's Revolution and the Chinese Political Culture.* Berkeley: University of Cali-
          fornia Press.
Sorenson, Jay B.
   1969   *The Life and Death of Soviet Trade Unionism, 1917–1928.* New York: Atherton.
Starr, John Bryan
   1971   "Conceptual foundations of Mao Tse-tung's theory of continuous revolution."
          Asian Survey 11 (June).
Teiwes, Frederick
   1971   "Rectification campaigns and purges in communist China." Unpublished doctoral
          dissertation. New York: Columbia University Press.
Townsend, James R.
   1967   *Political Participation in Communist China.* Berkeley: University of California
          Press.
Tsou, Tang
          "The Cultural Revolution and the Chinese political system." Unpublished manu-
          script.
Union Research Institute
   1968   *CCP Documents of the Great Proletarian Cultural Revolution, 1966–1967.* Hong
          Kong: Union Research Institute.
Vogel, Ezra F.
   1969   *Canton under Communism: Program and Politics in a Provincial Capital, 1949–*
          1968. Cambridge: Harvard University Press.
Walker, Kenneth L.
   1968   "Organization of agricultural production." In A. Eckstein, W. Galenson, and T. C.
          Liu (eds.), *Economic Trends in Communist China.* Chicago: Aldine.
Weber, Max
   1964   *The Theory of Social and Economic Organization.* New York: Free Press.
Wheelwright, F. L., and Bruce McFarlane
   1970   *The Chinese Road to Socialism: Economics of the Cultural Revolution.* New York,
          Monthly Review Press.
Whyte, Martin K.
   1970   *Small Groups and Political Rituals in Communist China.* Berkeley: University of
          California Press.
   1973   "Bureaucracy and modernization in China: The Maoist critique." *American Socio-*
          logical Review 38 (April): 149–163.
Yu, Frederick T. C.
   1967   "Campaigns, communication and development in communist China." In Daniel
          Lerner and Wilbur Schramm (eds.), *Communication and Change in Developing*
          Countries. Honolulu: East-West Center. Pp. 195–215.

Index

A
B 7
C 8
D 9
E 0
F 1
G 2
H 3
I 4
I 5

STUDIES IN SOCIAL DISCONTINUITY

Under the Consulting Editorship of:

CHARLES TILLY   EDWARD SHORTER
University of Michigan   *University of Toronto*

William A. Christian, Jr. Person and God in a Spanish Valley

Joel Samaha. Law and Order in Historical Perspective: The Case of Elizabethan Essex

John W. Cole and Eric R. Wolf. The Hidden Frontier: Ecology and Ethnicity in an Alpine Valley

Immanuel Wallerstein. The Modern World-System: Capitalist Agriculture and the Origins of the European World-Economy in the Sixteenth Century

John R. Gillis. Youth and History: Tradition and Change in European Age Relations 1770 – Present

D. E. H. Russell. Rebellion, Revolution, and Armed Force: A Comparative Study of Fifteen Countries with Special Emphasis on Cuba and South Africa

Kristian Hvidt. Flight to America: The Social Background of 300,000 Danish Emigrants

James Lang. Conquest and Commerce: Spain and England in the Americas

Stanley H. Brandes. Migration, Kinship, and Community: Tradition and Transition in a Spanish Village

Daniel Chirot. Social Change in a Peripheral Society: The Creation of a Balkan Colony

Jane Schneider and Peter Schneider. Culture and Political Economy in Western Sicily

Michael Schwartz. Radical Protest and Social Structure: The Southern Farmers' Alliance and Cotton Tenancy, 1880-1890

Ronald Demos Lee (Ed.). Population Patterns in the Past

David Levine. Family Formations in an Age of Nascent Capitalism